CW00960232

In Search of Truth

The Story of the
School of Economic Science

In Search of Truth

The Story of the
School of Economic Science

BRIAN HODGKINSON

SHEPHEARD-WALWYN (PUBLISHERS) LTD

First published in 2010 by
Shepheard-Walwyn (Publishers) Ltd
107 Parkway House, Sheen Lane,
London SW14 8LS

British Library Cataloguing in Publication Data
A catalogue record of this book
is available from the British Library

ISBN: 978-0-85683-276-5

Typeset by Alacrity,
Sandford, Somerset
Printed and bound through
s | s | media limited, Wallington, Surrey

Contents

Acknowledgements

IT IS IMPOSSIBLE to acknowledge by name all the numerous students of the School of Economic Science who have effectively contributed to this book. Many kindly agreed to be interviewed or to send information about various aspects. To all of them I am especially grateful. In addition, however, I must mention Hugh Venables for his continuous support and encouragement, Derek Aldous for his readiness to help with the archives, Anthony Werner for his advice as the publisher, Jean Desebrock for her patient work on the proofs and Donald Lambie for his generous attitude to the whole project.

The picture research was carried out by Richard and Odile Wythe, and Martin Lubikowski designed the plate section. The photographs were provided by Alan Marshall, Ian Murray, Nathan Gaydhani, Richard Wythe and Martin Lubikowski; and the Robert Schalkenbach Foundation in New York supplied the image of Henry George. I am grateful for their assistance and permission to reproduce their photographs.

The Index was prepared with the help of my son David. As always, my wife Catherine has borne stoically the demands made on her by so much of my attention being given to the book. Thank you to them both.

CHAPTER ONE

Origins

WHEN Leon MacLaren was in his seventies, he gave a talk about the School of Economic Science. These were his opening words:

> I am coming to speak to you about the beginnings of the School. I wish I could, because the School like everything else begins in the Absolute. Of that beginning only the Self knows. In this, as in many other things, we are forced to speak of what comes into manifestation, what appears and then develops.

He then described how, at the age of sixteen, he was sitting by a lake in Wimbledon Park when:

> It became very clear to me that there was such a thing as truth, and there was such a thing as justice, and that they could be found and, being found, could be taught. It seemed to me that that was the most valuable thing that one could pursue. So I resolved to pursue this when I was twenty-one.

That these two words, 'truth' and 'justice', should have been heard in this way at that particular time bears witness to what MacLaren often said about how certain schools or teachers arise to meet a need of humanity, when conditions threaten to become unbearable. The First World War had seen millions dead or maimed in the horrific circumstances of trench warfare. Weapons of destruction were developing by the application of modern science to the stage where the machine gun was giving way to the tank and the bomber, and nuclear missiles would soon succeed these. Mass unemployment and revolution had followed the war in many countries. In Russia Bolshevism was established, and already showed signs of turning into totalitarian dictatorship. In Germany the fragile Weimar Republic was soon to be undermined by a Nazi movement that would condemn the world to another conflagration.

In Britain itself the General Strike of 1926 was evidence of deep unrest and of dissatisfaction with the whole structure of the economy and society. Amongst the people themselves there was disillusion, fear and doubt. Yet it was in Britain that MacLaren's insight had occurred. For all their suffering in the war of 1914-18 the British had not lost a deep-seated belief in their native freedom. The traditional institutions that guaranteed it – the monarchy, Parliament and the law courts – remained intact. Despite economic injustice in the form of huge disparities of wealth, low wages and endemic unemployment, the population retained a belief in a way of life that at root was Christian, albeit without much outward observance of that faith. Hence it was in Britain, a country where the need was as insistent as elsewhere, yet where a response based on lasting and proven values might be elicited, that these words 'truth' and 'justice' came with prophetic force to a man capable of ensuring that they would be heard and acted upon.

Leon MacLaren (christened Leonardo da Vinci MacLaren) had been brought to Wimbledon at the age of four in 1914. His family had moved from Glasgow, where his father Andrew had been an active campaigner for the land reform movement inspired by the teaching of the American economist Henry George. This involved shifting taxation off labour and capital and onto land values, as a letter written by Andrew in 1912 shows:

> The great difference between land and capital, which Socialists seem to overlook, lies in the fact that land is not a product of human exertion, and the value of land arises not from individual exertion, but from natural differences of productivity, made potent by social growth and necessities, while capital is the result of individual exertion performed singly or in co-operation with others.
>
> To tax capital is to increase the cost of living and hinder productivity; to tax the value of land is to shatter a monopoly, and increase the productivity and employment of labour and secure to labour its just reward.[1]

Not long before the revelation at the lakeside in 1926, Leon MacLaren had asked his mother what book it was that his father so often turned to in preparing his speeches. The book was Henry George's major work, *Progress and Poverty*, and Leon had read this by the time that 'truth' and 'justice' came to him with such potency.

1 Quoted in John Stewart, *Standing for Justice*, Shepheard-Walwyn (Publishers) Ltd, 2001 p10.

In so far as ideas appear to pass from one mind to another, one can find many references to truth and justice in George's writings that anticipate their appearance in the first stirrings of MacLaren's thought about Economics and humanity. For example, near the end of *Progress and Poverty* we find them juxtaposed:

> In permitting the monopolization of the opportunities which nature freely offers to all, we have ignored the fundamental law of justice… But by sweeping away this injustice and asserting the rights of all men to natural opportunities, we shall conform ourselves to the law – we shall remove the great cause of unnatural inequality in the distribution of wealth and power… What is it but the carrying out in letter and spirit of the truth enunciated in the Declaration of Independence?[2]

How did Henry George arrive at these conclusions? As a poor young man he had come to New York from San Francisco to set up a small news bureau, only to be crushed by the power of monopoly press interests. Roused to seek the cause of such monopolies, he realised, when he saw the flagrant contrast in the city between the glittering rich in their fine apartments and the paupers in the streets outside, that they arose from the unbridled private ownership of land. From that time onwards he devoted his life to the land issue, writing several books and making speaking tours in the USA and abroad.

Contesting the theories of orthodox economists, including famous contemporaries like Alfred Marshall, George argued that land cannot be assimilated to capital, since it is not man-made, is in fixed supply and, above all, generates rent when any particular site has beneficial advantages, such as greater fertility, mineral deposits or superior location. If equal labour and capital is applied on all sites, rent is the excess value created by these advantages over the value arising on the least productive sites. For example, a retail store on Madison Avenue creates many times the value created by a similar store in a small town fifty miles away. This differential rent, said George, underlies the huge disparities of income and wealth in modern societies, for as economies develop the growth of output is distributed more and more unequally, as landless workers are forced

---

2 Henry George, *Progress and Poverty*, Robert Schalkenbach Foundation, New York, 1962, p.545.

to compete for jobs and wages, whilst landowners reap greater and greater rewards from the same fixed amount of land.

What George emphasised was that this rent of land is not produced by individuals. It is the result of the very existence of communities. They give rise to the demand for the products of land, to the advantages of location and to the development of public services, like transport and law and order, which make land valuable and nourish the growth of rent. Therefore, concluded George, the rent of land belongs to the community that creates it. Those individuals who claim it through a title to the land where it arises are stealing the birthright of the nation, the common wealth that naturally provides for the needs of the community. Thus taxation should be drawn from rent and not from labour or capital, both of which are entitled to the income derived from work or ownership. The proper rights of private property are invaded by taxes on these, whilst taxes on rent take nothing of private property, for the land is given by God or by Nature to the whole people. From the natural fund of rent all the communal needs of the nation can be met. No other taxes are required.

Support for Georgist ideas had grown rapidly round the world after the publication of *Progress and Poverty* in 1879. George himself had lectured in Great Britain and elsewhere in Europe. Glasgow in particular had become a hotbed of land reform, not least perhaps because of an atavistic memory amongst the congested and impoverished population of the land enclosures in the Highlands that had brought their predecessors there.

Andrew MacLaren's father was a choirmaster at a Catholic church near the Gorbals, the heart of the crowded working class area of the city, so the young boy grew up under the contrasting influences of widespread poverty and the church music of Palestrina and Mozart. Andrew himself was artistic and devotional by nature, but left school for an engineering workshop in order to help support the family. Although for a time he considered art, or even monasticism, as his vocation, his engineering training in fact stood him in good stead later in life. What drew upon his varied talents, however, was the call to the mission of the land question that then dominated much of the political life of Edwardian Britain.

In the election of 1905 the Liberal party of Campbell-Bannerman won a landslide victory, and strove to put land value taxation through Parliament. To some degree they succeeded in the famous 'People's Budget' of 1909, that brought in its wake a drastic curtailment of the power of the House of Lords, but the land clauses were ill-drafted, and moreover the First World War prevented the legislation being implemented.

Meanwhile Andrew MacLaren, after campaigning fiercely for the same taxation principle, joined the Independent Labour Party in 1914. A pacifist during the war, he found the land movement greatly weakened in post-war Britain. Nevertheless he battled on, entering the Commons as MP for Burslem in 1922. Soon he was the most ardent speaker on fundamental tax reform in the House, taking over the role of greater public figures, like Lloyd George and Winston Churchill, who had championed Georgist proposals before the war.

By the early 1920s the land question had receded into the background. The Liberal Party had split, following Lloyd George's coalition with the Conservatives, and the Labour Party, increasingly influenced by Socialist ideas and by the prospects of power after its brief spell in office in 1924, followed Karl Marx in believing that the real issue was a struggle between capital and labour. They did not listen to voices, like MacLaren's, that reminded them that the denial of access to land forced workers into an apparent subservience to the owners of capital. Although some more radical MPs gave support to MacLaren, he became almost a lone voice for his cause, speaking at every opportunity in debates on land or taxation. He continued to serve his constituents in Burslem assiduously, especially by providing frequent meetings about land reform!

Small in stature, but with a bony frame and jutting chin that matched his fiery nature, MacLaren tried often to rouse the House out of what he felt to be a torpor of forgetfulness. Often he was taunted for his adherence to a cause that few understood. Such treatment only strengthened his resolve. During the inter-war period, he saw a second devastating war approaching, whilst the underlying causes of human conflict were ignored. What must he have made of the German claims of 'land-hunger' and the concomitant demands for more territory in Europe, knowing that it was the enclosure of land in unrestricted private ownership in areas like the Junkers' East Prussia and land speculation in Berlin that gave Hitler the opportunity to exploit the frustration of the people of Germany? Yet MacLaren's humanity prevented him from venting his anger without discrimination. His friendships were not inhibited by party politics. He shared with Stanley Baldwin, the Conservative Prime Minister, an interest in calligraphy, and when Baldwin visited Burslem Andrew got into trouble with local Socialists for greeting him warmly and with due respect for his office.

These qualities of indifference to abuse, controlled anger, and a reverence for law and the Constitution were not lost on his son Leon. They all had a significant influence on the later development of the School. So too did the sense of humour that passed likewise from father to son. Some of Andrew's jokes could be ribald, but one perhaps illustrates the amusement he got out of politics itself. The fact that he had an Irish grandmother – who, he said, introduced him to the land question – did not prevent him from telling stories that nowadays would be politically incorrect, such as one that concerned an Irish trade unionist, who was reporting to his members the result of negotiations with the bosses. 'I'll give you the bad news first. We've got to take a pay cut of 10 per cent!' 'What's the good news?' they shouted. 'Ah!' he retorted. 'I've got it backdated to last January.'

With such a father Leon MacLaren could hardly fail to take up the cause of land and tax reform himself as the practical and apposite form of the justice that he sought. A great deal more was to follow from this initial impulse. He was to find that truth and justice would draw him far beyond the confines, however broad, of Economics; yet for some time he would devote most of his energy to this mission that he inherited from his father. Nor has the School that he founded ever ceased to follow the path of economic justice.

By 1931 the economic situation had darkened further. The Wall Street Crash had sent its malign shock wages beyond America. Unemployment in Britain was growing fast. Families went hungry, charities were overwhelmed with work and more State assistance was demanded, whilst in Germany economic collapse was bringing the Weimar Republic to its knees. Leon MacLaren was now 21; the time had come to implement his resolution made five years earlier.

The wealthy widow of Lewis Jacobs, a leading Georgist, had opened an office near Trafalgar Square to promote the idea of taxing land values. It had, said Leon MacLaren, 'neon signs, posters and a secretary'. There he met about a dozen other young enthusiasts for the movement. Free lectures were instituted, which were well attended; though it may have been the free tea that brought many in. In fact, interest was probably aroused by the gloomy economic conditions, for the Labour government of Ramsay MacDonald was grappling with a huge outflow of funds as bankers and speculators lost confidence in the government's power to deal with mounting problems.

The government soon fell, to be replaced by an improvised National Government, mainly of Conservatives, led by the Labour Premier himself. Ironically enough the Labour Chancellor, Philip Snowden, assisted by Andrew MacLaren, had introduced into his budget earlier that year clauses that provided for the taxation and rating of land values as 'a potent instrument of social reform'. The National government soon repealed these measures. It was a mark of how deep the vested interests attached to land ownership were embedded in British life and politics, and a clear sign to the small group of people struggling for economic justice with their free lectures and tea that something beyond the reach of politics was needed. Andrew, for example, had begun to run regular evening classes in Economics and a Sunday evening discussion group. Even he, and certainly his son, was beginning to look to education as the way forward.

CHAPTER TWO

Establishment of the School

ONE ASPECT of this new approach became evident to Leon MacLaren soon after the Georgist classes began. He noticed that people heard different things when words were spoken. They changed the sounds into something else. This recognition of a confusion of tongues was never afterwards lost by the School's founder. It was to focus his mind first upon the clarification and absence of ambiguity in the terms used in Economics, words like 'land', 'capital', 'credit', 'margin' and others, a rule that Henry George himself had practised. Later it informed the introductory Philosophy course, and then it gave emphasis to the School's interest in the study of language, notably of Sanskrit. Indeed the gulf that opened between the studies of the School and those of other institutions, especially in the field of Economics, was derived largely from disparities of meaning. Land, for example, has loosely been called capital in a great deal of academic literature, whereas the School has always insisted on their fundamental differences.

As a practical consequence of this discovery, Leon MacLaren came to a decision. He would start a School for enquiring into truth and justice, following his initial insight when he was sixteen. He had no idea what form a School should take, except that in some inchoate sense it should be Socratic. How it would teach truth and justice he did not know. Nor was he impressed with the erudition or eloquence of the teachers at his disposal, including himself! Such a situation was to recur again and again, both in his own life and in those of his students. Once a member of the School told him that he was deeply troubled by having to address an important meeting without knowing what he was going to say. MacLaren's answer, delivered with characteristic force, was, 'You are not expected to know!'

Outside help was at hand. In September 1936 the
Union for the Taxation of Land Values and Free Trad
ference in London. A United States contingent, calle
George School of Social Science and founded by Os
professor of Philosophy, were using a question and an
of teaching. The questions were written by Geiger, whilst the
answers were to be elicited from a perusal of *Progress and Poverty*.
Geiger had also written a teachers' manual that enabled otherwise
untrained teachers to take classes, provided that they were well
acquainted with the works of Henry George. Students attended for
an evening a week for ten weeks. By November 1936 there were no
less than eleven classes in cities throughout the UK. Question sheets
were now prepared by Leon MacLaren and his associates, though
some did not welcome the new method. This caused difficulties with
the committee that was running the British classes.

By the following year, 1937, there was a split. MacLaren and some
other members were asked to leave. In the reorganisation of these
individuals, the beginnings of the School emerged. Andrew
MacLaren gave a powerful series of lectures, question sheets were
once more rewritten, and all the breakaway members completed a
course that they called Part One. Meetings were held in a Parliamentary committee room, arranged by Andrew, who had recovered
his seat in the Commons in 1935 after four years of absence. (He had
promoted a Land Values (Rating) Private Member's Bill in 1937,
which failed by only 23 votes.)

By now the new group had adopted the title of the Henry George
School of Economics, and in the Autumn of 1937 they offered
evening classes to the public. A London restaurant was booked and
166 people attended. Tea and coffee were available in the break – one
of the ongoing features of School meetings to the present day. Parts
2 and 3 were soon developed. By 1939 about three hundred people
were coming. All the work was done by a handful of devoted members. A small office over a garage was obtained. The Economics
material, now written by Leon MacLaren, was modified to take
account of the observations of students. Some tutors, upset by
constant revisions, walked out!

These were early signs of the leadership that Leon MacLaren was
to assume with such authority as the School grew. There can be no
doubt that he had already found his true vocation in founding a
School dedicated to truth and justice, but at 29 years of age he could

not ignore the need for a career and what was perhaps the siren call of a public life in politics. In 1938, after some years of study, he was called to the Bar at Inner Temple, where he began to represent the London County Council at transport tribunals; and in 1939 he was nominated as Labour candidate for Epping, with the extraordinary challenge of standing against Winston Churchill, himself once an ardent land tax enthusiast, but now diverted by more urgent matters. Fortunately perhaps for MacLaren, the election was cancelled with the onset of war in September.

Meanwhile the members of the new School formed themselves into a Henry George Fellowship, holding their first Annual General Meeting in January 1939. This was to pursue activities beyond that of running public classes. Andrew MacLaren, for example, put forward a political programme. The School and its teaching organisation were to be controlled by the Fellowship. The Chairman was the Labour MP for Ipswich, R.R. Stokes.

A meeting two months later gave a flavour of the character of the Fellowship at this time. A speech, delivered by Colonel Josiah Wedgwood, included the following:

> The land which God intended for all has been made the private property of a few. Unemployment only means the stopping of useful productive work which comes from the land. It is wrong to call our remedy a tax. We do not propose to tax; we recover. Taxes on commodities raise their price because the tax is always passed on to the consumer, but a tax on site values will make land cheaper because it will compel its use.

He went on to tell a story of Tolstoy, in which cattle penned in a small enclosure begin to gore each other. A sympathetic passer-by gives them grass, which Tolstoy likened to the charity that ignores the basic cause of the problem. An appropriate tale, as the landless masses of Europe were about to slaughter each other once again!

At the same meeting no less than 36 MPs were proposed as Vice-Presidents of the Fellowship, including such prominent figures as Hugh Dalton, George Lansbury, Aneurin Bevan and Arthur Henderson. It is not recorded whether any of them accepted. Talks, however, were arranged by MPs and others on such matters as war policy and agriculture. About this time there were over fifty MPs pledged to support land value taxation and, according to Fellowship records, 'seven who thoroughly understand the Philosophy of Henry

George'. This was encouraging, but a far cry from the days of the Liberal government's 1909 budget.

When war with Germany began in September 1939, the School inevitably was forced to curtail its activities. Some members of the Fellowship joined the armed forces – Leon MacLaren was given the low medical class of C3 and undertook civil duties – and for a while no classes were held. Attempts to restart them were set back in 1940 by the Blitz on London. The annual report of the Executive described London as 'bright in the lurid glare of the burning docks'. When premises were found overlooking Buckingham Palace gardens, to be shared with another organisation, they were promptly bombed. Undaunted, the School booked evenings in a restaurant, and sent out advertisements to such bodies as Co-operative Societies, the Workers' Educational Association, the Labour Party, the Liberal Party, the Left Book Club, the Engineering Union, the Fabian Society, the City Literary Institute and the Peace Pledge Union. Lectures for the Fellowship were arranged, such as 'How to Pay for the War' by Josiah Wedgwood. When he failed to appear, Leon MacLaren, typically, gave an impromptu speech on the subject.

Groups gradually enrolled for the courses despite war conditions. Members of the armed forces, including some Canadians, attended. As the fortunes of war changed for the better, the School looked for new premises. In 1944 it found an attractive Regency house in the quiet cul-de-sac of Suffolk Street, just off Trafalgar Square, which became the School's home for about thirty years. Significantly, Adam Smith, generally regarded as the founder of the subject of Economics, had lived in Suffolk Street in the late eighteenth century, before the street was rebuilt by John Nash.

Now began the practice of caring thoroughly for School premises. Students laboured to overcome the water damage from the fire brigade's efforts to deal with incendiary bombs, to remove coal from the cellar and to clamber up scaffolding to decorate the frontage of the house. The basement was let to an actors' club. Sir Ralph Richardson became a firm friend of Andew MacLaren.

Serious work continued on developing the Economics material. This became essential when a decision was taken to offer a correspondence course, in view of the obstacles in the way of expansion of evening classes in wartime. Material was written in the form of a series of essays, accompanied by questions to which the student was asked to respond with answers posted to a tutor, who marked them.

A copy of Henry George's *Progress and Poverty* was sent with the material, and references to this helped with the answers. Model answers were also supplied.

The opening paragraph of the first essay gives a taste of what was offered:

> If any real social progress is to be made, there must first be a more general understanding of the great natural laws governing man's relations in society. In the modern complex world, social problems will only be solved if they are approached in a scientific manner, which will discover and clearly define the simple central principles of the intricate mechanism of present-day society.

Considerable space was given to criticising the nineteenth-century wage fund theory and the doctrines of Thomas Malthus. Academic Economics, of course, had moved on a long way from these, especially since the publication of J.M. Keynes' *General Theory of Employment, Interest and Money* in 1936, but what the School sought to eliminate were ideas that were still prevalent in society generally. In particular, the wage fund theory exemplified the idea that capital employs labour, with the implication that employment and output rest primarily upon the growth of capital, whilst the Malthusian assumption was that natural resources, or land, are scarce and severely limit the creation and distribution of wealth.

In contrast to these underlying ideas, the School taught that land and labour are the primary factors of production, that there would be no scarcity were these both free to co-operate fully, and that capital, defined accurately as 'wealth used to produce more wealth', is the servant of labour. Claims upon wealth, including shares, bonds and money, are quite distinct from capital, and merely draw their income, if any, from the output created by land and labour.

Some careful analysis supported these views. With the aid of diagrams, it was shown that when work is applied to land, rent is created as a surplus as soon as any inferior land is brought into use. Given that work is of a constant effort and quality, the product is less on the inferior land; hence the surplus on the better land cannot be attributed to labour but must derive from the superior qualities, such as fertility or location, of the land. This fundamental point, incontrovertible if not obscured by complications involving capital, money, etc, became the hallmark of the School's teaching on Economics. Its absence from the subject as taught and practised elsewhere meant

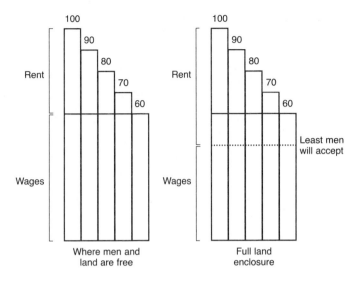

Rent and Wages

that there was little common ground on which the School could meet the world of outside economists and those trained by them, such as many contemporary politicians.

Why is this so fundamental? The material gave a categorical answer:

> In settling the law of rent, we automatically settle the law of wages. Where land is free, wages will be determined by what a man can obtain working for himself on the best natural opportunity open to use.

In other words, the full product of the marginal land, i.e. the least productive land in use, is wages, whilst the surpluses above this on all other land in use is rent. This holds true in industries where labour co-operates in large numbers and where capital is used on a large scale.

Land, however, is not free, certainly not in Britain in the twentieth century. The material acknowledged this:

> Where land is all enclosed by a few members of the community, wages are then determined by the least an unemployed man will accept for his work. Where, as during industrial depressions, unemployment sharply rises, competition for work will intensify, and wages will fall. During a trade boom, when men are absorbed back

into industry, the competition for work will be eased, and wages will rise, but as a man who has nothing but his labour is dependent on wages for his very existence, where all land is enclosed, wages must drop to a very low level. They cannot, of course, drop lower than the minimum return a man will accept in order to live, and what men will accept as a minimum will differ in different countries according to the traditions and education of the people…

It was emphasised that the law that determines the apportionment of output between rent and wages continues to operate, whether land is free or enclosed, i.e. in unconditional private ownership. The outcome, however, varies dramatically with the change from land being freely available to when it is withheld from use by private landholders. An analogy illustrated this. The laws of aerodynamics hold true for a well-designed aircraft, as for a faulty one that crashes. Societies can choose between free land with full employment and high wages, on one hand, and enclosed land with a minority of rich landholders, unemployment and low wages, on the other. This does not imply that wages cannot rise at all with technological progress, for example, under enclosed land. What cannot rise is the proportion received as wages. As societies get richer, rent as a share gets larger, if there is no free land.

Much care was taken with definitions, in accordance with Leon MacLaren's initial resolution to found a School whose members would not suffer from confusion of terms. Rent of land was distinguished from the rent paid for land and buildings. Payments for buildings cover the cost of depreciation, repairs, services and so on, and therefore do not include rent in the sense meant by economists. An example also demonstrated that a leaseholder may receive rent that is mistakenly identified as profits. In Regent Street a lease of fifty years expired; whereupon the landlords raised the annual payment from £45,000 to £540,000. The former 'profits' received by the leaseholders were now taken by the landlords. During the fifty years the rent received by the leaseholder, after paying £45,000 per annum, had steadily increased.

Wages were defined as all rewards for labour, whether called wages, salaries, fees, commissions or whatever. Capital was defined as 'wealth used to produce more wealth', whilst wealth itself is things produced to satisfy human desires. Money, bills of exchange, mortgages and similar certificates of title are not wealth but claims upon it. The consistent application of this distinction enabled the School to clarify many issues that have muddied the waters of economic debate, such as the proper role of credit and money.

Nevertheless, the treatment of interest in these early years of the public courses was more problematic, and needed to be revised at a later date. For at this point the definition given was, 'Interest is that share of wealth which a man obtains because of his control of capital.' Much play was made of the argument that the wage fund theory implied that wages and interest varied inversely. The material claimed that the opposite was the case, i.e. wages and interest rise and fall together as the trade cycle improves or worsens. It was argued, for example, that in the serious depression of the 1930s wages and interest both fell as a result of the lack of output and trade. Demand for both labour and capital was low. This definition of interest, however, led to complications. If money was borrowed to buy land, the interest paid to the lender was described as rent because it was paid out of the rent of the land. If it was borrowed to buy capital, then it was regarded as interest, as it was now paid out of the return on the capital. This view did not deal with the question of whether capital receives a return in its own right at all. Nor with the question of whether money loans receive interest as a return on the money lent, rather than on whatever assets are bought with the loan. The clearing up of these difficulties took some time, yet demonstrated the School's readiness to revise its teaching with further study and experience.

Searching questions were asked of the students following the correspondence course. For example: 'If the user of the land is also the owner is there rent?' 'Can any piece of land have a value if there is other land of equal productiveness that can be had without cost?' 'Can increasing population raise rent without reducing the margin of cultivation?' 'If the worker is engaged in an enterprise the product of which cannot be put into exchange immediately, are his wages advanced from capital?' 'During a strike what happens to capital, to labour, to land?' The model answer to the last question was typically concise: 'Capital wastes, labour is starved and landowners wait.' An explanatory note, however, was added.

Henry George's *Progress and Poverty* was often quoted. His evocative 'Savannah Story', telling how the USA developed with the westward movement of settlement, became a leading demonstration of the law of rent and its implications for a fast-growing economy, where land ceases to be freely available. A paraphrase of George explained this:

> Where modern land law prevails, the owners of the farms situated in the centre of the community will have made a fortune, as happened in New York, Chicago, Sydney, Melbourne and other such places. Observing the great fortunes to be had for nothing, men will soon begin to appropriate large areas of land with the sole purpose of awaiting the growth of the community and gathering to themselves the huge rents resulting from this growth. This movement will have a disastrous effect on the fortunes of new settlers. They will find the land near to the centres of population appropriated for hundreds of miles, and they will be forced either to start new settlements or to compete for work in the towns. This competition for work and this forcing down of the margin of cultivation will put the new settlers back into the position of the first one. Poverty will arise, and wages will slump, with the inevitable result that rents will increase. When all the land is enclosed, new settlers, or the children of men already there, will not even have the alternative of opening up a new area. Their only means of livelihood will be obtaining work on someone else's land. Thus will grow up a great class of people who, having no means of livelihood but their bare labour, are reduced to want and distress.

Having established the basic definitions and principles of the subject, the correspondence course went on to deal with a matter still very much in the minds of students, despite the exigencies of war; namely the occurrence of industrial depressions as witnessed in the previous decade. An explanation was given based on the consequences of unrestrained private ownership of land. When the economy is performing well, speculators enter the markets for goods and land. As prices rise the production of goods responds with higher output that tends to reduce the profits of the speculator, but in the case of land there is no equivalent response, since the supply of land is more or less fixed. Land prices continue to rise and at a faster rate than those of goods and services, thus encouraging land speculation. But land prices enter into the costs of industry, both as rent paid to landlords and as payments for the capital cost of land. Firms must either raise their prices or close down. Hence inflation and closures impinge upon the apparent prosperity of the boom. Sooner or later speculation in land reaches a turning point, as land prices become unsustainable. Then a rapid decline sets in. Confidence evaporates;

credit is less available, production falls; heavy unemployment occurs. Some investors continue to buy land rather than invest in productive capital, which further delays any recovery. Eventually even land prices fall considerably, so that industry can begin to revive with lower costs of land, labour and capital. The key to this analysis is the unique status of land as unconditional private property. If it can become an object of speculation, it becomes the cause of industrial depression, whilst remaining the source of all production when combined with labour.

Following this, the course took up the question of property itself. Its conclusion was as follows:

> Every man has an equal right to land. Every man has an absolute right to the full product of his labour. Every man has a right of access to land and of exclusive use of it, provided he pays to the community the full rent of the land and keeps the land in good condition. The rent is the natural resource of public revenue and the foundation of public property... This is the law of property.

Behind this statement lay, not only the ideas of Henry George, but also the study by senior members of the Fellowship of such authors as John Locke, the French physiocrats (such as Quesnay), William Blackstone, Adam Smith and David Ricardo. The questions that arose from it were challenging, e.g. 'What constitutes the rightful basis of property?' 'What is the origin of land titles?' 'What is the difference between the robbery of rent and the robbery of an automobile or a sum of money?' The model answer to the last one was:

> The theft of wealth ceases with the act. A car cannot be twice stolen. But the robbery of rent goes on from day to day and grows more serious as the productive powers of labour increase.

In the light of these principles of private and public property the course went on to outline English land law, including features like tenants' rights and their infringement by landlords, and the question of security of tenure. It then discussed the proposal by Henry George for the taxation of land values. This was not seen as a panacea:

> It is a means of securing to the community the full rent of land, but in itself it does not secure to the individual the right of access to land, the right of security of tenure, nor does it have any relation to his rights against his neighbours and his duties to them.

Yet taxing the annual rent of land, when compared with the existing tax system in the UK was certainly exhorted on the grounds that tax should bear lightly on industry, fall equally on all citizens, be easy and cheap to collect, be certain, and not be capable of being passed on to others. Above all, it would enable the rent of land, created by the community, to be collected for the community.

The course ended with a warning that much was still to be learned about the fundamentals of Economics. Trade, prices, competition and monopoly, money, the role of government and other topics were still to be examined; and indeed the School has continued to investigate and teach the principles of these, whilst developing the central themes of land tenure and taxation. Ending with a radical flourish, the material claimed that were land and labour to operate in conditions of justice, and rent to be used as the natural fund of taxation, men and women would become free, independent and self-supporting, no longer needing public charity in the form of the dole, subsidies and all the apparatus of a Welfare State. Already the School was looking to the realisation of a full and rewarding life for all. It had begun with the study of Economics. It was soon to find that the path led beyond to yet broader and deeper fields of enquiry.

Outside London there were new developments. Classes in Economics were held in Stoke-on-Trent, under the energetic leadership of Andrew MacLaren, still MP for Burslem but also working for the wartime Ministry of Supply. Other branches were opened at Bath, Chelmsford, Manchester, Brighton and a few venues round London. In 1942 a significant change of name was made, reflecting the intention to promote a distinctive approach to Economics, free of association even with such a respected figure as Henry George. His name was dropped from the title, which became 'The School of Economic Science', the final word denoting a belief in the existence of natural laws in the subject and in a method of direct observation free from personal opinion and vested interest. In London there were now 350 students. About the same number took the correspondence course, whilst an ambitious Executive aimed at four thousand, and ran an advertising campaign in major cities. Meetings were held with speeches by both the MacLarens, R.R. Stokes and Josiah Wedgwood, and letters were sent to the press and to what were thought to be sympathetic movements, like trade unions and women's societies.

A new venture at this time was the publication of a journal called *Basis*, giving an analytical review of the news and explaining the economic basis underlying current problems. It was produced every few weeks from the Summer of 1943. The small editorial board was led, predictably, by Leon MacLaren. In view of wartime restrictions, *Basis* was remarkably well printed, and covered a wide range of subjects.

A report on the 1943 Finance Bill recorded an amendment proposed by R.R. Stokes condemning the absence of any tax on 'the economic rent of community-created values of all land – for which we are fighting.' The government's reply was that the treatment of land was a 'highly complicated matter on which no decisions had yet been taken.' Andrew MacLaren wrote an article on education, which, he suggested, should be concerned

> more with a way of life than a way in life. It has a twofold purpose: to bring out the latent faculties of a child and to impart to it the knowledge of past experience. Vocational training, though important, is secondary to the main objective: the quickening of the spiritual faculties.

A book on German economic policy was reviewed. It showed how the German government had used industrial cartels to control industry at home and to infiltrate foreign economies. The chemical firm I.G. Farben had become a 'business partner of the Nazis'. The League of Nations was seen by *Basis* to have failed by paying insufficient attention to Economics. Monopoly and cartels had grown without restraint: 'private monopoly of land and its minerals is a crime'.

Some editions of *Basis* carried brief pen portraits of great men. Winston Churchill, for all his endeavours in the Second World War, was praised as much for his efforts in the 1909 budget campaign, when he had 'correlated free trade with free access to natural opportunities' and had argued that 'if you have free trade and a vicious land system, the benefits of trading are nullified.'

Unfortunately the quality of the journalism and production of *Basis* was not matched by its sales organisation. It had several hundred subscribers, but nevertheless debts mounted, and it closed down after about a year. One of its final articles, entitled 'Planners Uber Alles', vilified the growing tendency in Britain towards a planned economy. Controlling factory developments, holding prices and wages down and directing workers' mobility between occupations and localities were all 'features of a Fascist system.' *Basis* was to have a second lease of life, but for now the war and a lack of marketing ability had struck it down.

In other respects, too, the later years of the war were difficult for the School. Many senior members joined the armed forces. Leon MacLaren served as a Labour councillor in Kings Cross. Despite the fact that course fees were now charged, finances were strained to the limit. A lease for No 11 Suffolk Street cost £750 with an annual rent of £350, which required a bank loan and generous contributions from members, notably from the President, Stokes. Lectures were given on subjects related to the war, like 'Transition to Peace', 'Economic Conditions in the Far East' and 'Central Control: is it Necessary?' but there was a fall in student attendance, particularly when the School refused to give certificates, which were demanded by people worried about post-war unemployment. Resources were found, nevertheless, to send copies of Henry George's *Social Problems* to British prisoners of war in Germany. The German authorities refused to take *Progress and Poverty*.

One response to the School's decline was the production of a textbook, written by Leon MacLaren. This work, his only major publication despite his writing a great deal of material for both Economics and Philosophy groups over very many years, was called *Nature of Society*, and presented a concise but comprehensive view of the distinctive Economics teaching as it had developed to date. The style was unadorned, the reasoning somewhat judicial and the terms and concepts gave scant regard to the theories of academic Economics. It marked, however, a definite advance in the School's contribution to Economics in several respects.

Firstly, it offered a systematic account of the principles already developed relating to rent, wages, capital, credit, money and taxation. All this was more or less in accord with the teaching of Henry George. But, in addition, as its title suggests, the book gave a central place to the relation of the individual to the whole community, emphasising that the very purpose of the latter is to give full expression to the inherent natural qualities of every man and woman. This is the end to be served by the removal of social impediments, such as the private appropriation of the rent of land. For free land and fair taxation release the creative talent of those who work.

A major step was taken also with the clarification of interest payments. This subject had been a stumbling block for many students.

MacLaren now corrected the view that interest was a natural return on capital. Instead, he showed that interest is simply a charge made for a loan of money:

> Clearly, the power of the lender to command interest has nothing to do with the use to which the loan is put. Whether the borrower uses it to build a factory or acquire a dwelling house, whether he spends it on tools of his trade or gambling on horses, will make no difference... The coupling of interest with capital has been an unfortunate error prolific in its progeny of falsehoods. It arises from confusing the power to exact payment for loans with the use to which some of the loans are put... It gives to the idea of a loan a quality it should not possess, a suggestion of productiveness and of social benefit, obscuring the indebtedness and dependence which the loan so plainly advertises.[1]

Such a view, implying that capital, as wealth used in the production of further wealth, is not a factor of production in its own right, but merely stored up labour and land, marked a definite break with Georgist doctrines. At the same time it opened up an understanding of capitalism that also became a leading feature of the School's economic principles. For, once interest was taken to be just a payment extracted from debtors for money loans, the modern structure of industry could be seen afresh. Capitalists become nothing more than lenders, or creditors, providing the money that the actual producers of goods and services lack. The true place of the entrepreneur as financier is revealed:

> No matter how brilliant and conscientious others may be, if their calling demands expensive equipment and they have not command of wealth with which to acquire it, they will, perforce, work as employees, (who) will be employed by the financier to manage and sustain the industries under his control... In a community where wages are depressed to the least labourers are willing to accept, but where labourers are not content to work with primitive or crude instruments, then the financier is bound to rank high in importance and his ideas and way of life will be one of the formative influences in thought and practice.[2]

'The complex and paradoxical structure' of the limited liability company, although now the dominant form of industrialised western

---

1 Leon MacLaren, *Nature of Society and Other Essays*, School of Economic Science, p.45.
2 *Ibid.*, pp.67-8.

economies, is really 'a fictitious personality separate from those of its members, built up primarily to protect borrowers from their creditors.' It encourages enterprising men to take on heavy responsibilities, raises funds to equip large numbers of employees, undertakes leases of land on onerous conditions and submits to heavy taxation. None of which would be necessary were wages at their natural level of the full product at the margin of production. This analysis of MacLaren thoroughly undermined the conventional view of capitalist economies as highly productive systems created by free enterprise and the accumulation of capital. On the contrary, they inhibit the potential growth that free land and free labour would yield with the benefit of modern advances in technology.

Yet *Nature of Society* never loses sight of the fundamentals of Economics. A story, similar to one told by Lloyd George, illustrated the irrationality of both the rating system and private receipt of land values. A house seller demanded a very high price for his house. The buyer enquired why it was so much. 'The site is bounded by two main roads, has main drainage, water, gas and electricity laid on, is near to the public park and close to the railway', was the reply. The buyer was impressed and agreed to the price. Shortly after he found a local government official assessing the house. When challenged, he said that he was valuing it for rates. 'What do I have to pay rates for?', asked the buyer. 'Why, for the main roads, the water, the public park and the other amenities,' replied the official.

Writing this book cost Leon MacLaren a considerable effort. For all its apparent simplicity, it was a profoundly original piece of work. Much of the course material on which it was based had in fact been written by him in the first place, but when he had nearly completed it, he experienced a crisis that he later described as 'standing before an abyss.' He saw no way of writing a conclusion. It was as though all his intellectual insight and energy was exhausted. He had nothing to say. His health was seriously affected, and he retired briefly to the country for a rest.

Once more seemingly chance events came to his rescue. He met a fellow author, named Peter Goffin, who was also just completing a book, called *The Realm of Art*. This was a quite learned and eclectic survey of a wide range of ideas about the nature of humanity, society, art, science and related areas, like religion, evolution, creativity and free will. These were rather loosely strung together by a very broad definition of art as all those activities that distinguish Man from other animals. It contained, unsystematically, elements of Philosophy, such as discussions of reality, mind and matter, knowledge and, perhaps most importantly in view of the later development of the School, of consciousness.

What particularly appealed to MacLaren when he read the book were the quotations. Goffin drew upon these almost as though they were collectively what inspired him to write. They included both Eastern and Western sources, such as Tao Te Ching, Radhakrishnan, Chuang Tze, Einstein, Jeans and, significantly, P.D. Ouspensky, the pupil and successor of George Gurdieff. Amidst this medley of ideas were some that struck a note in accord with what MacLaren himself was experiencing at the time. Perhaps it was the emphasis upon Man's potential for growth and creativity; or the concept of human nature as rooted in love and harmony rather than in hatred and conflict; or the evaluation of Eastern ideas; or simply the centrality of consciousness. Certainly quotations like that of Sir James Jeans must have appealed strongly to the musician in MacLaren, who was a pianist of some ability and much later a composer:

> The laws which nature obeys are less suggestive of those which a machine obeys in its motion than of those which a musician obeys in writing a fugue, or a poet in composing a sonnet.[3]

A quote from Ouspensky may also have made its mark:

> Noumenal means apprehended by the mind; and the characteristic property of the things of the noumenal world is that they cannot be comprehended by the same method by which the things of the phenomenal world are comprehended... It is necessary to remember that the noumenon and the phenomenon are not two different things; but merely different aspects of one and the same thing. Thus, each phenomenon is the finite expression, in the sphere of knowledge through the organs of sense, of something infinite.[4]

There were two vital outcomes to this meeting of two authors in search of an ending. Most immediately, MacLaren completed his book with a chapter called 'The Law of Human Progress'. Its

---

3 James Jeans, *The Mysterious Universe*, Cambridge University Press, 1931, quoted in Lindsay Drummond, *The Realm of Art*, 1946, p.107
4 P.D. Ouspensky, *Tertium Organum*, Kegan Paul, 1937, quoted in Lindsay Drummond, *The Realm of Art*, p.82

opening sentence – 'The purpose of being born is to live, and of living, to live more abundantly' – echoed one from *The Realm of Art*. It continued by moving beyond any notion of Economics as normally conceived, for it briefly examined the means of knowledge, the importance of practice and the power of choice. The conclusion pointed the way to the next step that the School was to take, a step into philosophical enquiry that would lead its members into a world not envisaged by students of Economics:

> Though a society is at war with itself, the retrogression may be arrested and the conditions of progress restored if the members of the community will use their natural powers to understand their predicament, to discover in which elemental respects they are deny-ing their own nature. There has been of late a welcome flowering of philosophical thought, drawing its inspiration largely from those old eastern civilizations which gained such deep understanding in the subjective mode, and, if this prospers, it may enrich and balance the intensely objective knowledge of the natural sciences.[5]

The second outcome was an invitation to Peter Goffin to give a series of lectures on Philosophy. The School's executive committee reported that these were successful. By their means 'a common ground for all human activity may be found and people of creative ability may be attracted.' What became clear was that the School could not mark time by limiting its studies to the field of Econom-ics. Having progressed to the level of natural law, it now experienced the ineluctable necessity to investigate human nature itself, to ask philosophical questions about mind, spirit and existence. Leon MacLaren, and the School of which he had become the intellectual leader, were together ascending from the study of Man in society to the study of Man in himself.

Amendments to the constitution of the School in August 1944 reflected this development. All references to the specific teaching of Henry George were removed, notably the advocacy of a tax on land values, now seen as just one way, albeit a beneficial one, of collecting the rent of land for the community. The new primary objective became 'to promote the study of the natural laws governing the relations between men in society and all other matters ancillary thereto.' Political activity by the School itself, though not by its members, was now explicitly rejected.

5 Leon MacLaren, *Nature of Society*, p.169.

This last amendment may not have pleased Andrew MacLaren. Whilst continuing to give lectures in Burslem and elsewhere, he remained in Parliament, though increasingly at loggerheads with the Labour Party. In 1942 the Beveridge Report had appeared, written by the erstwhile director of the London School of Economics and an enthusiastic follower of John Maynard Keynes. Its strong recommendation of a programme for the amelioration of poverty, rather than the removal of its causes, infuriated the elder MacLaren. How often had he exclaimed that the rich will do anything for the poor except get off their backs! For him, charity offered to those who were able-bodied yet unemployed was an insult and an injustice. Only those unable to care for themselves should receive charity. Every fit man or woman should find work readily available either on their own account or as an employee. If they did not, then there were obstacles in society that stood in the way. And unconditional private property in land was the principal one.

In March 1943 Andrew wrote to Arthur Greenwood, chairman of the Parliamentary Labour Party:

> For a number of years in the House of Commons it has been noticeable that in parliamentary action the Labour Party has attempted to mitigate the results of poverty by compromise and political expedients which did not fundamentally challenge the root causes of poverty and economic insecurity... Believing that all men have equal rights to life, which implies the equal rights of all human beings to the enjoyment of those gifts freely provided by nature and necessary to man's existence – land, light, water and air – I hold that it is the first and primary duty of workers' representatives in Parliament to destroy utterly the private ownership in any of these elements... If these principles are no longer vital to the Party then I have no alternative but to withdraw from the Party in the House...[6]

His letter went unheeded. The Labour Party had indeed lost sight of its origins in Christian Socialism and in the early Fabian Society, which had for a while adhered to the teaching of Henry George. In 1945 Andrew MacLaren stood for Parliament as an independent, and lost his deposit. Never again would he sit in the Commons. They had lost their only unflinching advocate of free land. He had sacrificed a political career for a principle. A Burslem newspaper recorded the following extract from a speech he made in the town that Summer:

6 John Stewart, *Standing for Justice*, p.81.

This land of ours would have been the property of the German invaders had it not been for the effort of the common people of this country. Whose land is it now – now we have saved it from the invader? England is God's free gift to the people of England.[7]

At this time, too, there was the threat of legal action by the London School of Economics concerning the name 'The School of Economic Science'. When the School took legal advice, it was assured that there was little danger of a successful action, which led it to the conclusion that the underlying reason for the dispute was the belief amongst academic economists at the LSE that the School was a propaganda vehicle for the Henry George movement with a dogmatic and biased approach to the subject of Economics. No doubt the School's views of what the LSE taught was a kind of mirror image of this. No one considered whether any reconciliation of their opposing theories was possible. In the twentieth century, academia sidelined Henry George as an outmoded amateur, whilst more or less ignoring the School; and on its part, the School, particularly Leon MacLaren, insisted that academic Economics was beyond the pale of reason.

With the devastating use of two atomic bombs at Hiroshima and Nagasaki, the Second World War came to an end. Britain rejoiced at the triumph of the Allies, but the people knew that hardships still lay ahead, as the country adjusted itself to the austerities of an economy shattered by war and a new world order dominated by the USA and the Soviet Union. A Labour government, led by Clement Attlee, would set about implementing an enlarged Welfare State, nationalisation of utilities and controls on many aspects of the economy, such as foreign exchange. When Andrew MacLaren asked Ernest Bevin, the dockers' leader now made Foreign Secretary, what had happened to the old Labour belief in taxing land values, he was told that the Labour Party had moved on beyond such outdated policies. Both World Wars had taken their toll of the understanding of many social and political issues, even though, chastened by suffering and hardships, people were perhaps more compassionate. Henry George had become little more than a footnote in histories of economic thought.

What then of the School? Attendance at the Economics classes had fallen off in the last years of the war. Would it revive? The small

7 *Ibid.*, p.85.

beginning made with the Philosophy classes based on Peter Goffin's book offered a new direction. Those who had struggled to keep alive the light of comprehension of natural law through the darkness of world war, who retained a faith in reason whilst the recognised authorities seemed to have lost it, realised that the School required a new impulse that would meet the needs of the post-war world. It was to come from unexpected sources.

CHAPTER THREE

The Development
of Economics

L IKE BRITAIN itself, the School in the immediate post-war
period struggled to make ends meet. Debts of £3,000 had
accumulated, whilst fees remained at one guinea per term.
Such problems led to the demise of some of the courses in the
provinces. The Treasurer even proposed that the School should close
down. But devoted work in London, plus some financial help from
the President, Stokes, kept the courses going there, and even enabled
special lectures to be given that raised extra revenue. Subjects
covered included 'The Road to Recovery', 'Is Civilisation in
Decline?', 'The End of Art', 'English Law in India' (by the Chief
Judge of Karachi), 'The Economic Crisis' and the policies of the
three main political parties. A Philosophy course tutored by Peter
Goffin or Leon MacLaren attracted a modicum of students, whilst
Economics numbers built up to several hundred a term. By 1949
debts were paid off. New poster advertisements appeared on the
London Underground, and proved a long-term success with their
unadorned appeal to the reason of metropolitan commuters.

The MacLarens were not alone in the School in their forceful
advocacy of economic principles. Other senior members played
significant parts, though not without some friction. Ronald Burgess,
for example, was a professional economist, later to work with the
well-known Professor Colin Clark and to lecture at York University.
As Treasurer of the School, he disapproved of Leon MacLaren's
tendency to spend money whenever he thought it was necessary.
Kenneth Jupp, a barrister with an Oxford classics degree and an MC
from Anzio, and later a High Court judge, became too reliant, in
Leon's opinion, on the philosophy of Plato. Both Burgess and Jupp
helped to develop the Economics course by original research. They

gave lectures on such subjects as the economic state of Britain, raw materials, the development of economic thought, monopolies, land enclosures, and industrial history.

This was indeed a time of consolidation before the decisive step forward in the development of Philosophy. Andrew MacLaren did not approve of this incipient change of direction, but Leon realised that the School's Economics teaching led naturally towards an enquiry into the essence of Man, and that such a philosophical venture would fulfil the desperate need of those who found the scepticism and rootlessness of the twentieth century oppressive. Victory in the war had made possible a life of enlightenment and hope for the people of Britain. Was this opportunity to be wasted, as it had been in the locust years between the wars? And yet, as the dawn of a new Philosophy approached, there were few signs of its imminence. In the Autumn of 1947, for example, only four students enrolled for the Philosophy course.

Leon MacLaren, now in his late thirties, still hankered after political action. He stood as a Liberal candidate at Yeovil in 1950 and at Hendon South in 1951, but the Liberal Party was at its nadir. Moreover, he did not have the common touch of his father on a political platform. This was demonstrated after his defeat at Yeovil:

> [MacLaren], before stalking off the platform in disgust, having lost his deposit, declaimed 'People of Yeovil, you have been handed the keys of liberty and you have dashed them to the ground!'[1]

Some time later marital failure also beset him, when he was divorced from his first wife Joyce – they had two daughters.

His unfailing promotion of equity in Economics was shown with great clarity by a lecture on justice that he delivered at Christmas 1951, which was published fifty years later. Trying to remove one injustice by introducing another is useless, he argued. The Welfare State is a means of plundering some to relieve the poverty of others. 'The whole frightful mechanism is bred of injustice.' Justice is to render to every man his due, which we acknowledge in the field of the civil duties not to assault, imprison, steal or libel, but ignore in economic life, where we lack a clear concept of duties. It is unjust that some work to maintain those who do not:

1 Paddy Ashdown, *A Fortunate Life*, Aurum Press, 2009, p.192.

The pathetic masses, still loyal to their erstwhile leaders, are so restrained as to be truly British. Their claims for more pay are arbitrated upon for months, at the end of which they get half of what they ask. Meanwhile prices rise to swallow the whole of their claim before it is granted. Just to make sure, the government puts the bank rate up and swells unearned income.[2]

Few people own houses, few are tenants of land where they work. Their tools and materials are not their own. 'They are strangers in their own land.' Whilst in the British colonies the injustice is compounded by alien rule:

> In Africa a terrible game is being played out slowly. British governments have taken the best of the land in many parts of Africa and reserved it for white people only. The rich mineral resources of the continent have been acquired by two powerful industrial groups, so that they own all the minerals except those still under public control and some part of the coal.[3]

Our nation is divided into two mutually incomprehensible parts. Yet our political and legal traditions, he concluded, preserve the peace. In that remains our chief hope:

> Britain has led the way. She has shown how simply, how beautifully, political justice can be created and maintained, and how all the tussles and tyrannies that are associated with political tyranny can be removed. With our freedom of speech, our tradition for restraint, our understanding of political justice, we are in an ideal position to carry our work one step further forward, and say, 'Here is the way economic justice may be created and preserved.'[4]

This lecture was delivered shortly after MacLaren's defeat in the general election at Hendon South. It demonstrated the breadth of outlook and enquiry into causes that made him an unsuitable candidate in the eyes of an electorate looking for quick remedies and accustomed to a two party system. By now it must have been clear to him that his vocation lay, not in politics, but in making available to the whole nation a new way of life.

For the time being, however, Economics continued to be the main subject that the School had to offer. In the early fifties about

2 Leon MacLaren, *Justice*, School of Economic Science, 2001, p.14.
3 *Ibid.*, p.15.
4 *Ibid.*, p.20.

twelve hundred Economics students came each year. *Basis* was launched again; now as a weekly journal demanding a great deal of work. It was advertised in the *Manchester Guardian* and the *New Statesman*. A young journalist called John Allen, who would play an important part in the School for fifty years, became the editor. In the first copy a leading article claimed that workers' participation in the firm of Scott, Bader and Co. Ltd., manufacturers of paint and plastics, could become a model for the reform of industrial structure in Britain. Employees owned 90 per cent of the shares and one half of a general council was elected by workers.

Later editions included articles on Asia and Africa:

> The shadow of Malthus has fallen upon Asia. The pernicious doctrine that the growth of population is outstripping the means of subsistence is still being advocated. What is happening is that everywhere people are being prevented from using the natural resources which would provide them with a living. In no Asian or Middle Eastern country is there a lack of land to cultivate... but there is a vicious system of land tenure which robs the peasant farmer of the fruits of his industry... The peasant farmer exists from season to season on money lent by the landlord at usurious rates of interest.
>
> The treasures of Africa could be opened up to an impoverished world. The way to do this is to let the Africans get at Africa and assist them with knowledge of new techniques and new ideas to fit them for the competitive life of the modern world. The way it will not be achieved is to enslave the people for the benefit of a few foreign concessionaires and moneylenders. Can a handful of rapacious and ruthless men be allowed to check the development of a continent? The tensions which are turning Africa into a melting-pot of hatred, suspicion and greed must be relaxed. The relief may be found in access to land. There is certainly plenty of it in Africa.

And in Malaya, where Britain was fighting Communist insurgents, the British government could end the war by giving to the people of Malaya the land held by the Sultans and by Europeans.

As before the new *Basis* only lasted a year. The last edition in April 1952 dealt with the inflation that was creeping into the British economy now that it was released from Socialist controls. The cause was explained in simple but penetrating terms: 'Inflation arises when money – i.e. titles to wealth and services – is put into circulation, but no wealth and services are made available in exchange.' Increasing taxation, it continued, forces marginal industries to raise their prices.

If the margin were relieved of tax, new output would break the monopolies and cartels. Such a reform would render superfluous the harmful monetary policies favoured by Conservative Chancellors. An article in the *Financial Times* had said that within twenty-five years British industry would either be under complete oligarchical control or the government would have nationalised all institutional investors. *Basis* recommended, as an alternative, that workers become owners.

But once more the quality of the writing was not backed up by proficiency in marketing, and so, despite a readership of about five hundred, *Basis* ceased as a journal and became instead an in-house news sheet. As such it was to continue for five more years.

In what turned out, in view of his subsequent pursuit of Philosophy, to be almost a swan song for Leon MacLaren's devotion to Economics, he gave a lecture in July 1952 entitled *The Function of Economics*. Its first lesson, he proposed, is that we seek in nature the bread of life – food, materials, knowledge and inspiration – and the more advanced our civilisation the more complete our dependence. Without electricity there would be immediate chaos. Men and women bring to nature their natural gifts, he continued, which can be cultivated only through a community in which each may specialise. In thus giving we may receive back what we need. But all who levy tribute from their fellow men disturb this balance, for when land is enclosed poverty is inevitable. The landless many are forced into dependence on the landed few. Then workers cannot equip themselves without recourse to a moneylender. Entrepreneurs, skilled in the art of borrowing on one hand and employing a workforce on the other, become the new masters of industry:

> All these dependencies on landlord, moneylender and employer, and the tribute of rent, interest and unearned profit, grow out of the first and continuing injustice, the enclosure of land. This is the substratum, the cause of weakness in the many and the power of tribute in the few. Without it, all would have to work for their living… The law of property in land is the most important economic institution in any community. If this is wrong, little will be right. It is fundamental.[5]

There followed a conclusion that explains how MacLaren was led naturally to an enquiry into Philosophy. If people are denied the use of their special gifts, are forced to do work they dislike and to live in

5 Leon MacLaren, *The Function of Economics*, The School of Economic Science, 1997, p.12.

poverty, nature may intervene to render them unaware of their anguish. 'How many of us walk about in a kind of twilight sleep, neither waking nor sleeping, our sensibility dulled?' Already, it seems, he had met a teaching that spoke of different levels of consciousness, of the prevalent state of 'waking sleep', from which only a special kind of memory and effort could draw one to a better condition.

Meanwhile, economic forces continued to play their inexorable game of successive cycles, induced by the speculative withholding of land from productive use:

> Now see where it has led us to. Watch the corrective forces of nature at work. Unearned incomes have gone too high, our economy is out of balance. How are they to be reduced? Simply by smashing industry. Let industry stop and then there is no unearned income, and that is what happens in every depression. The balance is restored by depression or war, one of the other, or revolution.

The revolution that was to come for Leon MacLaren and the School of Economic Science was of a different order. Out of the need to study the causes of injustice had arisen the prospect of a system of knowledge that transcended Economics and even justice itself. The search now was for nothing less than the truth itself.

6 *Ibid.*, p.18.

CHAPTER FOUR

Meeting
the Fourth Way

IN 1953 Leon MacLaren was introduced to Dr Francis Roles, the leader of the The Society for the Study of Normal Psychology (The Study Society) in West London, an organisation based upon the teaching of P.D. Ouspensky. MacLaren attended lectures at the Study Society, and was particularly struck by the use of diagrams that were similar to those he was developing for the School of Economic Science classes in Economics. The search for a wider and deeper understanding of Economics was clearly leading the School into new areas of philosophical thought.

Ouspensky was a Russian intellectual, who had written several books on esoteric ideas. In 1915 he had met G.I. Gurdjieff. Ouspensky described the effect of this meeting:

> Very soon I realised that I had met with a completely new system of thought surpassing all I knew before. This system threw quite a new light on psychology and explained what I could not understand before in esoteric ideas and school principles.[1]

Gurdjieff, a Greek-Armenian, had travelled extensively, especially in Central Asia, looking for a secret teaching that he believed contained the key to the meaning of human life. Ouspensky, too, had visited many places in Egypt, the Near East and India, but felt that he had failed in his quest, until he met Gurdjieff. Fragments of an unknown teaching were all that either man claimed to have discovered, but it was enough to inspire them to gather pupils and to form an organisation.

1 *The Bridge*, No 12, The Study Society, 1997, p.251.

Perhaps troubled by his master's erratic and impromptu style of teaching at the Institute for the Harmonious Development of Man at Fontainbleau, Ouspensky left Gurdjieff in 1924, and eventually opened his own school in London in 1931. During the Second World War he went to America and taught in New York. Shortly before his death in 1947, Ouspensky returned to gather together his British followers, instructing Dr Roles to look for a vital missing element in the system that he had refined since the first meeting with Gurdjieff.

Like the book of verbatim conversations published after Ouspensky's death, his teaching was known as the 'Fourth Way'. Gurdjieff had explained how a fakir trains himself through physical, often painful, disciplines, a monk though devotional methods, and a yogi through intellectual exercises. All of these require retirement from ordinary life. The Fourth Way, drawing on all three aspects, is for those not suited to withdraw from the business of earning a living and having a family. It is the way of the householder. Yet it is an ancient way, employing ideas and practices embodied in many of the great teachings of both East and West – the Sufis, the early Christians, the Brotherhood of the Common Life, the Masons and others. For at the heart of the Fourth Way are schools for those who seek escape from the meaningless charade of a life spent wholly in the pursuit of ephemeral ends, like pleasure, wealth or fame. Ouspensky portrayed the aim of his teaching in a brilliant analogy:

> Man is in prison, so what can he wish for, what can he desire? If he is a more or less sensible man, he can wish for only one thing – to escape. But even before he can formulate this desire, that he wants to escape, he must become aware that he is in prison. If he does not realize that he is in prison, he cannot wish to escape. Then, when he formulates this wish, he begins to realize the possibilities of escape, and he understands that, by himself, he cannot escape, because it is necessary to dig under walls, and things like that. He realizes that first of all he must have some people who would like to escape with him – a small group of people. So he realizes that a certain number of people can perhaps escape. But *all* cannot escape. One cannot and all cannot, but a small number of people can. Again, in what conditions? He comes to the conclusion that it is necessary to have help. Without that they cannot escape. They must have maps, files, tools and so on. So they must have help from outside.[2]

2 P.D. Ouspensky, *The Fourth Way*, Routledge & Kegan Paul, 1960, p.13.

To escape from the prison of ordinary life one must begin, asserted Ouspensky, with study of oneself. We think we know all about ourselves, whereas in reality we know very little. Why is this? The answer, upon which his whole system revolved, was that we are asleep. We think we are awake, when we are in fact lost in a kind of waking sleep. How often are we daydreaming, imagining, or living in the past or future, rather than being consciously present here and now, in this very moment? Therefore the first and cardinal direction of the teaching is to wake up:

> So, at the same time as self-observing, we try to be aware of our-selves by holding the sensation of 'I am here' – nothing more. And this is the fact that all Western psychology, without the smallest exception, has missed. Although many people came very near to it, they did not recognize the importance of this fact and did not realize that the state of man as he is can be changed – that man can remember himself, if he tries for a long time.[3]

One consequence of this prevalent sleep is that each person ascribes to himself an I, a selfhood, when in practice there are as many I's as there are desires and ideas. I intend one thing and do another. I want this, and a moment later want something else. There is no constant awareness, no single centre of one's existence that can properly be called I. This profound observation leads to a recognition that there are different levels of consciousness in Man. His inconstant 'waking' state is merely one stage above that of genuine sleep. Above it lies self-consciousness, when a man or woman has a permanent centre and higher powers, and above that is objective consciousness, of which we only have glimpses through great art, literature or other truly creative works.

Study of oneself reveals much more of what we ordinarily ignore. There are, for example, four centres that control all our actions, emotions and thoughts: the instinctive, moving, emotional and intellectual. In the state of relative sleep we confuse these, and interfere with their proper functioning. They work at quite different speeds, as we find if we try, say, to think our way into walking, which is controlled naturally by the moving centre. Observing, but not interfering with, these centres, helps to correct their operation.

Ouspensky laid great emphasis upon the malfunctioning of the emotional centre. In particular, negative emotions, like undue fear,

3 *Ibid.*, p.5.

anger, envy, shame and so on are highly destructive, and completely unnecessary. To deal with this he instructed his pupils to stop all expression of negative emotions. This was not to suppress them, merely to refrain from their outward expression. By so doing, he claimed, enormous saving of energy would take place, and emotion could in time be transformed into something positive and permanent that could inform a lifetime.

Underlying this practice was a principle that Ouspensky regarded as perhaps the most important of all his ideas, apart from that of simply waking up. This was to do and say nothing unnecessary. Especially he condemned unnecessary talk, which he saw as a huge waste of energy:

> Another useless function is talk; we talk too much. We talk and talk and talk, and we never really notice it. Generally we think we talk very little, much too little, but particularly those people who talk most think that they never talk. This is a very useful subject for watching. You will see how your day passes, how many mechanical things you say in certain conditions, how many other mechanical things in other conditions.[4]

Unnecessary also is what the system called inner considering. This is the habit of thinking and feeling about other people in ways that have no practical consequence, such as asking yourself what someone thinks of you, whether they like or dislike you, whether you are better or worse than them, and so on. Outer considering, on the contrary, is a valuable practice. By this one takes account of other people's needs, their situation and how they may be benefited. Indeed much of Ouspensky's teaching, paradoxically perhaps, was concerned with turning outwards and away from an introspective world of imaginings and false opinions. The latter led to what he called identification, the loss of self in identifying with some thought or feeling that takes over the consciousness in an individual, and ascribes to itself the name of I. 'I am miserable; I am clever; I am ignorant.' None are true.

How then are such obstacles as negative emotion, unnecessary talk and identification to be dealt with? Ouspensky had many practical answers, of which the most powerful was probably the giving of attention:

4 *Ibid.*, p.43.

A certain control of attention is necessary even in ordinary life. But attention can be drawn, or it can be controlled, and that is of quite a different value.[5]

This control of attention could be developed by physical work, so Ouspensky set his students many tasks at Lyne Place in Surrey, a substantial house and estate bought by his students, where he lived for many years. Such work yielded practical knowledge, as opposed to what he called theoretical and philosophical knowledge, which contained general ideas divorced from life itself. Practical knowledge gradually allowed the student to develop a 'magnetic centre', which kept him or her connected with the system itself and his or her own inner potential.

Work on oneself needs to be complemented by an understanding of the fundamental laws that govern the universe, including mankind. Modern science, claimed Ouspensky, has ignored two laws that determine how all events occur and how a sequence of events develops. Every event whatsoever requires three forces: active, passive and neutral. Usually it is the third of these that is overlooked, whereas action and resistance, for example, are usually recognised. In the case of human actions, the state of one's being or consciousness is the crucial third force.

Whilst the law of three controls a single event, a series of events comes under the law of seven. In a sequence there occur two critical points at which the direction changes. The musical octave is an illustration: between *mi* and *fa* and between *si* and *do* there are missing semi-tones. If this law is understood, account can be taken of it in one's own actions.

The Law of Seven explains that, if you know how and at what moment to do it, you can give an additional shock to an octave and keep the line straight. We can observe in human activity how people start to do one thing and after some time do quite a different thing, still calling it by the first name without noticing that things have completely changed. But in personal work, particularly in work connected with this system, we must learn how to keep these octaves from deviating, how to keep a straight line. Otherwise we shall not find anything.[6]

5 *Ibid.*, p.114.
6 *Ibid.*, p.17..

In an activity, like writing a book, there certainly occur periods when an extra effort is required to keep the work proceeding, most noticeably to bring it to a final conclusion.

Ideas about time were a major feature of Ouspensky's system. He taught that time has not one dimension but three. The first is the procession of time in a straight line from past to future. The second, only occasionally noticed in specific circumstances, is the dimension of cycles, the tendency of events to turn back to their origin and recur in a succession of similar cyclical phases. Most importantly for his practical teaching, Ouspensky emphasised the third dimension, the moment now. This moment is ever present; even our apparent excursions in thought into past and future occur in the present. Hence now is eternal; through it we find eternity, not by looking for an infinite future, which is no more than a dream based on a one-dimensional idea of time.

Gurdjieff is said to have remarked of Ouspensky that he could not rid himself of absorption with the idea of recurrence. The Russian had indeed written a novel about it, and his system made reference to it with considerable ingenuity. For example, when asked to explain the difference between reincarnation and recurrence, he replied:

> Recurrence is in eternity, but reincarnation is in time. It supposes that time exists apart from us and that we continue to exist in this after death. For instance, in Buddhism they take it that a man dies and is immediately born again, so that one life follows another, because this is easier to understand for ordinary people. But we have no evidence for the existence of time beyond our life. Time is life for each person, and it includes in itself all time, so that when life ends, time ends.[7]

As always, Ouspensky dwelt upon the practical aspect. How a student responds to school teaching will influence his next lifetime, and enable him to escape from a purely mechanical succession of lives. This doctrine drew upon a distinction between influences upon human life. They are of three kinds: A influences are the ordinary features met in daily life; B influences are those of a higher, more conscious, order, as found in great art, literature and religion; whilst C influences are those of special schools containing esoteric knowledge. Most people meet only the first kind; contact with the second

7 *Ibid.*, p.415.

may lead in a few cases to the third. 'A certain number of people can perhaps escape'.

There is no doubt that Ouspensky, affected perhaps by having personally witnessed some of the worst excesses of the Russian Revolution in 1917, was scornful about ordinary life and common people. Yet he did assert that, whilst not all could look for full development and freedom, anyone could who responded to the right influences and was prepared to work on themselves and with others. For humanity as a whole, he envisaged the strange function of forming an essential part of organic life on earth in transmitting energy within what he called 'the ray of creation'. This stretched from the Absolute to the Moon through All Worlds, All Suns, the Sun, the Planets and the Earth. To appreciate the significance of this one has to have a concept of scale:

> Without understanding how everything is connected and in what way the life of man on earth is connected with the planets and the Sun, we cannot understand man's position and his present life as it is.[8]

Ouspensky was a cultured man, who had worked as a journalist in Russia before the First World War, and written several books that embodied ideas of considerable scope, based on both artistic and scientific research. His deep insight into the need for humanity to wake out of a complacent sleep came at a time of enormous upheaval and suffering on a world scale, evinced by revolution, war and economic catastrophe. He had shown much courage in dangerous situations in Russia and immense perseverance in pursuing his studies and supporting his students. A personal friend described his appearance at meetings:

> He looked very stern. He would come into the assembled group, adjust his pince-nez, scrutinize the room and say: 'Well, any questions?' He was intelligent, a bundle of knowledge and energy… You had to be wary, for if the question was too theoretical he would ignore you and move on to the next.[9]

Physically Ouspensky was rather short and stocky, with a broad head and a look of serious concentration that, at least in photographs, gave an appearance of frowning. As he admitted to Dr Roles,

8 *Ibid.*, p.197.
9 Dorine Tolley, *The Power Within*, p.14.

there was something missing from his system that perhaps left it with a severity reflected in Ouspensky's own character. And yet the care for his students and the determination to pass on all that he had discovered were evidence of a love that was not overt. On first meeting him, Dr Roles realised 'that because he never put on any sort of an act he was the first man I could really trust.'[10]

---

10 *The Bridge*, No. 12, p.235.

CHAPTER FIVE

The Emergence
of Philosophy

I N THE 1950s the School crossed the frontiers set by its devotion
to the study of Economics. With the introduction of Philosophy
classes derived primarily from the principles of the Fourth Way,
it embarked upon a journey not yet ended, a pursuit of the holy grail
of the ultimate truth about Man. Nevertheless, this decade saw the
Economics courses continue, albeit with a growth of students much
eclipsed by the rapid expansion of those of the new subject. *Basis*,
reduced to an in-house news sheet, remained as an indicator of the
School's broad interest in economic matters. Between 1952 and 1957,
when it closed down, it published articles on a very wide range of
issues that reflected the state of economic and political life in Britain
and beyond.

The Conservative governments of the 1950s partially reversed
the nationalisation policies of Labour, but found themselves beset
by new problems of inflation and burgeoning wage demands. *Basis*
had a clear response: 'Taxes are probably the largest single factor in
inflating prices,' a remark only to be fully appreciated by those
who had learnt of the impact of existing taxation on the margin of
production, where prices and wages are determined. Nor was *Basis*
impressed by government attempts to control the economy by
means of the high interest rates introduced in 1957. Housing,
agriculture, pensions, the motor industry, health and new towns, all
came under scrutiny from the standpoint that underlying conditions
of land tenure, taxation and credit were being ignored. Not that a
Labour government could be expected to improve matters. A *Basis*
prediction, that has perhaps been proved true half a century later,
accused Labour policy of leading to 'the State and big industries

becoming partners – a super welfare State provided by employer and government.'

Basis had some potent criticisms of government policies overseas. As the British Commonwealth divested itself of colonialism, usually with efforts to pass on valuable institutions of democracy and common law, it was seen by *Basis* as avoiding the equally fundamental issues of land ownership and economic justice. In Northern Rhodesia concessions of mineral rights by the Colonial Office were 'a clear and glaring example of how natural revenues of rich colonial territories have been delivered into private hands', i.e. those of British commercial companies. In Kenya the violence of the Mau Mau movement was viewed as the inevitable result of white farmers occupying 'as much land as they could get, not what was needed.' The Kikuyu tribe had been forced into reservations as a source of labour on white farms. 'Mau' meant literally 'the promised land'. Even justice was administered unequally, with inferior standards for Africans. Apartheid in South Africa got similarly short shrift.

Yet *Basis* was by no means a kind of soft left news sheet. It advocated an agreement with Egypt concerning tenant rights over the Suez Canal, but when the Suez crisis broke in 1956 it supported Anglo-French action, on the grounds that without it the Arab world would become wide open to Soviet influence. Furthermore, when the Russians forcibly suppressed the Hungarian uprising in the same year, *Basis* even wanted Western intervention, perhaps allowing its principles unduly to override political realism. Closer to home, one of its final articles was on surer ground in attacking a landowner's right to receive the full development value on the sale of land to public authorities. Despite the expansion of Philosophy classes, Economics in the School was alive and well!

More evidence of this came with the publication of Leon MacLaren's *Further Essays in Economics*. These were carefully reasoned developments of such aspects of the subject as costs of production, credit, profit and landlords' claims. A chapter on monopolies neatly sums up their causes:

> These, then, are the powers by which monopoly is sustained: control of natural resources so as to exclude others; the force of law; control of public services; the concentration of wealth in the hands of a few; and agreements in restraint of trade.[1]

1 Leon MacLaren, *Nature of Society*, p.246.

The beneficial effect of a tax on rent in allowing new forms of industrial organisation to emerge is highlighted:

> As the weight of the tax on landlords' claims rises, land will become readily available, and any man who so wishes may easily acquire a piece for himself. People will no longer pass out of industry into the care of the Ministry of National Insurance, but will pass out of industry to set up in competition with their former masters. The astonishing conditions under which the majority of the people have no right or title to the land on which they work will steadily change. Forms of industrial structure developed to suit conditions where all land is enclosed, wages are reduced to the least a man is willing to accept, and capital equipment is provided by loans, will give way to forms of organisation suited to the new conditions. The relationship of master and servant will become much less common and some new form of joint enterprise or partnership will take its place.[2]

The vexed questions of value and price are reduced to the simplicity of value as a subjective concept and price as 'all that is given, done, and promised to one party to an exchange in return for all that is given, done and promised by the other.' Upper and lower limits of price are fixed between the vendor's and purchaser's respective values. Finally there is this appraisal of the current state of Economics:

> So far removed has the study turned in practice from its true sphere and proper function, however, so strongly has the accent shifted from human life to the production and distribution of wealth, that economists have come to regard human beings and human life as a means towards the end of producing and distributing wealth. Men, woman and children are spoken of as labour, units of demand, manpower and so on. In the process the study has deteriorated from a liberal art, one of the humanities, to a sordid and arid calculation of dead numbers, materialist and confessedly unethical.[3]

There was further evidence of the breadth of the School's interest in society and government. In the early fifties courses were running on Economics, The Development of Economic Thought, The Machinery of Government, and the Economic History of the English People, in addition to the brave new subject of Philosophy. A day school was also held for the Union of University Liberal

2 *Ibid.*, p.265.
3 *Ibid.*, p.276.

Societies. Behind the scenes, however, there were potentially dangerous upheavals. Leon MacLaren was voted out as Principal in 1953. He said later that he had felt it was time to hand over to people who were now capable of leading the School, but there may have been pressure from some who found his leadership dominating and his handling of finances rather cavalier. His first wife said of him that she feared his love of power. Some senior members of the School did not take easily to the introduction of Philosophy – Andrew MacLaren agreed with them – and perhaps foresaw that this would become the chief interest of the man whom they had followed zealously as an Economics teacher of genius.

Leon, however, could certainly not be sidelined. He was an inspiring thinker. After his introduction to the Study Society, he began to write new Philosophy material. This did not come easily to him:

> Being a perfectionist it had to be right. He would sit down with a blank piece of paper and learned to write what came through him, knowing nothing. After a few paragraphs had been written, he would reread them and take out all unnecessary words, sometimes leaving just one sentence. It would take him all weekend and Sunday night to get it ready for Monday, when the groups met. There is no doubt he left an invaluable heritage with that material. In later life he became so fluent that he would dictate the material without having to change a word.[4]

A new relationship between MacLaren and the School was required that relieved him of most administration. Later this was formalised as 'Senior Tutor'. Meanwhile, the rule that precluded any payment for services to School members was suspended in his case, enabling him to conduct research to develop the School courses. The need for this was essential in view of the fact that within a few years the number of students would be no less than 3,700, of which 2,900 would be enrolled for Philosophy. Students were staying longer, and new material had to be provided for them.

As Principal the Fellowship elected Kenneth Jupp, the barrister whose interest in Plato has already been noted. Ronald Burgess was granted the same exemption as MacLaren, and carried forward research in Economics. The new leadership was presented with an acute problem of finding space for classes. With increased attendance finance was no longer a difficulty, but now premises such as

4 Dorine Tolley, *The Power Within*, p.55.

Church House, Westminster and the Newton Institute, just off Leicester Square, were rented. Once again branches were opening outside London. All this was managed with the help of just two employed secretaries.

The Principal's annual statement to the Fellowship in 1958 gives a sense of the task that was being undertaken:

> From the outset, the purpose of our common work was conceived as the creation of a School, in the ancient sense of that word, in which men and women might be brought under the power of truth, to be raised by it in being, knowledge and understanding, and through which a leaven might be brought into society by which it, too, might be raised in being, knowledge and understanding.

More evocative is the description given much later by a student who had joined the classes at Suffolk Street in the 1950s:

> There were smiling people, serene and self-confident. Something special was going on. People had questions about life, how to find a fuller life. This was where we had to be. One came into the real world, a world that seemed bigger, exciting, new. One was going on a journey to truth, together in a group.

In these early days of the Philosophy classes the room at Suffolk Street was often quite crowded, with people sitting close together on the dark green canvas, steel-framed chairs that were characteristic of the School at that time. The method of instruction followed that used from the beginning of the Economics classes: the tutor read a few lines, then asked for comments or questions. Everyone was encouraged, but not required, to speak. Gradually students warmed to the discussion, and there were moments of insight that might be remembered for years afterwards.

In the refreshment break conversations would begin that were free of much of the clutter of habitual thoughts about other people, like 'What are they thinking of me?', as though the spirit of what was being offered somehow permeated the very atmosphere of the place. Some people continued the course as much for the kind of open-hearted friendship and good company as for the content of the teaching itself, though these were indeed very closely related.

Leon MacLaren, himself, if he were not tutoring that evening, would usually be there. On one occasion, as he stood quietly by the wall during the break, a new student approached him and said 'What do you do here?' To which MacLaren promptly replied, 'Oh, I am the entertainments manager.'

The speed with which the Philosophy classes expanded during the nineteen fifties undoubtedly reflected a widespread feeling amongst people of very varied social backgrounds that something was missing from their lives; that despite a general recovery from the war weariness of the forties and rising material prosperity for the majority, there was a kind of emotional or spiritual emptiness for which conventional culture and religion did not provide. It was the decade of the 'angry young men', of a frustration, especially amongst the young, at the rigidity of society and the absence of real creativity in art, literature and the theatre. Some turned to breaking the conventions, to defying the respectable norms, to ignoring traditional morality. Others, just a few in relation to the population, turned to the School of Economic Science, which also shocked some of its more staid members by apparently teaching Philosophy in the name of Economic Science!

CHAPTER SIX

The Pearl
of Great Price

B Y 1954 the tentative steps in Philosophy that had been taken
since the end of the war were transformed into a full series
of courses, based largely upon the teaching of Pyotr Ouspensky. The School material, however, was written by Leon MacLaren,
who brought to it a unique blend of legal acuteness and intuitive
penetration. It appealed strongly to a generation looking for a new
way of living in an age of growing materialism. As always the written material only came alive when spoken with understanding and
experience, and when heard and discussed on the spot. In fact,
although MacLaren himself frequently tutored the early parts of the
course, some of the other tutors were but a few paces ahead of their
own students.

MacLaren's material was not systematic in having a clearly defined
framework and order. Rather it was inspirational, and followed a kind
of inner reasoning that introduced ideas one by one with a connecting thread that made them easy to assimilate. Usually each idea
or practice was repeated later, but in a different form or with new
examples, so that the student became familiar with them, rather than
learning them in the conventional sense. This technique was vital,
because the whole object was that the teaching should be practical,
that it should be put to use in people's lives. The ideas had to be
absorbed into one's being, not memorised in the intellect. This is also
why the method was to create a dialogue between tutor and student
in the hope that, as the *Taittireeya Upanishad* says, discourse joins them
and knowledge arises between. For real knowledge, practical knowledge – so the School teaches – is not held in the head like a bookful
of words. Nevertheless, plenty of words were offered, particularly in

the liberal use of quotations from a very wide range of sacred and profane sources, exemplified below.

For many years the Part One course remained exactly as first written. It began with the simple statement that the word 'Philosophy' means the love of wisdom, and argued, with Plato, that a specialist, like a doctor or sailor, might be wise in his or her own field of activity, but that the real question was 'What is a wise man?' Aquinas, following Aristotle, answered that the wise seek the highest causes, the end of the universe itself. So what do we, as students of Philosophy, now seek? Do not all people at heart have three basic questions: What is this creation? How did it come to exist? What is my relationship to it?

To begin to find answers, we must be here and now, in this room, in this present moment. We are in a room in 11 Suffolk Street, in the West End of London, in Great Britain, in the world, in the solar system, in our galaxy, in all galaxies, in the universe. This moment of this minute, this hour, this day, lies between the weeks, months, years, centuries before and after.

Such an introduction led naturally to an exercise that became one of the most potent of all the practices given by the School. Students were asked to sit upright but comfortably; to let the mind become still; to be here and now; then to feel the feet on the ground, the weight of the body on the chair, the pressure of clothes on the skin and the play of air on the face and hands; to see colour and form without making any judgments about what is seen; to smell; to taste; to hear the sounds within the room; then to let the hearing go out to sounds outside, to the furthest sounds of all. And finally to rest in the deep awareness of the present moment. For about two minutes the room became a haven of stillness and silence, even in the midst of the clink of coffee cups downstairs and the buzz of passing traffic outside. Students were asked for their observations of this exercise, and encouraged to practise it two or three times every day.

The exercise alone had a profound effect. A new dimension cut through the hassle and confusion of daily life in London, in the office, on the tube, in the home. After the class one emerged into a world that was brighter, endearing, more immediate, and yet less intrusive and demanding. One looked upon the vista of Trafalgar Square, the busy cabs and buses, the wet pavements shining under the street lights, with new eyes, like a child on its very first trip to the great city.

With the exercise came an explanation of why it was so effective. Before anything can be done, it was said, one must be aware. But are there not levels of awareness? A diagram illustrated this: successive levels run from deep sleep, through waking sleep – our usual state – to self consciousness, objective consciousness and finally to an unnamed and unlimited level above them all. From the common experience of students, examples were drawn of imaginings and dreams that are rife in waking sleep, and of occasional glimpses of self consciousness, in the sense of being conscious of oneself and all about one. Little was said of the higher levels, except that in objective consciousness one knows objectively what is present, free of any subjective interference.

The course built upon the initial impact of the exercise and the recognition of levels of awareness. Work was needed on both knowledge and being. Only through the development of being can the latent possibilities of a man or woman be realised. You can only observe what you are equipped to observe. Even modern technology depends entirely upon this fact. A slow motion camera produces images that the human eye can naturally see. A mechanical digger only works when the human arm and brain are properly employed. For the state of the human instrument, the mind and body, is the crux. Provided knowledge is also available, everything depends upon this state at the very moment of action. How often did Jesus speak of wakefulness, and its absence, of those who have eyes, but see not, who have ears, but hear not?

> And he cometh, and findeth them sleeping, and saith unto Peter, Simon, sleepest thou? Couldest not thou watch one hour?[1]

What is this wakefulness? A mother in deep sleep awakes to the needs of her child. How does the call of one's name awake one from sleep? Something within us hears. Even within each level of awareness there are degrees of wakefulness. We may be aware of dreaming; we may sleep walk; we may get to work in the morning without knowing how we got there! Between waking sleep and self consciousness there is a kind of awakening consciousness. By means of the exercise this may grow, as we move out of the common waking sleep.

What is this creation? In the pursuit of this question, the material turned to the French philosopher, Blaise Pascal:

1 *Mark* 14:37.

For, in the end, what is man in nature? Nothing in relation to infinity, all in relation to nothing, a central point between nothing and all. Infinitely far from understanding these extremes, for him the end and principle of things are impregnably hidden in an impenetrable secret. He is equally incapable of seeing the nothingness from which he is drawn and the infinity in which he is engulfed.[2]

What thoughts, what feelings, what memories, students were asked, does this passage evoke? Modern science easily overlooks the sense of wonder at nature and man's place in it. Looking out further and further into space and inwards at ever and ever smaller particles is no way to study the world. Look first for the laws, like Isaac Newton, who saw the law clearly, then verified and demonstrated it for years afterwards. From a quiet mind comes depth, as we see also in artistic creativity. Witness Mozart:

When I am, as it were, completely myself, entirely alone and of good cheer ... my ideas flow most and most abundantly. Whence, and how, they come I know not; nor can I force them ... All this fires my soul, and, provided I am not disturbed, my subject enlarges itself, becomes methodised, and defined, and the whole, though it be long, stands almost complete and finished in my mind, so that I can survey it like a fine picture or a beautiful statue at a glance. Nor do I hear in my imagination the parts successively, but I hear them, as it were, all at once. What a delight this is, I cannot tell![3]

And yet, whilst the ideas of a Newton or a Mozart spring from the unknown depths of nature itself, they retain an individual character, as though they are the product of one man, as well as of one humanity, one organic life, one earth and one nature. Thus law at every level is available for each of us to find, if we will but use the faculties with which we are endowed.

All this led into a fundamental idea taken from the teaching of Ouspensky: that man's nature is threefold, for it consists of head, heart and guts; a reasoning principle, a feeling principle and a principle of action. Then came a key instruction. For this to be practical knowledge and not just theory, these principles must be observed. Watch them, without interfering, during the week ahead.

How was this advice to be followed up? The observations of students were vital. The development of the School itself depended

2 Blaise Pascal, *Pensees.*
3 Edward Holmes, *The Life of Mozart*, p.268.

on them. They were its life-blood. 'Learn and teach' was of the essence. From what students reported back from their testing in practice of the tutors' instructions, the School learnt how to advance, enlarging what was useful, withdrawing what was ineffective. Students saw how reason could be ignored under the impulse of strong feelings, how an over-anticipated meeting would lose its freshness and spontaneity, how action could be stultified by thought. And yet also how life could be guided by reason, enlivened by feeling and made efficient by action, if these naturally became harmonious.

People are predominantly centred in one of these three principles, so that effort is required to keep a balance between them. There is a time to be reasonable, a time to feel, a time to act, as *Ecclesiastes* assures us. A most valuable aspect of the reasoning principle is 'the watchman' that, for example, sees a hasty word before it is spoken; but reason also forms and stores ideas and has the capacity for clarity, precision and silence. Feeling is the function that may cleanse the mind with laughter, look to membership of a greater body, and indeed recognise the need to wake up, but it needs the watchman to avoid excess. The active principle has three parts: sex, movement and instinct. Sex is the source of power, not just of reproduction. Instinctive reflexes deal with unconscious movements, conditioned reflexes with activities like walking and reading.

What upsets the balance between these principles is when one tries to do the work of the others. The head may interfere with the heart by thinking too much about matters of emotion; the heart may give rise to misplaced imaginings. 'The imagination of man's heart is evil from his youth'.[4] The active principle may create circling thoughts, causing rage or depression, or endless inner conversations and associations of ideas. We see a familiar object, like a suitcase, and immediately think of a time when we saw it before, perhaps when we were on holiday abroad. So we spend the next five minutes on the beach in the south of France.

Worst of all are imaginings about ourselves, such as what other people think of us. How often do we imagine what the boss thinks of us at work, what a friend thinks about something we have said, what a stranger thought when he or she greeted us? As one tutor said, 'Whenever you find that you are thinking about yourself – stop!' The view that such thoughts present is always false.

4 *Genesis*, 8:21.

Misuse of the three principles is especially damaging in relation to emotion. We need to be clear about what emotion really is. It is not excitement on one hand, nor depression on the other. True emotion is silent, still and detached, constant and without thought for oneself. St Paul says this of it:

Charity suffereth long, and is kind; charity envieth not; charity vaunteth not itself, is not puffed up, doth not behave itself unseemly, seeketh not her own, is not easily provoked... Beareth all things, believeth all things, hopeth all things, endureth all things. Charity never faileth.[5]

First see the misplacements of ideas, feelings and movements, then stop them. They are false. True ideas, feelings and movements need to comply with nature, to produce the intended result, not something else, like a tea-cosy knitted instead of a baby's cardigan! Let the exercise put the watchman in place. Cut out unnecessary movement. When true principles prevail, the truth itself may be found. It lives within every man and woman, yet may be seen in everything that exists. It lives as Spirit, as the *Kena Upanishad* asserts:

That which makes the tongue speak, but needs no tongue to explain,
    that alone is Spirit; not what sets the world by the ears.
That which makes the mind think, but needs no mind to think, that
    alone is Spirit; not what sets the world by the ears.
That which makes the eye see, but needs no eye to see, that alone is
    Spirit; not what sets the world by the ears.
That which makes the ear hear, but needs no ear to hear, that alone
    is Spirit; not what sets the world by the ears.
That which makes life live, but needs no life to live, that alone is
    Spirit; not what sets the world by the ears.[6]

Why is Spirit hidden? – because darkness lies within, obscuring the light of consciousness.

To find one's true Self what price has to be paid? The price is simply to give up all that is false. We cling to what is false; we even justify it. If we are offended by someone, we dwell on the offence. To find happiness, give up being miserable! To give up false action, give attention to your work, to simple tasks, to movements of the

5 *1 Corinthians*, 13:4-8.
6 *The Ten Principal Upanishads*, translated by Shree Purohit Swami and W.B. Yeats, Faber & Faber, 1960, p.20.

body. Then we may see that the love of wisdom attracts powers of which we are hardly aware; they come like iron filings to a magnet, from a scattered field to a magnetic centre.

Who is the central figure of our imaginings? Me! At one time 'me' is brave, strong, heroic; at the next moment he is timid, weak, trivial. Now he is assertive; then he is bashful. Now he is successful, even triumphant; then he is a failure, a defeated man. Always 'me' wants to be the centre of the picture, even at the cost of being blamed or disliked. He claims everything – body, feelings and thoughts, virtues and vices, talents and defects. I am loved, hated, admired, despised, clever, stupid, kind, unkind, pleasant, unpleasant, beautiful, ugly... But who am I? What am I? Of what are the principles of ideas, feelings and action the parts or functions?

Philosophy is concerned with wholeness; we are mainly trained to analyse. One part of ourselves may claim wholeness for itself. But where are we looking from? In observation there is an observer, observation and an object. Who is the observer? Instead of just observing, we evaluate what we see; we have preconceptions, likes and dislikes. The most intrusive of these is 'me'. Yet this 'me' can itself be observed. I am the observer, not what I see.

At this point the material introduced a practice that has run through the School's teaching ever since, namely the giving of attention. This was presented as a practical choice that we all face many times a day. Our attention is open to impressions from both within and without. It may be held by one particular impression, say of a sensation or a sight or sound. It is captured by this, and we are lost in it, until something else brings us out of it. But there is a choice in all this. In the moment when the impression first appears, we may give our attention to it, or not, as the case may be. In other words, we may control the attention, rather than let it be held or taken away. Clearly what happens depends upon our level of awareness at the time. If the attention is controlled, then order may be brought into the operation of the principles of thought, feeling and action. On them the light of attention may be shone, for attention is a kind of beam of consciousness itself.

So the practice is to control the attention, and to find out what captures it in order that the habitual loss of attention can be avoided. By means of the exercise the general awareness may be raised, so that all this becomes easier. Attention is the ladder to bring man to higher consciousness, concluded the material, words which echoed the ancient teaching of the Orthodox Church in the *Philokalia*.

By control of attention one gains strength. By its loss one degenerates, as the *Bhagavad Gita* explains

> When a man dwells on the objects of sense, he creates an attraction
>   for them; attraction develops into desire, and desire breeds anger.
> Anger induces delusion; delusion, loss of memory; through loss
>   of memory, reason is shattered; and loss of reason leads to
>   destruction.[7]

When in observation we identify with the object observed, we say 'I am sick or well'; 'I am cross, happy, confused', and so on. We disappear in the object. What is the remedy? Remember that you have a body. Be aware of it, and of all around; of the room, the house, the street, the city, the nation, the earth, the planets, stars, galaxies. Man is at the centre. All are without, but also within. Hear the *Chandogya Upanishad*:

> In this body, in this town of Spirit, there is a little house shaped like
>   a lotus, and in that house there is a little space. One should know
>   what is there.
> What is there? Why is it so important?
> There is as much in that little space within the heart, as there is in
>   the whole world outside. Heaven, earth, fire wind, sun, moon,
>   lightning, stars; whatever is and whatever is not, everything is
>   there.[8]

A diagram of concentric circles illustrated the relation of Man at the centre to the greater and greater entities beyond. How do we see life, students were asked. At what level do we see its purpose or significance? If all one knows is the body, then that is what one sees everywhere, just material things. Yet even this contains billions of cells, all descended from one, each containing a set of genes, all given order by a life intelligence. The instinctive part of the moving principle acts under this intelligence, as we see if we watch its speed and potency.

If the intellect is clear, external movements appear slower, colours brighter, more is seen. One student gave a remarkable observation of this. When climbing a mountain, he had fallen down a rock face.

7 *Bhagavad Gita*, translated by Sri Purohit Swami, Faber & Faber, 1965, pp.25-6.
8 *The Ten Principal Upanishads*, p.107.

As he fell, he experienced everything slowing down. He saw a piece of rock jutting out below him, and had time to seize it and hang on. Danger had cleared his mind.

The enemy of the clear intellect is mechanical thinking, especially the way we tend to think in terms of opposites, such as 'Ought I to do this or not?' Look for a third point. Turn the attention away from duality. The third point may be to do nothing, or to wait.

What then is the enemy of feeling? It is involvement, captured attention. Very often it is 'me' that captures it, my beliefs, my family, my work, my ability... Hear what Thomas a Kempis wrote about real feeling:

> Love watches, and sleeping slumbers not; when weary is not tired; when straitened is not constrained; when frightened is not disturbed; but like a lovely flame passes through all opposition. Whosoever loveth knoweth the sound of this voice.[9]

What is the enemy of movement? It is idle repetition, especially idle talk. Do not chatter, as St James warned:

> If any man offend not in word, the same is a perfect man, and able also to bridle the whole body.
> Behold, we put bits in the horses' mouths, that they may obey us; and we turn about their whole body.
> Behold also the ships, which though they be so great, and are driven of fierce winds, yet are they turned about with a very small helm, whithersoever the governor listeth.
> Even so the tongue is a little member, and boasteth great things. Behold, how great a matter a little fire kindleth!
> And the tongue is a fire, a world of iniquity: so is the tongue among our members, that it defileth the whole body, and setteth on fire the course of nature; and it is set on fire of hell.
> For every kind of beasts, and of birds, and of serpents, and of things in the sea, is tamed, and hath been tamed of mankind:
> But the tongue can no man tame; it is an unruly evil, full of deadly poison.[10]

Another key practice was now introduced: listen to the sound of the voice, both of others and of oneself. One will notice much unnecessary talk, like saying things one does not really know, giving offence to others, even talking when no-one is listening. Stopping all

9 *The Imitation of Christ*, Book III, Chapter V.
10 *The General Epistle of James*, 3:2-8.

this can bring a recognition of a deep and silent power within one-self; whereas talk like flattery and offensive remarks attenuate one's power. When 'me' is dominant, ordinary intellect and feeling are cut off from the higher intellect and feeling that are associated with self and objective consciousness. These higher principles are the king-dom of heaven of religions:

> Again, the kingdom of heaven is like unto a merchant man, seeking
>   goodly pearls:
> Who, when he had found one pearl of great price, went and sold all
>   that he had, and bought it.[11]

> If you wish to seek the Buddha you ought to see into your own nature; for this nature is the Buddha himself… The Buddha is in your own mind, make no mistake of bowing to external objects. Buddha means 'Enlightened Nature'. This nature is the mind, and the mind is the Buddha, and the Buddha is the way, and the way is Zen. To see directly into one's own original nature, this is Zen.[12]

How did the material deal with the sex centre as a part of the active principle? Sex, it said, is the powerhouse. Procreation is but a small aspect of it. It is the force that drives homes, careers, sustained endeavour of many kinds. It may turn to destruction, to recklessness, ambition, even to warfare. Cycles of excitement and depression may arise from it. Yet, if correctly used, it is creative. Here, too, to find the truth give up what is false:

> For the things that commonly happen in life and are esteemed among men as the highest good, as is witnessed by their works, can be reduced to three – riches, fame and lust – and by these the mind is so distracted that it can scarcely think of any other good.
>   But love directed towards the eternal and infinite feeds the mind with pure joy, and is free from all sadness. Wherefore it is greatly to be desired, and to be sought after with our whole mind…[13]

Students were asked not to accept or reject anything that is heard in the School. Wait and see whether it is verified. That advice was given near the conclusion of the introductory course. By this stage most students had seen much verified. As the material said, we begin to realise that we lack unity, consciousness, will and choice. Our

11 *Matthew*, 13:45-6.
12 The first patriarch of Zen.
13 Spinoza, *De Intellectus Emendatione*, quoted in Robert Bridges, *The Spirit of Man*.

intelligence is lost in an imaginary world. Yet moments of greater awareness increase with practice. We learn from each other; others are mirrors in which we see ourselves. The view from the speeding train becomes tempered by a broader vision from outside.

Of the four levels of consciousness, the highest is governed by higher intellect. It is described in St Luke's Gospel:

> And when he was demanded of the Pharisees, when the kingdom of God should come, he answered them and said, The kingdom of God cometh not with observation:
> Neither shall they say, Lo here! Or lo there! For, behold, the kingdom of God is within you.[14]

The third level of consciousness is governed by higher feeling, the charity that never faileth, the love that is not constrained. Ordinary feeling governs the intermediate state of awakening consciousness; external events and movement govern waking sleep; and deep sleep comes under instinct. These levels are the holy mountains of religions.

When the heart is cleansed of impurities, a gate opens through the barrier erected by 'me'. This work begins in the intellect, when it guards against the power of unnecessary thought or excitement, and brings order. 'Blessed are the pure in heart; for they shall see God'.[15] On this note the course that introduced thousands of students to practical Philosophy came to an end.

14 *Luke*, 17:20-1.
15 *Matthew*, 5:8.

CHAPTER SEVEN

Meditation

BEFORE he died Pyotr Ouspensky had told his students that there was a key piece missing from his system that they should try to find. Dr Roles did not forget this injunction. In 1959 he heard of the arrival in Britain of Maharishi Mahesh Yogi, an Indian teacher whose intention was to spread the practice of meditation far and wide. The Maharishi had been a pupil of Sri Brahmananda Saraswati of Jyotish Pitha, known as Guru Deva, a great teacher in the tradition of Advaita (non-dual) Vedanta. About twenty years previously a group of Indian master teachers had set out to develop a form of meditation that was simple and suitable for the West. What they created was a method that had the same power as Patanjali's ardous system of yoga, but was much easier to practise. Dr Roles was initiated into this meditation, recognised it as the missing element, and promptly advised his students to follow suit. When Leon MacLaren was initiated, he too decided to introduce meditation to the senior students in the School.

The Maharishi planned to speak at a public meeting in the Albert Hall. About five thousand people crowded into the building. The School had agreed to provide attendants. They met him first in one of the School houses, recognisable as 'an unusual gentleman with long hair and a beard, wearing Indian clothes and invariably carrying a bunch of flowers, who smiled or laughed most of the time.' This was the Maharishi, who would later be world famous as a friend of the Beatles and the instigator of palatial meditation centres around the globe. In the media the phenomenon of 'flower power' became a frequent attraction, especially for young people looking for some brightness in the bleak world of Cold War materialism. At the Albert Hall hundreds came forward to be initiated, giving the School and the Study Society a major task for some time.

Indeed, with the agreement of the Maharishi, the School promised to set up an independent body called the School of Meditation,
to offer introductions to meditation and to care for students who
came forward. Under the leadership of William Whiting, this new
School took premises in Holland Park, and at present continues to
administer meditation courses. Soon it began to run evening classes
to meet the needs of meditators who asked for greater knowledge of
the system to which the Maharishi's practice was related, namely the
Philosophy of Advaita Vedanta.

Meditation, of course, takes many forms; both Eastern and Western religions and other systems contain meditative techniques. Dr
Roles had examined some, such as the Jesus Prayer, before he met
the Maharishi. Most, if not all, use attention as the focus of the practice, but this may be applied through any of the senses or inwardly.
Meditation as imparted by the Maharishi uses a mantra heard silently
in the mind and given to the student at an initiation ceremony. He
insisted that the tradition of this ceremony should be adhered to as
a condition of passing on the system to any organisation. Naturally
the School has kept strictly to this condition ever since, even though
critics of the School have sometimes regarded it as an unnecessary
intrusion of Hinduism.

Later there was a troublesome incident, when the Maharishi
proposed that both the School and the Study Society should be
absorbed into his organisation, with Leon MacLaren becoming chief
administrator and Dr Roles international initiator. The two leaders
did not succumb to this proposal, preferring to maintain the independence of their respective bodies. A connection with the master
teacher of both men, Sri Shantananda Saraswati, head of the tradition to which the Maharishi adhered, had already been made by this
time.

Henceforth all students in the School would be offered meditation after about two years attendance. Its fruits were soon apparent.
Most students took to the practice with ease, assisted by care from
those who had gone before them and now acted as advisers after initiation. The meditation works by turning the attention away from all
distractions – sense objects, bodily sensations, thoughts, imaginings,
feelings, worries, expectations, problems, memories, indeed anything
whatsoever, except the mantra – so that a movement can take place
deeper and deeper into the being, into oneself. As one goes deeper,
movement becomes less, mental 'noise' is reduced, and finally there

may be stillness and silence, like water from which all impurities have subsided. In this state nothing is there but the Self, without an object, without space and time, without even knowledge. In reality this is not even a state, for the depth is infinite, the existence eternal, so there is no state to arrive at or recognise.

Students may reach this pure stillness after just a brief time practising, or more likely after many years. It may come frequently or just once. Ultimately a 'realised' man or woman may find it always available. For the stillness, the presence of the Self, is always there. The question is only one of connecting with it. In the movement towards it, many beneficial side-effects may occur, as students have borne witness:

> Meditation has changed my life. Nothing drastic or dramatic. No flashing lights, no visions in the night. Nothing but a gentle, though seemingly inexorable, turning away from what was. There is a lessening of tempo, of temper; a gradual flowing towards people; an understanding of the underlying unity between me and all created things... An appreciation of what Matisse called 'the lived-in silence of empty rooms' – the furniture speaking, the seemingly deserted room vibrant with echoes.
>
> (A social worker)

> It's a foundation, a base, a calm centre from which I can do whatever needs to be done in the normal course of my life... I know that this foundation cannot be harmed. It isn't mine, so I need not fear that something or somebody will take it away from me; neither did I grasp it from somewhere outside myself, so I need not worry about losing it. It is just there – not me, yet within me. It has been there all the time, really. Meditation did not add it to me, but helps to put me in touch with it.
>
> (A computer programmer)[1]

The word 'meditation' is derived from the Old English *metan*, meaning measure, and also has a common Indo-European root with the Latin *meditari* to consider, ponder or contemplate. One effect of meditation is to bring measure into the inner and outer lives of practitioners. Inwardly the three functions of intellect, heart and movement are brought closer to harmony, nearer to the unity of the whole man. Outwardly a sense of union, or communion, with other people, with other creatures and with the world at large gives life a new simplicity and meaning. Happiness, as exemplified by the

1 Quoted in William Whiting, *Being Oneself*, The School of Meditation, 1985, p.1.

Maharishi himself, becomes a feature of lives previously beset with worldly problems and anxieties. In particular, students in the School have found a mutual understanding and genuine friendship that extends far beyond the relatively narrow associations made within single groups or teams. It is as though a burden were lifted. Whence comes this great relief, this rest from the weariness of the world? Clearly it is from the very centre of one's being:

> He that hath light...
> may sit in the centre
> and enjoy bright day.[2]

As the School had taught for many years, the centre is the creative principle, the very essence of Man, not an individual ego but a universal reality, pure being. Meditation is the means; the Self the end. Whilst the meditator follows whither the mantra takes his or her attention, levels of awareness are transcended. As the Philosophy teaching had adumbrated, these levels are both inner and outer. Through the sensual feelings, dreams and imagination one penetrates to the level of sleep, without in fact identifying with that state, and beyond sleep to an underlying and permanent condition of unity:

> God made sense turn outward, man therefore looks outward, not into himself. Now and again a daring soul, desiring immortality, has looked back and found himself..[3]

This inward turn is not introspection, the mere observing of mental phenomena, for it brings with it the recognition of an inner unity that is the same in the seemingly external world.

For students who were initiated there came, too, a greater degree of non-attachment. The demands of the world became less pressing; the claims upon family and friends, the clinging to possessions, the desire for wealth and success were attenuated. As the centre became closer, the attractions of the perimeter were more remote.

> The Wheel of Time rotates, but its axis is ever at rest... Where would you rather be? I say to you, slip from the rim of Time into the axis, and spare yourself the nausea of motion. Let Time revolve about you; but you revolve not with Time.[4]

2 *Ibid.*, quoting John Milton, p.viii.
3 *The Ten Principal Upanishads*, p.33.
4 *The Book of Mirdad* by Mikhail Naimy, quoted in William Whiting, *Being Oneself*, p.35.

To the constant meditator time indeed seemed to change. Being in the present moment became a practical proposition more frequently, and the wheel of time, the endless and repetitive cycle, could be observed for what it is, a passing show, a play of creation for the delight of the observer who is not part of it. So, too, events seemed too occur at a slower pace, as though the projector in the cinema was retarded. There was time for things to take their place without rush or undue effort. Those students who had feared the loss of one hour a day spent in the two regular half hours of meditation found themselves with time on their hands, time to give to people, to work in the School, to new studies.

When in the 1960s School students undertook meditation it was seen in society generally as a strange Eastern practice, alien to Western culture. One spoke of it with a hushed voice. Today it is widely available in university courses, in city lectures, in airport quiet rooms. Medical experts have subjected it to empirical tests. They have shown how it reduces the oxygen intake with a lower rate of breathing, slows the heart, and increases the alpha rhythm of brain impulses, a sign of deep rest. The metabolic rate falls, and there is a reduction in anxiety, reflected in greater skin resistance. Electro-encephalograph readings show the same degree of restfulness and, at the same time, greater inner alertness. Post meditation tests register faster reactions. Meditators also learn quickly, owing no doubt to clarity of mind.

Other tests have shown that the right hemisphere of the brain begins with meditation to function more in relation to the left hemisphere. The latter deals with the logical, sequential and often scientific forms of thought that are verbal, descriptive and explanatory; the former with intuitive, creative and wholistic thinking. As Whiting has written:

> The scientifically orientated West has been suspicious of the East, which emphasizes the importance of the other modes of consciousness. The East has not followed the same scientific development, is relatively inefficient in the production of material things but has a depth and perception not seen in the West, and the last decade has seen many Eastern teachers arriving in Western communities to teach methods which give access to the still inner-perceiving, unifying mode of consciousness latent in everyone. To have access to a sphere of consciousness which gives stillness, depth and inner perception is to transcend the ever-moving logical mind

and discover a new dimension of mind and a new concept of reality.[5]

For most students who met the meditation the world that they experienced became quieter, more beautiful and less demanding than before. One student remarked that on a day when meditation was missed a brightness had departed. Another found relief at last from depression. Yet another, whose professional work had provoked unremitting anger in him, discovered that the anger could be transformed into love. A lady who had a stroke said that she sounded the mantra for long periods whilst in hospital, and saw her time there become a play, with herself merely a person playing the part of having had a stroke.

There were occasional mistakes. One student had forgotten the mantra, and was found to be meditating upon a Sanskrit word that meant 'concrete'. Another, who found it difficult to practise for two half hours a day, was told by his tutor to practise for six periods instead. The student returned later, looking even more worried, and said that he found six half hours a day even harder!

Leon MacLaren himself clearly noticed some effects in himself of meditating. He asked a question to Shantananda Saraswati, who became his teacher soon after the meditation was introduced:

> Nowadays, when someone needs help, I seem to disappear and there is only the watching. The ordinary mental processes are very quiet and seem to be controlled by the watching, playing their part as it were. Ordinary mechanical physical movements take place, like changing posture, lighting a cigarette and so on, but do not seem to matter or affect what is in hand. Is this right? Are these experiences related and do they signify anything of value? If so, can they be developed?

The answer elucidated what had been seen:

> When one is attentive and still, one finds that pure 'I' emerges out of the mass of impure 'I's. This will facilitate proper action in the presence of pure 'I' acting naturally in everyday work. This is a manifestation of meditation in action. This is good.

Such were a few of the benefits of this extraordinary new practice brought from the East, like gold, frankincense or myrrh. For

5 William Whiting, *Being Oneself, ibid.*, p.45.

the School it was truly a kind of gift that conferred immortality. Without it the teaching of Philosophy might have been a brilliant but heartless exercise. For, as Dr Roles and Leon MacLaren knew full well, wisdom was the fruit of work on both knowledge and being. Meditation was work *par excellence* on being. It plumbed the depths of existence. Those who practised it assiduously were sure to enter the fathomless deeps and to emerge renewed in body, mind and spirit.

CHAPTER EIGHT

Know Thyself

THE Philosophy material developed further, still based primarily upon what had been learned of the Fourth Way, but influenced greatly by Leon MacLaren's own insight and by sources drawn from past philosophers of East and West. A diagram showed Man as three concentric circles, labelled Nature, Mind and Body with, at the centre, the Creative Principle. Each circle was said to interpenetrate those outside it, like water permeating wood, air water and light air. Thus the outer circle – the body – is permeated by the mind, body and mind by nature, and all three by the creative principle. Each one is bound by the effect of those within it; so the creative principle gives Man existence in time and space; nature limits how the mind and body may develop – what man can add one cubit to his stature? – and mind controls the body.

Students were asked, especially, to note the position of mind. It acts as a kind of reflector both ways between nature and body. Through it the creative principle and nature may be brought to bear upon human actions; or, on the other hand, the influence of the physical body may be allowed to obscure the deeper sources of our being. Much depends upon the state of mind as a reflector. Is it cleansed to enable consciousness to flow out into the world, or muddied by the impurities of common life? Do we go about identified with our bodies, or awake to inner resources of light and happiness? Recalling the diagram may be sufficient to bring us back to a proper view of our condition.

Our nature leads us to search for knowledge, happiness and a greater fullness of life, for these are essential attributes of our being. In numerous forms this search is the mainspring of human life. And yet these three ends are not Man himself. They leave open the most fundamental of all questions: What am I? We have forgotten what we really are. Hence the deeper quest that has run through history,

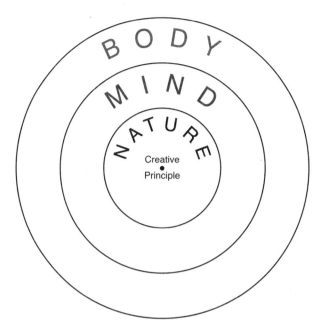

The Human Form

from those who inscribed the words in stone above the temple at Delphi – 'Know Thyself' – to those now in this room in London. What barrier cuts us off from knowing who or what we are?

Discipline and training are required. The barrier is ignorance, which requires a constant effort not to see, not to understand. We can be assured, however, that the strength to overcome ignorance is always sufficient. It is always available in the present moment. The creative principle may light up with consciousness just one part of the mind – one idea, one feeling or one desire. The man believes that he is this one small part, for that is all that he is aware of at the time. He is identified with it. 'I am intelligent'(or angry, hungry, etc). The spotlight shifts to other parts. Now he believes he is this, now that. Thus we may spend our days. Let the diagram remind us that we are in truth the creative principle itself, the origin of the consciousness, not the object upon which the light plays.

The material then turned to a closer look at the mind. It was represented as a circle full of dots, each one representing an idea, thought, feeling, sensation and so on. Any unit may fall within one's attention. They are created largely by outside influences, such as

education, imitation or public opinion. Occasionally an influence of
a special kind, perhaps from the Gospels or Plato, a work of art, or
simply a person we have met, may stir our memory of truth, and
bring us to a School.

Look for these units in the mind. Each is a view of the same
person at different times. 'My name is legion.' We talk to ourselves,
one unit to another. We have no single will, only wilfulness. They are
dust motes, illumined by the shaft of light of the creative principle.
Nature obscures some of the light. The greater the nature of the
person, the less is obscured.

What is the world for me now? It may be the next three paving
stones under one's feet, or the room one is sitting in, or a particular
idea in the mind. What world does the whole Man inhabit? What
is the world for organic life, for the earth, for the Sun? Beyond all
these lies a final unity, which we may call the Absolute. It depends on
no other thing. Remember the question: What is the world for me
now? By its use we may see the myriad units of the mind for what
they are, so that we are not deceived by them. Each of them may
claim to be 'I'. Their strength comes from this identification with
the whole Man. Ralph Waldo Emerson had a clear view of the real
mind:

> There is one mind common to all individual men. Every man is an
> inlet to the same and to all of the same. He that is once admitted to
> the right of reason is made a freeman of the whole estate. What
> Plato has thought he may think; what a saint felt he may feel; what
> at any time has befallen any man he can understand. Who hath
> access to this universal mind is a party to all that is or can be done,
> for this is the only sovereign agent...[1]

Such a view of the universality of mind is completely hidden, if
one identifies with a thought, a feeling or, like Shakespeare's *Hamlet*,
with a mood. Lost in a terrible depression consequent upon the murder of his father, Hamlet yet manages to see his condition objectively
for a moment, and to rise above it for a magnificent view of what he
and mankind itself really are:

> What a piece of work is a man! How noble in reason! How infinite
> in faculties! In form and moving, how express and admirable! In
> action, how like an angel! In apprehension, how like a god! The

1 Ralph Waldo Emerson, *The Universal in Man.*

beauty of the world! The paragon of animals! And yet, to me, what is this quintessence of dust?[2]

Practising the exercise clears away gross thoughts, feelings and sensations to make space for knowledge of oneself. What is this Self? It is the creative principle at the centre that creates a great store of energy to form the nature of each person, like the tiny mustard seed that grows into a mighty tree. Jesus spoke of this innermost principle, calling it, as he always did, by the name 'I'.

> I am the light above the All, the All came forth from me, the All returns to me. Life up a stone and I am there; cleave a piece of wood and you will find me there.[3]

For a man who makes the connection with his real Self, body, mind and even nature become tools, instruments for his use. Believing that we are something else, a single unit in the mind, or perhaps a group of them, is identification, attachment or involvement. Our spouse, our work, our difficulties in life may become in turn what we are lost in. We even justify this by accusing ourselves of being callous if we are not so identified. When my wife or husband is unwell, I should feel miserable! When my work goes wrong, I am a failure! When problems beset me, I am troubled or confused! Thus the dots in the mind grow strong, given life by the power of oneself, by consciousness.

Particularly when we are criticised, the identification may become ferocious. 'I' seems to be under attack. 'My whole world is collapsing.' Yet if these imposters, these mere dots that lodge in the mind under false pretences, can be dislodged, then the force that sustained them is available for greater purposes. A professional singer in the School said that she reacted strongly to criticism, but when she saw this reaction clearly as stemming from identification, her anger and dismay turned into joy at offering songs to others. Her world enlarged from 'me' to all those who heard her sing.

The story of the prodigal son is that of a man caught up in attachment to worldly pleasures, whose energy is drained away, until he turns in despair to the source that gave him all that he had and still awaits his return. And then his father restores him to his rightful place. We, in our ignorance, are all prodigal sons. The creative

2 *Hamlet*, Act 2, Scene 2.
3 *The Gospel of St Thomas*.

principle – consciousness – within us awaits our return. Only by both observation and knowledge, under the memory of truth itself, will this take place. Observation alone may lead to 'justification' of our state, like blaming one's spouse for one's own mistakes; whilst knowledge alone is merely theoretical.

As students progressed they were reminded of the importance of being members of a group. 'The group is the smallest unit in the School' was the rule. As Ouspensky used to say: there is always someone awake in a group at any one time! In the group there is freedom to speak, to be heard without criticism, and to ask questions without fear. Through the power of the group persistent habits could be overcome. People recognised this strength that came from unity. It could be called to mind during the week when the individual's life threatened to become overwhelming. 'Remember the group' was a kind of lifeline.

One was reminded again not to speak outside the School of what was said in a group, nor to criticise other students either openly or in one's head. In the course of time, the latter instruction came to have a remarkable effect on everyone. Such criticism did not totally disappear, but its comparative absence made relations between people a great deal easier, and created an ethos of lasting friendship, even of love. Students were told also that all service in the School was without payment. No financial benefit and no public reputation were to be gained from work within the School.

Once more following Ouspensky, the material elaborated the division of mankind into inner and outer circles. Men and women of the outer circle have forgotten who they are. They speak with many tongues, as in the Tower of Babel. Nor do they truly listen. Those in the inner circle are the heart and brain of humanity, who prevent a complete relapse into self-destruction and barbarism. They speak a common language. In the world they are rarely recognised. When they are, they are usually persecuted, like Osiris, Socrates and Jesus. Yet no one begins in the inner circle of mankind. Those who enter it have first received help from those who went before, the makers of myths and parables, the wise, the master teachers.

Nevertheless, every man or woman contains all that is necessary for Man. In each the whole universe is reflected. As above, so below. The strength of a man lies in his universality. No one is in truth the part he plays, as father or friend, lawyer or businessman. What is great cannot find satisfaction in what is small, the infinite in the finite. Some apparent limitation may have brought us to the School, but that is not the truth of the matter. Limitations are set by the false activity of the mind, by false images graven on the mind:

> I am the Lord thy God, which have brought thee out of the land of
>   Egypt, out of the house of bondage.
> Thou shalt have no other gods before me.
> Thou shalt not make unto thee any graven image…[4]

Without these graven images of ideas about oneself, the mind is naturally peaceful. It reflects the peace of the Self, of the 'I am' that exists before all the superimpositions that we place upon ourselves. Jesus repeated the same truth; 'Before Abraham was, I am.'

Anticipating the emphasis upon the Self that would be given later when the connection with Advaita Vedanta was fully made, the course developed further this theme of false images. The picture that each has of himself or herself is a limit. We say 'I am tired', then we receive an invitation to a party, and the picture changes instantly. Once these false pictures are seen, our real study begins. We cannot just change them at will. They must be observed, if possible without any motive at all. Then change may come, for these pictures do not like the light of observation. They prefer to hide in the darkness of ignorance.

Imaginings are a serious drain on our available energy. So too are physical tensions, and the excessive use of energy. When we practise the exercise, we may notice unnecessary tension in the body; for example, in the shoulders or in the face muscles. It can be released. When we turn a door handle, we may see much greater force being exerted than is required. Energy saved can be put to a finer use. As for imaginings, they can burn up fine energy itself. Ignore them, deny them attention, turn to something else.

There is the story of a man who went to see a sage in the hope of becoming his disciple. The sage asked him what he had seen on the way. 'A dead donkey' was the reply. 'Then you must go away and get the image of this dead donkey out of your mind', he was told. The man spent hours trying to remove the image, but he could not do so. The harder he tried, the stronger it became, so he returned to the sage in despair. 'If you cannot remove the image of this donkey,

4 *Exodus*, 20:1-4.

how can you remove all the thoughts you have harboured for years and years?' said the sage. 'Do not try to remove them. Just ignore them, neglect them, and they will go of themselves.'

Most, if not all, of what we think we are has been acquired from outside. The child begins to imitate its parents. Thoughts, emotional states and learning of all kinds are picked up. None of this is truly ours. What we are and what we have acquired are two distinct things. 'Sell that thou hast and give to the poor.' said Jesus. Yet we must not judge; self-criticism is deadly. Observation and knowledge do the work; judgment need play no part at all. Watch especially such remarks, spoken aloud or inwardly, as 'I cannot...', 'I always do...', 'I like or hate...'; looking for others' opinions about ourselves; what we think others expect from us and so on: all these are unnecessary. Let them go.

A useful practice in this connection is to pause between activities. Then play the part fully, but realising that it is a part, however seemingly important. Before we can begin to be what we are, we have to come out of all that we are not. We are what we have always been; we are not what we have acquired.

This distinction can be seen in terms of nature and personality. The latter means wearing a mask, like an actor. We wear what we have acquired. But if we forget that it is only a mask, we give it the force of existence. We think it is what we are. Nature is what we are: knowledge, happiness and fullness of life. A reflection of this nature may appear in the profession that we choose. But how we follow it is determined by personality. Yet personality is not to be despised. The mask helps us to deal with the world. Indeed it may protect our nature until that has developed sufficiently. What interferes with this development is identification with personality, believing that we are the mask.

In support of this the material quoted from a Vedic discourse:

> He is said to be the greatest actor who performs deeds as they occur to him, whether joy giving or otherwise, without any fear or desire for fruition.
> He is said to play his part well who performs his duties without fuss or anxiety, and maintains his reserve and purity of heart without taint of egoism or envy.
> He is said to perform his part well who is not affected by any person or thing, but regards all objects as a mere witness.
> He is the greatest actor who looks at his own birth, life and death,

and upon his rise and fall, in the same light, and who does not lose equanimity of mind under any circumstances whatever.

Personality is what one has become as a result of past actions. It is like a second nature superimposed upon the real nature. When we first awake after sleep, the very first experience is a feeling of existence. That is the real nature, what we really are. In truth it is not individual, for existence is universal. Remember that the body – and the mind – are ' instruments for my use.' In a moment of action realise that one is not the dominant group of feelings. 'I am not this fear, this pleasure, this expectation.' The power of past actions to become this second nature arises from the force of existence given to them at this very moment

The initial feeling of existence, on the other hand, is not attached to anything. It gets related to something, to this or that. Notice how the present moment itself does not dominate. Past and future dominate, if we let them. The past holds limitations; the future holds possibilities. At the moment of action, do we do what has been done before, or do we face the unknown? Do our habitual roles determine what we do, or do we act according to nature, ignoring habit? It may be uncomfortable, but 'the good is one, the pleasant another … who follows the pleasant, drops out of the race', says the *Katha Upanishad*. It needs courage to be in the present.

When virtue is dead, right action appears; when right action is dead, propriety appears; when propriety is dead, chaos appears. Who will move in the other direction? Whoever hears great ideas and acts upon them commands the future. Let the exercise help us. It brings us into the present. Only then is there escape from bondage.

Living in the present moment has always remained the simplest and perhaps the most potent of all the School's instructions. At this point it was recalled in terms of meeting the present situation, rather than wanting to know the future or to imitate the past. Each time one meets people or events it is in reality for the very first time, for every occasion is unique. A diagram about time supported this contention. On a circle of passing time the present moment was represented by a radius, touching the circle at 'now', but passing inwards to the timeless, unmoving centre. Only through the ever-present moment 'now' is connection made with eternity. The circle, seen as a human life, was divided into three equal parts: ten months in the womb, a hundred months as a child, and a thousand months as an adult. To

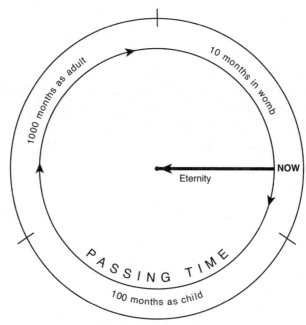

live only on the circumference is to live out the futility of MacBeth – 'Tomorrow and tomorrow and tomorrow, creeps in this petty pace from day to day...'

Leon MacLaren, like Ouspensky, gave much consideration to questions about time. He even made a film about it:

> The film, called *The Surface of Time*, consisted of images filmed from real life, people on the escalator of the London underground, traffic in Piccadilly Circus and also animated images, as well as various diagrammatical representations. The text was spoken by Dr Roles and a mixture of classical music and parts of *My Fair Lady* were played in the background. *My Fair Lady* had just opened in Drury Lane in 1958. This mixture of new technology, contemporary music and ancient knowledge was a real surprise to watch. The camera work was obviously limited and the animated pictures primitive by today's standards, but it was an attempt to bring the teaching alive in a new way and in a medium that was rapidly taking over the world.[5]

There were hitches. At one point the cameraman spent hours filming a moving snail, only to find that he had forgotten to remove the cover from the lens.

5 Dorine Tolley, *The Power Within*, p.56.

As the material explained, the English language is more or less limited to one word for time; whilst the ancient Greeks, for example, could distinguish between passing time (*chronos*) and the moment now (*kairos*). In the present moment everything is connected, in particular body, mind, nature and the creative principle. When we are awake, we may choose to move inwards towards the centre of our being or outwards, beyond the circle of passing time into the outer darkness of imagination, of dreams of yesterday and tomorrow.

If we give attention to something, mind and body are at the same time and place. Attention emanates from the creative principle itself, for it is the force of consciousness. When we do not give attention, many things come between the observer (oneself) and the object observed. Dreams intervene; they become the object in place of what is actually presented to us. So we need to take great care about what we present as an object. Most dangerous of all are pictures of oneself; for they are all false. The mind feeds on these objects, on what appears before it. Is it to grow strong on the real stuff of the present moment, or to weaken and die on the rotten food of false imaginings? We shall be asked how we spent the present moment. That is the real Day of Judgment.

A remarkable conclusion followed from this discussion: all our difficulties stem from believing that I am an object. On this principle hinged the teaching that the School presented at that time. Nor was it to be refuted by the later introduction of Advaita Vedanta. Remember, the material added, that whatever you are looking at, you cannot possibly be that. You cannot see yourself:

> You cannot see the seer of the sight, you cannot hear the hearer of the sound, you cannot think the thinker of the thought, you cannot know the knower of the known.[6]

Often this false 'me' that is allowed to be an object of our attention is really some function, some role to be enacted, at work or in the home or when we meet someone. The function should not be disregarded, but it is not oneself. If we see it truly for what it is, it can be performed more efficiently, not less so. A student went to an important business meeting, but forgot to take the reports and other papers that he had prepared. All he could do was to give his atten-

6 *The Ten Principal Upanishads*, p.138.

tion to what went on at the meeting. He performed his role there most efficiently.

When such barriers are dislodged from the mind, the horizon broadens. The natural desire for knowledge, happiness and fullness of life replaces the demands of pleasure, success and whatever else we want for ourselves alone. For the law of our nature denies a separate existence. In truth we desire knowledge, happiness and life for everyone, for every creature.

Things get done, however inefficiently! Involvement is even seen as efficient. But see how much more efficient is attention freely given. Attend to listening, to eating, to getting dressed in the morning. The senses give very precise information. Listen to silence. It contains strength and the memory of truth itself. As for the mind, it needs to be still. Let it rest on a problem. Watch the rapid impressions that pass through it. It will select some items and reject others. If the time is right, knowledge may enter. All this requires patience.

When Leon MacLaren first met the Study Society, he had remarked on the similarity between their diagrams and those used in the School's Economics classes. This arose from a mutual recognition of both the laws of three and of seven, which Ouspensky had expounded. In Economics the law of three appeared, for example, in the co-operation of land and labour in production: land as the passive force, labour as the active, with the third neutral force acting at the point where they meet, in the form of conditions like the laws of land tenure, of employment of labour and so on. The law of seven was seen in recurring trade cycles, for the number seven generates repetitive cycles. Seven divided into one gives the recurring decimal 0.1428570'.

These two laws were introduced into the early Philosophy material. Students were asked to watch for their action in simple events. When kicking a football, for example, one leg is active, the ball is passive, and the other leg gives stability as the neutral force. In the account of man's nature as threefold, the law of three is apparent. In work of all kinds the law of seven governs the sequence of actions. Intervals near the beginning and end require an extra input of energy to keep the job going and to bring it to fruition. Without this knowledge how many tasks falter at the first hurdle or fail to reach completion? Most homes and offices are littered with such false starts and uncompleted business. Endless repetition is the law of passing time. Only conscious intervention at the right intervals can maintain continuous action. Later on these laws would be confirmed in the context of Advaita Vedanta.

Meanwhile, the teaching was described as being as old as mankind, yet new for every current situation. The few who have ears to hear are the leaven in humanity, making the connection with its source. Nevertheless, the work begins on oneself. It becomes work with and for others, and eventually may become work for the work's sake. Help is always available from those further on. Thus did the Philosophy course progress. It was soon itself to receive a fresh impulse that would set it upon a new direction towards the same truth.

CHAPTER NINE

A Decade of Expansion

'ALWAYS the work is to be prepared for moments of destiny when great things are possible.' Thus spoke the Chairman of the School's Executive in his annual report for 1961. The following decade confirmed his precautionary words, for the School developed in a remarkable variety of ways under the impulse of the connection made soon afterwards with a great Indian teacher. Meeting Sri Shantananda Saraswati was undoubtedly a moment of destiny.

Yet the rapid growth of the School and its expansion, both geographically and into several new activities, was a kind of reverse image of the public life of the decade. For it was a period of superficial, even degenerate, change:

> Britain remained an industrial society and apparently a world power, whose future was believed to depend on factories churning out cars, engines, washing machines and electrical goods for export, and whose major cities were relics of the industrial revolution... Little islands of change were all around. Immigration was changing small patches of the country, the textile towns of Yorkshire and parts of west London, though it had barely impinged on most people's lives. There was a growing snappiness and lightness of design, in everything from clothes to the shapes of cars, an aesthetic escape from the seriousness of the immediate post-war period, which took different form year by year, but was experienced as a continuum not a revolution... In poetry, politics and incantation were returning. In painting, pop art and the pleasure principle were on the attack.[1]

Whilst the governments of Harold Wilson sought to shift the

1 Andrew Marr, *A History of Modern Britain*, Macmillan, 2007, p.233.

economy onto a higher plane of production by a technological revolution, and to free society from restraints like censorship, divorce and abortion laws, yet greater turbulence was experienced on the international stage. The world came very close to nuclear war in the Cuban missile crisis of 1962. President Kennedy was assassinated in the following year. The Cold War continued, focussed on the divided city of Berlin, and later in the 1960s the brave Czechs of the 'Prague Spring' were beaten down by Soviet tanks and the Brezhnev doctrine.

In the mirror of the School, such confused and violent events were reflected in a movement towards reason and tranquillity. The starting point for this was the recognition by both Dr Roles and Leon MacLaren that they had at last found a master teacher, whose words could be completely trusted. In 1961 Dr Roles went to India to help the Maharishi set up a centre for meditation. One day the Maharishi announced that he would be meeting the head of his tradition, Shantananda Saraswati, in the nearby city of Dehra Dun. On his return he said that the master would be coming to stay. Dr Roles described his arrival:

> First of all a car arrived with some of his entourage who unpacked a great throne of gold and silver, and a great red and gold umbrella which fitted into the back of it, two silver maces and two great plumes to keep the flies away, and tridents with drums of Siva; and then a big estate car drove up after it. Meanwhile, much of the population of the surrounding country had gathered there, when out of the second car stepped this man with his closest people around him. He looked like a great Kahn, more Tibetan to my ignorant eyes than Indian, with jet black hair, long greying beard, square, very firm step; a little bit frightening at first; and immediately he stepped out of the car there was this press of people putting garlands over his neck, trying to kiss his feet, pressing and pushing forward, gongs, bells, conches blowing, and he was completely 'withdrawn'. You could see that he was holding himself unaffected by it all.[2]

An audience followed:

> A chant would begin with the high tenor voice taking up each verse and the deeper refrain sung by all the Indians who knew it, and this chant rang such a strangely familiar bell in me. It came from one of

the Vedas, not the Rig-Veda, but the Ayur-Veda, and absolutely
stirred something deep in me... He answered questions immediately, without having to think at all; very precisely and tersely; often
in one sentence; beautiful formulations; he didn't change his voice
very much, but you could tell by the happy laughter which went up
that the Maharishi was enjoying them as much as anybody, before he
translated them to us. Those answers were very witty and his stories
were absolutely beautiful, almost anything could be illustrated by
some story, and if the atmosphere needed lifting, he would tell a
story that made us all laugh, and if it was the right atmosphere we
would speak about serious things and so on; but we all had a little
fun poked at us in a very benign and gentle way if we exaggerated
or dramatised! These terse and beautiful formulations, said in this
soft voice, said in a very modern way, very simple language, made an
extraordinary impression on all of us.[3]

This experience profoundly affected Dr Roles. On the same
occasion his belief that he had found the source of the teaching
inherited from Pyotr Ouspensky was confirmed by a remarkable
statement from Shantananda Saraswati:

> The whole thing is that we never remember ourselves. All our
> troubles come from not remembering ourselves, only we can't talk
> about this at the beginning because it is never understood. You will
> have to reach realisation before you can understand it.[4]

For the next few years the Shankaracharya[5] and Dr Roles were
frequently in touch, and other members of the Study Society also
accompanied Dr Roles to Allahabad for audiences.

Meanwhile Leon MacLaren had been given transcripts of the
Shankaracharya's conversations, and immediately recognised them as
the words of a man of real knowledge. He sent him some questions
that had arisen from the practices introduced in the early Philosophy
groups. One student, for example, had experienced a state of 'not
doing', in which actions were performed as though by themselves.
Another had spoken of being an 'absolutely still point of existence',
whilst the world seemed like a play. MacLaren himself had observed
meditation taking place throughout the space of a room and all its

3 *Ibid.*, pp.247-8.
4 *Ibid.*, p.256.
5 The great eighth-century AD philosopher, Shankara, who had revived the whole tradition
of the Vedas, set up four seats of Philosophy in India. Shantananda Saraswati was the
latest in the line of Shankaracharyas of the North. *Acharya* means teacher.

contents, and on another occasion, in New Zealand when students were meditating in a hotel by the sea, he experienced meditation extending around the whole bay into the hills and trees.

The Shankaracharya's reply to these was to confirm that such experiences may occur in places of special beauty or devotion, and to introduce the idea of *guna*. When *sattva* is predominant at such times, deeper levels of experience are easily available.

A question referred to a student's extreme thirst for the truth; to which the reply described only the *Atman*, the Self, as the truth, never changing, indestructible, neither improving nor decaying. When MacLaren wrote that, if the 'watchman' is present, 'I' disappears and thoughts, feelings and the rest become 'public property', the Shankaracharya told him that the watchman is not separate from the Self; that if one is attentive and still, one 'I' emerges out of many 'I's, pure *Aham* out of *Ahankara*.

Later, questions were asked about students' meditation. Several had experienced the need to stay on a line, which sometimes ran ahead or in a circle. Others discovered 'inner rooms' or spheres that contained events and people from the past. Such experiences emanate from the heart and move towards the head, was the reply. In some cases dirt from the past had to be blown away! When asked about the feeling of 'I am', the Shankaracharya said that *Aham* is the form of the *Atman*, and is neither the actor nor the experiencer. When 'I am' corresponds to *Atman*, the whole creation is seen as a play. To a question about essence, he replied that it takes in the substance of actions, both useful and useless ones, to determine the form of being and hold possibilities for the future.

Some questions about science from John Allen were sent. What is the true method of research? What is the true idea of the atom? Is the material of the whole universe organised like a kind of table of elements? The answers were forthright: the real search is for causes, not for more manifestations in the physical world, which show only the relationship of movements. Truth is only found if one is still and looking inward. The real cause is *Brahman*, like clay causing the pot.

All these questions had arisen from members of the School, and they elicited practical answers to be put to work and to bear fruit in the lives of students. Their outcome was that in 1965 the Shankaracharya invited Leon MacLaren to go to India, and on 11 December they met in Allahabad. The dialectical method that preceded the visit was to be continued for thirty years. It drew forth a system of knowledge that precisely met the needs of the West at this time, a unique version of the ancient tradition of Advaita Vedanta, not given in that form even to the master's disciples in India.

A crucial part was played by Sitaram Jaiswal, an Indian member of the School, who acted as translator for both Leon MacLaren and Dr Roles. He gave up his work as a commercial artist in order to have time for this. The Executive waived the rule about students being paid, and gave him an allowance to finance study in Benares and London of Sanskrit and Hindi. At times the relationship between Jaiswal and MacLaren was difficult, but there was great mutual respect. The role of translator was very demanding. Although conversations with the Shankaracharya were recorded, Jaiswal had to provide an immediate version, so that the dialogue could take place. A revised account was prepared later, and became the text used by both MacLaren and senior students in the future. Jaiswal also helped MacLaren to learn Sanskrit terms and to begin upon a study of the language itself, for, although the Shankaracharya spoke Hindi, his own learning encompassed the Veda and other Indian scriptures in their original Sanskrit. Jaiswal has served the School loyally for no less than half a century. In more ways than one, he has been a link between East and West, at a time when the transmission of ideas may prove critical to the survival of both cultures.

This meeting in Allahabad in 1965 transformed the School. Now it had acquired a sure foundation, a teaching that drew together the philosophical sources drawn upon previously, from Plato and the Gospels to the Fourth Way of Ouspensky. These were not to be abandoned. On the contrary, they were enlivened by the light cast on them by Advaita. But henceforth the School would concentrate upon the words of the master in India. He would be the guide of Leon MacLaren, and his answers would become the gist of the material that would be offered to students.

The context in which this transformative event took place was a general expansion of the School. By the early 1960s the London School was holding a hundred classes per week. By 1965 it achieved a record attendance of three thousand students, including five hundred for Economics. Pressure on buildings was inexorable. In 1959 a fine Victorian house in Chepstow Villas, Notting Hill was purchased. Five years later a larger house, amongst the tall, stuccoed terraces of

Queens Gate, near Hyde Park, was bought. In 1966 the lease, with a peppercorn rent, on a country house with extensive grounds, called Stanhill Court, at Charlwood in Surrey, was obtained. This was to be used for residential courses. Then followed, in 1970, Sarum Chase on Telegraph Hill by Hampstead Heath, a fine house built for the notable portrait painter, Frank Salisbury, in a style sometimes called 'Hollywood Tudor'. Meanwhile, the newly formed art group was granted a house in Harlem Road, West London, followed by Augustine Studios in Fulham.

All these houses were financed mainly from gifts and interest-free loans from students. They were to give the School holdings in the London property market that were to appreciate in value very considerably in the following decades. Ironically the School, founded on the principle that land is the common possession of all, and that land rent should be collected as public revenue, found itself a successful, if unwilling, player in the London land market. Why? The answer was very simple: it needed the buildings. No student, of course, has ever gained anything personally from their value.

Even these purchases were not the whole answer to the problem of space. Suffolk Street continued to be occupied, together with rooms in the nearby Newton Institute. Rooms were also rented from the Study Society, from the Housing Centre, from Church House, Westminster, from the School of Meditation, and in Earls Court Square. For a few years Embley Park, near Romsey, the home of Florence Nightingale, was used once a year for residential weeks.

The serial acquisitions of buildings in the 1960s was almost matched by the serial acquisition of School Principals! Iain Bowerman became Principal in 1961, Kenneth Dunjohn in 1963, Ian Berry in 1964 and finally Peter Green in 1967. He was to remain until 1998. Leon MacLaren continued throughout as the effective leader of the School, but growth had led to a practical division between philosophical leadership and administrative responsibilities, which by the 1960s were becoming very considerable. MacLaren's treatment of the short-lived Principals, however, probably hastened their departure. Foremost in his mind was always the spiritual development of all members of the School. The office of Principal gave no exemption, when it came to the need to confront false ideas about oneself. Moreover, even on administrative issues, MacLaren's status inevitably meant that his views prevailed if he chose to intervene. Peter Green's longevity in the post owed much to his tact and diplomatic ability.

He once appositely said that he felt like a French Prime Minister serving under General de Gaulle.

Nor did everything run smoothly in other areas. Ronald Burgess, the long-standing Treasurer and Senior Tutor in Economics, was not happy with the relationship between Leon MacLaren and Dr Roles. The earlier co-operation between them had been replaced by more single-minded developments of their respective organisations. Burgess attempted to read a letter from Dr Roles at an Executive meeting, but this was ruled out of order. Later he opposed the purchase of Queens Gate, claiming that the School was 'three months off bankruptcy'. When he was not consulted over an appeal made to some students for gifts and loans, he angrily retorted that confidence in him as Treasurer had been undermined. In 1966 he resigned, and left the School soon after. As a professional economist of some note, he was a serious loss. In fact, the financial position was sound enough. Peter Green replaced him as Treasurer, and oversaw a surplus of £10,000 in that year. Endowment income from students amounted to over one third of total revenues.

Alongside the development of the London School came the growth of branches. In rapid succession they were opened, usually by students who had moved out from London, in Wellington, Preston, Amsterdam, Johannesburg, New York – where the opening was hit by a violent snow blizzard – Sydney, Malta, Dublin, Auckland, Boston and Manchester. These all had to be furnished with Philosophy – and in some cases Economics – material from London, a task organised by a lady who was becoming very influential, Shelia Rosenberg. Some branches, notably Amsterdam, grew at a remarkable rate.

Besides the growth of London and the branches, what gave proof also of the depth that the study of practical Philosophy brought to those who took it seriously was the introduction of wider activities into the School. These arose primarily from the needs of students. Creative ability appeared spontaneously, apparently in a random way, and was met by a response from Leon MacLaren, not only to encourage but to offer guidance. In this he himself began to show a highly creative feature of his character, a capacity to see the essential principles of subjects, like art or music, that ranged far beyond his own training in law and economics. As students came to him asking searching questions about such subjects, usually when disillusioned with what they had found in the world outside, he would give perhaps only a few germinal words of advice, and then arrange for an appropriate group to be formed – for he had little faith in the power of unaided individuals. His first words to the new art group, for example, were 'Paint what you see'. Too simple perhaps? – but how many artists were actually doing that in the 1960s?

Groups began to study music, drama, mathematics, calligraphy, printing, anatomy (for the artists), and, possibly most significant of all, Sanskrit. In 1968 a group embarked on the translation of the letters from Latin into English of Marsilio Ficino, the Renaissance philosopher. Impetus was given to the music group when a student gave a grand piano to Stanhill Court, enabling MacLaren, who was a gifted if unconventional pianist – earlier he had played jazz, but now eschewed it – to entertain residential students with Mozart sonatas.

These activities greatly enriched the School, broadening its appeal beyond the hard core of Philosophy and Economics, and satisfying the desires of many students whose talents, often hidden by neglect or personal circumstances, could now begin to flourish. Some students found themselves impelled to change their careers. One went from being a business executive to become a headmaster. A professional chemist returned to a London music academy and became a music teacher and choirmaster. Many more became enthusiastic amateurs, contributing both to the School and to local communities through their developing ability with hand or tongue. Others, of course, found a new creativity in their existing professions, as artists, performers and teachers, or in areas where new ideas and practices could be introduced. And in small, influential ways the activities entered people's lives: speech became refined, handwriting more beautiful, homes better decorated, clothes more decorous.

To accommodate these developments the rules of the School were amended slightly. Rule 1 became:

> To promote the study of natural laws governing the relations between men in society and all studies relating thereto *and to promote the study of the laws, customs and practices by which communities are governed and all studies related thereto.*

In mind perhaps was Plato's famous dictum that, when the laws of music change, so too do the laws of society.

As the School evolved, so did Leon MacLaren. He had become a kind of intermediary, or bridge, between the ancient wisdom of India and twentieth-century Britain. He sat at the feet of a wise man in India as his loyal disciple, and at the same time he was like a master teacher himself to students in the School. As an English barrister, he had prepared in a way for such a role, standing in court between the learned judge and the public gallery! It was at this time – in 1963 – that he finally vacated his chambers in the Temple. Earlier he had sacrificed the opportunity to travel to judiciaries in the British Commonwealth to investigate the creation of a new Commonwealth Court of Appeal, in which he strongly believed. His travels now were strictly on behalf of the School: to Amsterdam, New Zealand, South Africa, New York, and, of course, to India. Meanwhile, his second wife Peggy left the School in order to remain with the Study Society. There was a separation without a divorce. In Peggy's opinion, Leon was married to the School. To School students he was certainly the focus, the direct source of the teaching, and the one who never lacked enthusiasm for the ongoing search. With his wit and sense of fun, he made even learning the Sanskrit alphabet a thing of delight. At Stanhill Court in 1968, he touched the hearts of all present by referring to the Czech's fight for independence, then at its height. Did we know, he asked, that the Czech's President's name – Svoboda – meant 'freedom'? He remained a liberal in the best sense of the word.

CHAPTER TEN

The First
Conversations

A DESCRIPTION of Leon MacLaren in audience with the
Shankaracharya was given by Peter Green, the long-serving
School Principal, when he was present in India. Usually the
audiences were held at an ashram. The Shankaracharya sat in
the lotus position on a low dais, at first with his eyes closed, still and
serene, wearing an orange robe. Garlands were offered by the
visitors, who sat and waited. The chanting by attendants that had
greeted them stopped and, opening his eyes, the Shankaracharya
acknowledged their presence. He looked, said Peter Green, neither
Indian nor Western, without race or colour, ageless, the Self embodied. In reply to MacLaren's questions, he spoke in Hindi or Sanskrit,
in a clear voice, free of overlays, but rising and falling with unaffected
speech and gesticulating with his hands. Jaiswal translated immediately, though afterwards he would make a more thorough version for
MacLaren's perusal. When an audience ended a prayer was chanted,
they meditated briefly, and then the visitors withdrew, leaving their
teacher as they had found him. Strict formality had accompanied a
profound meeting.

From the beginning in 1965 the conversations between Sri
Shantananda Saraswati and Leon MacLaren covered a huge field of
philosophical topics. Any attempt to present them in outline can
never capture the spontaneity and depth of the Shankaracharya's
answers. Nevertheless, the general nature of the answers can be
summarised. Some of these confirmed what the School was already
teaching. Others ranged completely beyond any previous material.

The value of 'good company' was endorsed from the outset:
there can be no higher purpose, said the Shankaracharya, than to

bring men and women to a natural way of living, to help those who
have lost their way. Whatever the character a person has acquired by
past living, good company may correct it.

In relation to meditation various problems were dealt with. For
example, some students found an inability to control the body or the
emotions. The Shankaracharya emphasised the need to create a finer
energy by meditation, and then to put this to good use. Further
practices should be introduced to deal with this. How breathing
was related to meditation was explained. As the breathing slows, with
a longer rhythm, it reaches the base of the spine before turning back.
Energy stored there passes to higher centres. When the breath is easy
and natural it stills the mind, so that attention to the mantra may
improve.

Two analogies for meditation were given. Firstly, of life as a
drama in which one plays a part: the unwitting actor continues to
play his part at each performance without going back to rest and
to renew his costume. The wise actor repeatedly avails himself of the
opportunity to go backstage, and thus continues to play his part with
new energy and artistry. Secondly, the analogy of a well shows how
water is drawn and consumed during the day, but at night a fresh
supply must be allowed to run into the well to be available in the
morning. Meditation is the deep rest that revives not just the body –
as sleep may do – but the whole person.

In the original teaching of the School the concept of mind had
always strongly featured. Indeed most of the instructions given
had been concerned with correcting the operation of the mind. The
new teaching from India was in full accord with this, but gave a more
comprehensive view and a precise analysis.

First stands *citta*, which includes memory, emotion and reflection,
in general what may be called 'heart'. *Citta* determines one's attitude
to something – to a person, an event, indeed to life itself. Why this
is can be explained with reference to *citta* as a kind of store, in
particular a store of all that one brings into the world at birth – as
was explained later, from former lives – with the addition of the
effects of actions in this life. For any action has an effect on *citta*,
unless it is performed without any regard to one's own personal
benefit. These effects accumulate, so that together they exert an
influence on whatever the individual does later. It is as though the
citta, like glass, becomes stained with the colours of former actions,
and then reflects these on to all that happens afterwards. We see the

world 'through a glass darkly'. Hence the purification of *citta* should become a vital part of School work.

Below *citta* is *ahankara*, the sense of individuality or idea of oneself, the ego. From this, said the Shankaracharya, springs every experience that is called 'me' or 'mine'. The word is derived from *aham*, meaning simply 'I' or 'I am', and *kara*, meaning any kind of doing or event. Thus the *ahankara* is 'I' associated with something else, like having a sensation, feeling or thought, or performing an action. When 'me' or 'mine' is involved, there is necessarily an identification or attachment to something not in reality oneself, as when one says 'I am angry' or 'I am pleased'. *Aham* alone, on the other hand, represents the pure, unmixed awareness of oneself.

About the third aspect of mind – *buddhi* – the Shankaracharya spoke at length. *Buddhi* is broadly intelligence, but it has several functions. In these early conversations most attention was given to that of discrimination. Later more would be said about reason and creativity also. Discrimination he defined as the power to distinguish between what is true and what is false.

Coming from a society like Britain in the 1960s, many students were much in need of this ability. Old standards of behaviour were in question. Education, religion and political leadership were in varying states of confusion. Judgment lay in the street. This was not a matter of being handed a new moral code. On the contrary, the whole point of discrimination was that it came from oneself, from within. Everyone is in possession of it; the point was 'Is it being used?'

The Shankaracharya gave several examples. What are the most fundamental questions that we ask ourselves? Are they not 'What is this Creation?', 'Who made it?' and 'What is my relationship to it?' Discrimination raises these questions and persists in searching for answers. If it persists long enough, it arrives at the concept of an Absolute at the root of all three questions. For another example he turned to the *Crest Jewel of Wisdom*, written by the original Shankara. Five sheaths that obscure the real Self are discriminated one by one. The food sheath is the body, the breath sheath the movements or actions of the body, the mind sheath all mental activity, the intelligence sheath understanding and the bliss sheath personal happiness. Discrimination removes identification with each in turn. Once more the ultimate step is the realisation that only the Self remains.

At this time Leon MacLaren was concerned about students who had built up 'subtle structures' in the mind, which were obstacles to further progress. A journalist, for example, had constructed a whole mental apparatus for getting and reordering information, which was consuming his energy. Here was another practical use for discrimination. If the structures could be identified as the product of past actions reinforced by imagination, discrimination would recognise their falsity.

The Shankacharya added an invaluable rider. If a structure is destroyed, there may be harmful consequences if nothing is done to redirect the energy previously wasted. He drew the analogy of a dam. Once built, the dam saves water, but this will overflow dangerously if there is no proper channel for its distribution. The School could help to cut such channels. This is a matter of arousing emotion, so that the energy is willingly and usefully spent. How to do this? The answer was surprising. Students need to be introduced to the sacred centres of their own civilisation and culture. The beauty to be found there may awaken an emotional response, especially if it is remembered that consciousness is its source. Enjoyment may lead to a desire to preserve this beauty and the places that contain it.

When later this answer was given to students, many found a new interest in European culture. Sheila Rosenberg, Bernard Saunders – the leader of the art group – and others set about locating the sacred places: Chartres, Canterbury, Florence and Athens were soon selected. Both individually and in parties School members began visiting the great cathedrals and art galleries, studying history and practising various arts with fresh enthusiasm. For a while one could be sure to come across a friend from the School in the dim recesses of Chartres cathedral or in the long queue outside the Uffizi. A new dimension had been added that turned people's attention outwards and away from introspection. It was a valuable reminder that the Self is both within and without.

Several answers to questions about students with problems of health and mental disturbance referred to the idea of measure. A major function of discrimination is to recognise the measure or natural order in how the body and mind work, and indeed in all aspects of nature. This was a very powerful new concept, which Leon MacLaren quickly saw as a practical means of advancing the work of the School. Measure is recognised when there is both clear observation through the senses and discrimination based on an understanding of law. Food and sleep are two areas of life where correct measure is essential. Observation shows when enough food has been taken, and whether it is suitably fresh and tasteful. Discrimination restrains the desire for more when it is not needed. Similarly with sleep. On waking up naturally the rational choice is to get up. There were strong echoes here of the School principle derived from the Fourth Way of 'Do and say nothing unnecessary.' These highly practical elements of measure were soon to be widely disseminated amongst more senior students, notably through residential courses at Stanhill Court, often with startling results!

The Shankaracharya told the story of a greedy brahmin from Bombay, who was invited to dinner by a rich man. After a heavy meal the brahmin was offered five rupees for eating another sweetmeat. He accepted, then ate two more for ten and twenty-five rupees. As he was no longer capable of walking, he was taken home to bed. The food had swelled in his stomach, so that he could hardly breathe. A doctor was called, who prescribed a pill, but the brahmin indicated that, if he had space for a pill, he would have eaten another sweetmeat!

Measure involves both the quantity needed and a proper interval between enjoyment. This applies equally to food for the mind. Impressions through the senses should be those that are beneficial. Good pictures and good music are easily available, though even these can be taken to excess. A further example repeated an earlier instruction – avoid chatter! The measure of every activity is to be discovered. Food, for example, is seasonal; out of season its taste and freshness are lost. If measure is ignored, disorder follows.

In this regard, Leon MacLaren asked for guidance concerning physical health, particularly as doctors in the School could not relate their knowledge of biology and physiology to human development and to the real nature of bodily functions. The answer again referred to the importance of emotion. Modern medicine has much knowledge of the physical body, but tends to ignore the impact of emotion on, for example, body cells. This is determined in three ways: by inherited characteristics (*sanskara*), by company and by actions. Good company can neutralise bad or unhealthy *sanskara*; right actions can outweigh even bad company. Hence the School may help to purify the emotions, which in turn aids the recovery of damaged cells. The direction of causality, the Shankaracharya insisted, is always from subtle to coarse, from mind to body. Essentially the School's role concerning medical matters was preventative, rather than curative. Yet it would greatly ease the condition of those with bodily diseases to remind them that the Self is totally unaffected by them, and that the mind does not have to suffer with the body. Pain may be limited to the body alone.

All this was to do with the power of intelligence to discriminate. There remained the fourth aspect of mind, called *manas*, which the Shankaracharya described as 'the messenger boy'. Ordinary thinking, or what might be termed discursive mind, is one of its functions. In addition it controls the senses and, in particular, connects them with the higher functions, indeed with consciousness itself. When *manas* is absent the senses simply do not operate. We are absent-minded. Eyes may be presented with an object, ears with a sound, but unless there is a connection through *manas* with consciousness there is no experience. Thus 'the messenger boy' makes the connection. He is the interpreter between the world of sense experience and the ultimate Self.

Manas occupies a subordinate position. Its natural role is to obey *buddhi*, to be governed by intelligence. If *buddhi* is weak, *manas* may run wild. Uncontrolled it can cause havoc. One becomes dominated by the senses, by sensual appetites 'past reason hunted', when the mind does not properly restrain them. The senses need to be measured out in their use by intelligence, which *manas* lacks. It was evident that this simple explanation of how life may become natural and well-ordered, or on the contrary degenerate into coarseness and futility, comprehended much that the School had taught earlier by means of more disparate principles and examples.

In another respect the Shankaracharya's teaching about the four aspects of mind – heart, ego, intelligence and discursive mind – also coincided with what the earlier material had said. The ancient aphorism 'As above, so below' was already familiar to students. Man is a microcosm of the universe. Each of these four aspects of mind is really universal, so the individual sees only a kind of reflection of these enormously greater functions. Universal *citta* is the unmanifested storehouse of all created things, from which the Creation expands and into which it is finally dissolved. It is the universal memory. An individual similarly draws from memory all that has happened, and stores in memory everything that happens to him. Universal *ahankara* is the universal sense of existence that gives identity to the whole of nature. Just as the individual has creative power through *buddhi*, so too the whole Creation is made by universal *buddhi*. Finally universal *manas* is the link between sense objects and the intelligence of the Creator. Unlike the discursive mind of the individual, the world of nature never lacks intelligent control. At all times and places, down to the last detail, the universe remains under law, as every scientist knows.

Here in the conversation there was a reference to what the School had described as states of consciousness – sleep, dreaming, wakefulness, self-consciousness and objective consciousness. These are really only happening at the level of the mind, for consciousness is the permanent unchanging witness, whose light shines through all five states. What is experienced in them is nothing but a drama.

A fundamental error in common thought that the School had identified earlier was that ordinarily the mind is taken to be in some sense within the body, with the ego a central point within the mind itself. Each person imagines himself to be a conscious being looking out at the world from somewhere inside the head, with the mind and senses as intermediaries. The reverse is the case, as the Shankaracharya confirmed. The body is the smallest form of the man; the senses contain the body, the four levels of mind, starting with *manas*, are successively larger, and the Self as consciousness contains all. To undo this error would be to change utterly a person's view of himself and of the universe.

Leon MacLaren asked about the laws of three and seven. Once more the previous teaching was given a more extended and precise meaning. The law of three, it was said, is primarily seen in the three basic forces or qualities (*guna*) that appear from the very creation of the universe. These are indeed positive, negative and neutralising, but were given their Sanskrit names – *sattva*, *rajas* and *tamas*. At every level of manifestation they reappear, and accordingly the Shankaracharya was to refer to them many times in different contexts. *Sattva* is light, peaceful and full of knowledge. *Rajas* is the moving force, always active, sometimes agitating. *Tamas* is regulative, bringing rest or dissolution. For any event or state to occur there has to be some imbalance between the *guna*. One must be predominant, yet all three must be present to differing degrees. The particular combination determines the nature of what happens. Many examples were given. *Citta* in the *sattvic* condition yields memory of truth itself; in *rajas* it has knowledge derived from action and experience; in *tamas* it has knowledge merely of states of sleep. Faith similarly may be *sattvic*, which is unmoving love that 'looks on tempests and is never shaken'. *Rajassic* faith changes after some time and 'alters when it alteration finds.' *Tamassic* faith is fleeting, a thing of the moment.

In answer to further questions, much was said also about how the *guna* act in relation to meditation. The condition of the meditator may significantly affect the action of the mantra and the attention given to it. Obviously *sattva* is most conducive to meditation; *rajas* may seriously interfere with it; and *tamas* may reduce it to dreams and sleep.

A further development came with the idea that *guna* can take the form of obstacles, as what are called *kshaya*, *vikshepa* and *mala*. *Kshaya* is a screen, not opaque but creating a kind of fog in which one may feel nothing at all or a deceptive peace. Life may seem easy and enjoyable, but without any development. *Vikshepa* leads one to live always in the past or in the future. It means 'interference' and prevents decisions being made, so that one is always moving without knowing where to go. *Mala* is like a thick and impenetrable crust that produces a low state of life. These conditions were later easily recognised by School students! Those with *kshaya* need instruction to arouse genuine enthusiasm. For *vikshepa* the remedy is the company of people who live in the present and do not waver. *Mala* needs attention to physical work to bring body and mind into action and dissolve the *tamassic* quality.

Everything in the universe is subject to the three forces of *sattva*, *rajas* and *tamas*. Man as a creature on earth is no exception; yet he has within himself the one substance, consciousness, which is beyond the *guna*. This substance is the *Atman*, the Self, the principle of life itself. As the earlier material had foreseen, with its concept of the creative principle, this is the ultimate cause of all, including the *guna* themselves and all that they enter into. This natural essence of each man and woman gets covered over by accretions brought about by selfishness, greed and attachment, so that an apparent new essence overlays the real one, which remains dormant. If, by grace, good company is met with and memory aroused, then work may begin on revealing the truth within.

An amusing story illustrated this situation. A lion cub mistakenly followed a flock of sheep, and grew up with them, learning to eat grass and baa like a sheep. One day a lion appeared and roared at the flock. They all ran away, except the lion cub. Recognising the lion's form, he approached him with affection. The lion took care of him, and he grew up to be a real lion.

Although discrimination makes the law evident, there remains the choice whether to acknowledge it or not. Those who seek their own personal ends ignore the law. They try to force a result out of nature against the law, which can only lead to unexpected consequences of a lawful kind, perhaps some time later. Ignoring law at one level brings one under coarser laws. Those who obey the law go with the flow of events. For natural law is the undeniable will of the Absolute. The wise do nothing; nature does it all.

The account of the *guna* had been introduced as the principal instance of the law of three. When asked about the law of seven, the Shankaracharya replied that, whilst the law of three applies to every event, the law of seven explains the succession of events as finer substances become coarser, or vice versa. This enlarged on Ouspensky's proposition that the law of seven concerned stages in a process. The progression from fine to coarse begins in the Absolute, and runs from nature (*prakriti*) through the universal sense of existence (*mahattattva*), ether or space (*akasha*), air (*vayu*), fire (*tejas*) and water (*jala*) to earth (*prithivi*). Everything in the creation is made of these elements. Understanding this enables the student to discriminate the coarse from the subtle, and thus step by step to remain free from identification at coarser levels.

Each element contains those below it, but the qualities of each are only evident at their own level and below. For example, the quality of ether is sound, for sound expresses itself in space. Sound remains evident in air, which also expresses touch. Fire expresses light and heat, but also sound and touch, and so on. The special quality of water is taste; that of earth is smell. Thus earth expresses all five qualities. This account could easily have become a merely theoretical exercise for students. The Shankaracharya, however, added that each of the five lower elements has a subtle equivalent related to the senses. These subtle forces (*tanmatra*) turn out to be the qualities themselves as experienced by the human senses. This clearly implied a connection with the exercise that students had practised for some while. Awareness of the feet on the ground, the touch of air on the skin, sight, taste, smell and sounds near and far away were what had been directly experienced on first entering the School. Now these sense impressions could be understood as the subtle forms of what constituted the material universe itself, the five lower elements of earth, water, fire, air and space.

Leon MacLaren then raised the subject of science. Scientists regard the idea of five fundamental elements as a medieval view, long superseded by the findings of modern chemistry and physics. They also tend to dismiss the whole realm of inner experience as subjective and irrelevant. Could a system of number help them come to a deeper understanding? This question led to a lengthy discussion of number and the elements. Scientists place great trust in their five senses, replied the Shankaracharya. What gives them this trust? Whatever it is cannot itself be tested empirically by the use of the senses themselves Therefore they should be reminded that there is something that is completely trustworthy, yet beyond examination by the senses. To look into this subtle world an instrument is available – one's own being. This is the means of proof for that world, particularly the use of discrimination. For the causal world beyond that, the words of the Veda, spoken by enlightened men, are the means. By following causes back from the final element of earth, through the other eight elements, one arrives at the Absolute, for which there is no proof.

On this note the dialogue about number began. The laws that govern the universe are mathematical was the Shankaracharya's standpoint, one surely acceptable by most present-day scientists. Some, such as Erwin Schrodinger, would also have agreed with the Shankaracharya's statement that the elements are really activities, which merely appear to be observable forms. They are not material things or substances. This approach to the elements underlay the discourse that followed on number, for the numbers from one to nine were taken to be the very elements themselves. Hence the qualities of each number refer to nine fundamental activities that constitute the universe, not to fundamental things out of which it is built. It is for this reason, perhaps, that he said that modern scientists are looking in the wrong direction in searching for ultimate particles. They will always find more, since the varieties in the universe are infinite. Yet all are composed of the nine elements, organised in infinitely different forms.

The idea that the elements are activities is clearly demonstrated in the case of nature (*prakriti*). For it divides into the three *guna*, which are not separable entities, but three kinds of activity or force that always occur together, though in different combinations of intensity. So nature itself is one great activity, acting in three ways, both in the universe as a whole and in the microcosm of each human being. In terms of number, nature is indeed number three. Every event has a threefold aspect, for that is the nature of events.

Above nature stands its unmanifest form at number two, known as *avyakta*. This is the storehouse of the creative process, all things unmanifest or in potential, like the mustard seed from which the great tree grows. Space, time and the *guna* are all held within it, awaiting expression when nature itself comes to fruition. Its meaning as two is that when consciousness is aware of anything else at all there is duality. Thus everything present in *avyakta* exists as the 'other', making two with the consciousness that observes it. When an individual is aware of himself and an 'other', that also is duality.

The Self alone, of course, is one. In relation to the nine numbers it is one unmanifest, as well as being all nine, as the different levels of manifestation of itself. As the Self, it gets forgotten. A story of the Shankaracharya illustrated this. Ten men were crossing a swiftly flowing river. When at last they had all struggled over, they each counted, and could only find nine men. They were distraught at the loss of life. Fortunately a wise man came their way. On hearing their story, he counted them by tapping each in turn on the shoulder, once, twice and so on. On striking the last man ten times, he reminded them that each had forgotten to count himself. This ancient story highlighted the principal purpose of understanding the nine numbers. Lost in manifestations of consciousness at one level or another, we forget the Self that is observing.

One, two and three together constitute the causal world, beyond manifestation in mental or physical form. At four we enter the mental world, where the universal sense of existence (*mahattattva*) embodies all aspects of mind – *citta, ahankara, buddhi,* and *manas.* All that we are aware of through mind and senses – thoughts, feelings, and sense experiences – are held together here under the feeling of 'I' or 'mine'. The number four indicates this by its quality of firmness or stability.

At five is the transitional point between the physical world and everything intangible beyond it. It is the element of *akasha* or ether, of which space is the expression. The sense of hearing is associated with it through its quality of sound. Ether acts as an interpreter, said the Shankaracharya, between the physical and the subtle worlds. Here they make contact. Words, that take us into the mental and causal worlds, have first to be heard.

At six we find the element air. This is where physical movement begins. In the form of five breaths (*prana*), it enlivens the human body, governing not only inhalation and exhalation but also, for example, the digestive system. Seven is fire, arising from the friction caused by movements in air. At this stage the Shankaracharya demonstrated the threefold nature present in each element. *Sattvic* fire is the light of knowledge; *rajassic* fire is the great light of the Sun and stars; *tamassic* fire includes that made on the earth by artificial means, and is also the heat of the physical body. From the element fire men and women obtain their brilliance and energy. Water is number eight. It is the element that binds things together, the physical equivalent of love. If bonds of water are removed, things disintegrate, as when something becomes dessicated. Bonds also make limits, so that one may limit oneself to a particular form, and forget the formless reality of the Self in being identified with one's body or with an idea.

Finally at nine is earth, consisting of all the material of which physical things are made. This is at the same time both the coarsest of the elements and the glorious culmination or fulfilment of the whole creative process. From it all natural and man-made substances are created, even though all nine elements are present within it. It was salutary for the School to hear this encomium of the element that in terms of Economics means land, as though the studies that began with the ideas of Henry George had turned full circle.

It was indeed as a circle of nine points that the Shankaracharya presented this information on number. Number nine stood at the top, next to number one, which represented the beginning of a cycle of manifestation in nine stages. After nine, the number ten was said to represent one, or consciousness, alongside zero as the unmanifest, like the tenth man who is not evident because he is oneself. Ten was simply the beginning of a second repetitive cycle. There are only nine numbers, he insisted. Any more are merely repetitions of the nine, which can continue to infinity, like the infinite varieties of so-called scientific elements found in the universe. Apparent multiplicity beyond nine only occurs in the physical world.

Movement around the circle of nine points can be understood in both directions. Clockwise it represents the process of creation, with forms multiplying and forces diminishing. This is the outward thrust of creation from its origin in pure consciousness, the Absolute. Anti-clockwise it represents the movement 'against nature', the

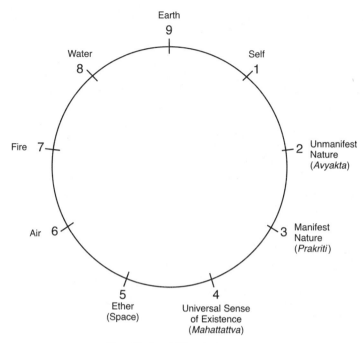

Earth
9

Water
8

Self
1

Fire 7

2 Unmanifest
Nature
(*Avyakta*)

Air 6

3 Manifest
Nature
(*Prakriti*)

5
Ether
(Space)

4
Universal Sense
of Existence
(*Mahattattva*)

The Circle of Nine Points

work towards self-realisation, whereby forms diminish towards one and forces are gathered together. This inward movement is that described in the *Crest Jewel of Wisdom*, whereby the five sheaths are penetrated one by one. The latter explanation, said the Shankaracharya, is more personal, whereas the circle of nine points is universal. In terms of the nine elements, we tend to identify with all the physical elements under the form of the body, rather than with earth or water etc. What is crucial is to see that non-attachment to any manifested element is the key to realising the Self.

As the School had already taught, real human development does not take place in passing time. Indeed its possibility is presented only in the present moment, and its movement is towards or away from eternity. Likewise, the circle of nine points does not describe movements in time from past to future. The outward creative process and the inward process towards self-realisation are not temporal. All the nine elements are present together. Their sequence moves from fine to coarse, or the reverse.

But questions about time would not be avoided, especially by Leon MacLaren, whose interest in them was second only to that of

Ouspensky. What the answers revealed was a surprising rebuttal of modern Western ideas about time and human life. Every man and woman has very many lifetimes. At birth one brings to a new embodiment the effects of former lives, stored in the *citta* and known as *sancita*. As explained earlier, these make for a kind of artificial nature or essence superimposed on the real permanent nature, which is pure consciousness. The present life is largely determined by this artificial nature. From it arises a person's character and traits, profession, favourable or unfavourable fortune and so on. The outcome is not inevitable, for as a conscious being, he or she may respond to good or bad company, or may choose to act well or badly. At every moment in a lifetime one is presented with a situation arising from both the store of *sancita* and from circumstances. This combination is known as *prarabdha*. It is like the part of a farmer's stock of seed that he uses to plant for the future. How one responds to *prarabdha* sets the pattern of future experience. Whatever the future then holds is called *kriyamana*. Thus everything depends on one's attitude in the present moment, a conclusion that vindicated all that the School had taught previously about time.

More surprises were in store. To a question about creation the Shankaracharya replied that the unit of time is called a *mahayuga*, which lasts for 4,320,000 years. Within this there are four periods: first a *satyuga* or golden age of 1,728,000 years, then a *dvaparayuga* or silver age of 1,296,000, then a *tretayuga* or bronze age of 864,000 years and finally a *kaliyuga* or iron age of 432,000 years. *Mahayugas* repeat 28 times, and this whole period occurs 81 times. Then the creation is withdrawn for a period of rest. Such a scheme is traditional in Indian thought. Sources could be found in ancient literature, such as the *Mahabharata*. In a later conversation the Shankaracharya explained that these four ages may be understood as occurring simultaneously, in the sense that a person may choose in which one he should live at the present time. Thus a wise man may live in the golden age, even amidst the multitude who live in the age of iron. Meanwhile this information raised searching questions for members of the School interested in history, evolution, geology and related subjects!

Although these introductory conversations covered a great range of topics, the Shankaracharya continually pointed out that the whole object of the teaching of Advaita Vedanta was to remind students of the Absolute (*Brahman*), and to show the way back to it. This

Absolute was nothing more nor less than the *Atman*, the Self within each person, one and the same. To this end he repeated the four great sentences of the Vedic tradition: 'That *Brahman* art thou', 'Knowledge is *Brahman*', 'This *Atman* is *Brahman*' and 'I am *Brahman*'.

In every creature *Brahman* is to be found as consciousness, which a story illustrated. A saint called Eknath was taking holy water from the source of the Ganges in the Himalayas to a temple of Shiva in South India, a distance of 2000 miles. On the way he saw a donkey lying in the road, dying of thirst. He stopped and poured all the holy water into the donkey's mouth. In a moment the donkey sprang up, full of energy. Eknath prayed to Shiva, saying 'I was asked to fetch holy water to pour over you, but you met me on the way, so I have performed my duty happily.' He heard the voice of Shiva, honouring his action.

This constant and universal presence of the Absolute was referred to both directly and in such stories. A favourite analogy was that of gold or clay as the material cause or substance of a thing. For example, a man possessed a solid gold statuette of his favourite god, Ganesha, attended by a mouse. Being short of money, the man went to a pawnbroker, who weighed the god and mouse separately, and offered more rupees for the heavier mouse than for the god. The man was upset. Surely his god was worth more than a mouse! But the pawnbroker was a realist; he measured value in gold, not in sentiment. Everything is made of consciousness. All the rest is mere form, which with discrimination can be seen as illusion.

Thus the final note of these conversations was that life itself is ultimately unreal. The only reality is the *Atman*, which is to be found within and without, the one eternal substance. Man himself is Absolute. Just as no man needs to hold in mind continuously the thought that he is a human being, but will respond instantly if his humanity is challenged, so a wise man does not have to keep remembering that he is Absolute, yet he knows it without any doubt. Towards this fundamental idea the School had been moving for many years. Now it was irrevocably confirmed by a man in whom the School leader had complete faith. Henceforward the teaching of the School would be founded upon this one cardinal truth.

Through this meeting of minds in 1965 and again in 1967 in India a connection had been made with a tradition of ancient wisdom. In written form it is to be found in the Veda and other sacred books of India, such as the *Bhagavad Gita*. But any practical understanding usually requires the words of master teachers, rarely to be found. The answers given to Leon MacLaren were unique. They arose from his penetrating questions to meet genuine needs amongst the students in London. What this teaching amounted to cannot be classified. It was within a tradition, but it was at the same time both peculiar to the Shankaracharya and of universal significance. As he himself said, it consisted of seeds that could germinate with unlimited possibilities.

CHAPTER ELEVEN

The Measure of
All Things

ANDREW MacLaren, at the age of eighty in 1963, was invited by
the School to give an end of term lecture on Economics at
the Institute of Electrical Engineers on the London
Embankment. This was the first opportunity for many younger
students to hear his unique brand of fiery eloquence on a subject
largely neglected by contemporary economists, namely economic
justice. Shortly afterwards he began to meet every Saturday morning
with a group of enthusiasts at Suffolk Street. The crowded room on
the first floor, with the genial figure of Roger Pincham chairing a
sometimes turbulent lecture and discussion, was long remembered.
Stories of confrontations at political rallies or in the House of
Commons, of Andrew's friendship with Stanley Baldwin, or of how
he helped a sick Neville Chamberlain leave the floor of the House
after his defeat in 1940 were interspersed with sharp reminders of
the land question, of the futility of the present tax system and of the
dangers of the Welfare State. His favourite analogies included those
of the goldfish who fight in their bowl if some water is removed,
and the heap of sand surrounded by a steel ring – like the rent of
modern cities on enclosed land, it would decline and spread out as
the enclosure was removed. Those mornings inspired by their penetration and wit a generation of students to continue his work in
teaching and publicising the economics of free land and fair public
revenue, a service for which his son Leon no longer had the time, or
perhaps the inclination.

No better evidence of the need for such instruction could have
been presented than the state of Britain at this time. The governments of Harold Wilson, Edward Heath and James Callaghan
grappled, largely unsuccessfully, with the unruly conditions created

by the widespread ignorance of natural law in economic and social relations. Behind the turmoil lay the enduring antagonism of workers and employers, forced into a false opposition by their desperate struggles for wages and profits. High wage demands and oil price rises by OPEC, the international oil cartel, pushed up UK prices, inflation weakened the pound in foreign exchange markets, a three-day week and strikes in vital industries undermined production, and the International Monetary Fund gave the UK loans against promises of damaging restrictions on the economy. No wonder that the 1970s ended with a 'Winter of discontent'!

Even more threatening was violence in Northern Ireland, as the IRA began their bombing campaign. Changes in the education system, whereby traditional methods of teaching gave way to 'child-centred' classrooms and the replacement of grammar with 'creativity' were more peaceful, but nevertheless deleterious. Ominous developments in popular culture hastened this trend towards oblivion. The comparatively harmonious music of the Beatles gave way to the raucous sound of the Rolling Stones and Punk. Drugs and promiscuous sex condemned many of Britain's young people to later lives of insecurity and despair. Rarely could the need for intelligence, self-discipline and measure have been greater.

Members of the law group in the School were fond of quoting a remark by Edmund Burke that was most pertinent at this time of declining standards in society: 'For the triumph of evil, it is only necessary that good men do nothing.' One good man who was doing a great deal about conditions in Britain was a Christian trade union leader, called Tom Chapman. He was introduced to Leon MacLaren some time in the late 1960s. MacLaren recognised him as a man who was unselfishly dedicated to dealing with one of the key areas of conflict in Britain, namely that between employers and workers.

Industrial relations had deteriorated in the 1970s, partly owing to difficult economic circumstances, but there was a more sinister aspect to this, summed up in forceful terms, rather surprisingly by the left-wing Labour leader, Nye Bevan:

> Communism is not a party but a conspiracy, a deathwatch beetle destroying our institutions from within.[1]

In certain areas of the trade union movement Communists were hard at work infiltrating the leadership, getting seats on committees,

---

1 John Stewart, *A Promise Kept*, Shepheard-Walwyn (Publishers) Ltd, 2003, p.xiv.

becoming shop stewards and, sometimes by violent means, winning control of unions, often within industries vital to the British economy. One of these was engineering, then a very important industry in regions like the West Midlands. Chapman was a qualified engineer and a long-standing trade union official. He stood against a Communist candidate in an election to a major post in the Amalgamated Engineering Union (AEU), and won by one vote. He was a marked man, a vigorous opponent of a Communist takeover.

MacLaren gave him moral support and advice, whenever it was sought. Others in the School also recognised the high principles and worthy cause of this man, who perhaps even touched a nerve amongst those students, especially of Economics, who feared that they were becoming armchair critics of the system. People volunteered to help in a private capacity. Mainly this took the form of attending conferences over which Chapman presided. They were usually held at Church centres around the country, including Church House, Westminster, where he became employed as liaison officer to the Church of England's Board of Social Responsibility. Lessons were given in public speaking, and Chapman himself always gave moving addresses, inspired by his simple but profound faith in God.

Some students agreed to help more actively. Teachers, in particular, joined unions and even got elected on to local committees, where some were shocked to find them dominated by Communists or other left-wing activists, who promoted school reforms and teachers' strikes with equal zeal. A few students even joined Chapman in going to industrial areas, like St Helens and Barrow-in-Furness, where strikes threatened to ruin a firm or industry, and introducing Christian principles of conciliation. How far these efforts were fruitful cannot be measured. Chapman's personal influence, supported by the Church, undoubtedly affected some leaders on both sides of industry.

These actions were given a proper form by the establishment of the European Christian Industrial Movement (ECIM). Chapman had connections with Christian groups in, for example, Belgium, Portugal and Italy. A large opening conference was held in Brussels in 1973, with the help of, among others, Henri Schoup, leader of the School there and Margaret Bonstow, a senior student in London, who assisted Chapman for many years. The ECIM became known as the 'Bridgebuilders', a title that symbolised both his engineering background and the intention to bridge the gap between firms and their dispossessed workers.

When Tom Chapman's health declined with age, and he eventually retired, there was no one to fill the unique position that he had created. It may be that his work had performed a vital function at a critical point in British industrial history. Who knows what Communist domination of the AEU might have led to? How many ruinous strikes were prevented that might have brought the economy to a standstill? Were a handful of Soviet controlled agents ready to takeover if the right conditions prevailed? No one knows for certain. Yet the fact of Chapman's faith in Christ, and the example of his dangerous and demanding work, remains. Many members of the School learnt much from him. These were his words at a conference at Wadderton in 1969:

> It is a law that like is attracted to like and it is good that good men should gather together. Good company is all-important. It strengthens and refreshes as nothing else can, for it puts every good man in memory of what he really knows. It renews his confidence, strengthens his resolution and enables him to do what is needful.[2]

Within the School at this time Leon MacLaren was cautious in introducing students to the new material from India. Even modicums of it were not easily assimilated by students attuned to the concepts of Ouspensky and of traditional Western thought. The three positive, negative and neutralising forces, for example, became somewhat unfamiliar when given Sanskrit names. *Buddhi*'s control over *manas* seemed an alien way of describing the reasoning principle's mastery of feeling and action. Why did the simplicity of the exercise need to be complicated by speaking of five elements called *akasha* and the rest?

Yet gradually the greater depth found in these concepts of Advaita Vedanta and in the Sanskrit language was appreciated. The material written by MacLaren now spoke, for example, of the Self as *Atman*, just as before to be separated from whatever idea dominated the mind; of the body as *prithivi* i.e. the element earth at nine, which so easily is mistakenly put at one; of the unrestrained behaviour prevalent in society as *manas* out of control. He encouraged students to turn now to the Eastern literature of the Upanishads and the *Gita*; to read passages every day. Emotion was to be cultivated, as the Shankaracharya advised, by visits to sacred places and by study of the sources of Western civilisation, like the Bible, the *Cloud of Unknowing*

2 *Ibid.*, p.106.

or *Pilgrim's Progress*. One student who experienced the change of material said that previously there was a sense of incompleteness, almost of uncertainty, whilst afterwards there was a central core. Everything now seemed to arise from one point, from God or *Brahman*.

Above all, in the late 1960s, MacLaren introduced the idea of measure. This would mean nothing if it were not made practical, and so the decision was taken to begin residential courses as a permanent feature. Already senior students had spent one or two weeks at Embley Park, where they had concentrated on finding stillness away from the bustle of London. There they had listened to the 'old' material, walked quietly through the grounds, eaten tinned food and conversed happily around the sitting room fire in the evenings. Now, at Stanhill Court in Surrey, a new regime burst upon them.

The house was a slightly forbidding, red brick Victorian mansion, set amidst tall trees in countryside fairly near Gatwick Airport. Built in 1881, in accordance with the precise standards of such journals as *The Gentleman's House*, it contained on the ground floor a galleried central hall, surrounded by a dining room, library, drawing room, croquet-lawn lobby, billiard room and gun-room. Though perhaps tempted, the School did not pursue all these uses. Above the entrance porch was now displayed a Sanskrit inscription, and many of those who entered for the first time had the feeling that initiation into a new life was at hand. More immediately, however, the earlier students saw simply a grubby, shabby interior, cold, damp and most unlike a spiritual haven.

MacLaren was quick to turn these conditions to advantage. Had not physical work been prescribed as the cure for *mala*, the negative form of *tamas*? Few students could be regarded as quite free of this, especially the many office-bound professionals in need of exercise! The house was managed by a School couple, the Shelleys, who had a flat on the first floor, but the work on improving the building and grounds became a main ingredient of the residential courses. Years later the first waves of students remembered, almost with nostalgia, the long hours spent rubbing down walls, painting, varnishing banisters, whitewashing ceilings, erecting partitions, laying pipes and other heavy work in the garden.

The grounds were extensive, over thirty acres, with a large walled garden at the centre, stables where a few horses were still tended by local riders, and a big tool store that in some ways typified the standards set for all physical work. For after a long morning or afternoon spent digging, weeding or planting on the heavy clay soil, students would return with their forks, spades etc. to the cleaning area, and spend up to an hour meticulously washing, drying and oiling every tool until they hung in pristine condition in the tool shed. This necessitated a further lengthy period of bathing and changing in order to be presentable at lunch or dinner. The real object of such severe work, however, was certainly not physical fitness, nor indeed the improvement of the premises, but to give full attention to what was to hand, or as the School now put it, to the point where the working surfaces meet. Attention was the key, just as it had been for the Orthodox monks of the *Philokalia* and for Ouspensky's students at Lyne Place. Its practice yielded a host of acute observations. Students spoke of the power that arose as if from nowhere between the blade of a saw and the surface of wood, of the movement of a wheelbarrow driven not by pushing but by a force emanating from between the wheel and the path, of how the sound of a striking axe split a log in twain.

Those who had attended Philosophy classes for about three years were invited to spend an introductory week at Stanhill Court, where they underwent a programme of activities centred upon the new concept of measure. Afterwards they spent a week there once a year and a weekend once a term. Sleep and food were subject to precise rules. 'Get up when you wake up' was the only rule for sleeping, but it proved difficult to follow, even for willing students, when they were housed in bedrooms of up to twelve people. For usually someone would wake up in the middle of the night, and if they got up would wake several others. It was a difficult decision to make at two in the morning! Moreover, a few students would get to bed late, often those who had only just completed the washing-up in the kitchen, and thus prevent others from getting to sleep. It was suggested that about five hours sleep was all that a healthy adult needed. Some were lucky to get three hours! Nevertheless, the principle of measuring out sleep was generally established, albeit only after practising on returning home. Undoubtedly sleep would be deeper and less troubled by dreams when one avoided lying in on waking. Later on conditions in the School became more favourable. For example, bedrooms became better furnished and had fewer occupants, and washing-up teams finished earlier.

As for food, the general measure laid down was also simple: eat no more than is needed. This meant that one stopped when a little more could be comfortably eaten. The food at Stanhill followed the instruction of the Shankaracharya that it should be fresh, so nothing preserved was used. There was, however, no proscription of meat or of common recipes. Indeed elaborate cooked meals were served three times a day; so much so that large teams were needed to man the kitchen, and to be in charge of a meal for perhaps a hundred people was a daunting task.

This all changed dramatically after a year or so. Someone gave Leon MacLaren a copy of a potent small book, called *The Gospel of Peace of Jesus Christ by the Disciple John*, translated from Aramaic and Old Slavonic texts. Whatever its real provenance, this book contained a version of Christ's teaching that far exceeded the Gospels in its advocacy of austerities, especially as regards food. A brief extract shows its tenor:

> So eat always from the table of God: the fruits of the trees, the grain and grasses of the field, the milk of beasts, and the honey of bees. For everything beyond these is of Satan, and leads by the way of sins and of diseases unto death. But the foods which you eat from the abundant table of God give strength and youth to your body and you will never see disease.[3]

In following some of the prescripts of this book, MacLaren revealed a Puritanical side to his complex character. For the instructions that he then issued went beyond any that the Shankaracharya had given. Students on measure were to avoid cooked food, and to eat only fruit, milk products, nuts, bread and honey. All foods were to be not only fresh, but also grown as locally as possible. There was no breakfast. At any one meal only four foods were to be eaten. Even tea was only allowed once a day, a deprivation that was perhaps the hardest of all to endure, especially in Winter! Freshly squeezed orange juice, if more nutritious, was a poor substitute.

This abrupt sacrifice of an Englishman's usual diet struck hard. At Stanhill Court itself students accepted it, strengthened by companionship and a sense of humour, and by occasional cheating with chocolate, biscuits or a glass of sherry. Once back at home the response was mixed. A few kept to the new diet rigorously; more compromised, following it to a degree in accordance with their own judgment and self-discipline. For example, many became life-long

3 *The Gospel of Peace*, translated by Edmond Szekely and Purcell Weaver, The C.W. Daniel Co., 1969, p.51.

vegetarians, and few indulged in the full variety of foods previously eaten. Some, of course, left the School. What was certain was that a great number of students saw in themselves a tenacious greed that extended beyond the area of food and reflected the condition of society. From this recognition came a new respect for measure in life generally.

Shortly afterwards one further step was taken, when again in accordance with the same supposedly sacred text a fast day was introduced at the end of measure weeks. This revealed still further the strong attachment to food, even of students who had followed various self-disciplines for some years. Few made fasting a regular practice.

The Stanhill regime was by no means all about sleeping and eating, for the day itself was carefully measured out. The Shankaracharya had laid down that a precise relationship should be kept between meditation, study and physical work, since this would regulate the life of students in all three 'worlds': spiritual, divine (or mental) and material. One hour of meditation, three hours of study of the scriptures or similar activity and nine hours of ordinary daily work would establish a proper measure and remove the effects of *sanskara*. In plain terms it would cut across habits that stifled development. Accordingly a Stanhill day contained meditation morning and evening, two or three sessions of singing, chanting or reading sacred material, and about nine hours of physical work on the house and garden – cleaning, cooking, washing up, decorating and so on. Meditation was at sunset and sunrise, as the Shankaracharya referred to these as special times when *sattva* was prevalent. Around midsummer this last point proved to be challenging.

The culmination of the day was the evening meeting, held in the large drawing room with about five rows of chairs, usually in front of a roaring log fire, and taken by MacLaren himself, or later by the head of a particular level of students. Discussion would turn on the day's work, with observations of any kind from wheelbarrowing to pure consciousness. In these meetings MacLaren was in his element: profound, witty and sometimes fiercely angry. Students would be wary of speaking if they had anything to say that sounded critical. But the observations were essentially honest, and MacLaren very often would pursue them to reveal a deeper truth. Between him and the audience a kind of Socratic dialogue could develop. Often a student would be brought to realise that a false idea about him/herself had been lodged in the mind unknowingly, directing life for years. Heads of levels soon acquired a similar ability to let the fixed ideas of their students, stripped of their covering by practical work, reveal themselves by question and answer. Some indeed could rival MacLaren's repartee and even his anger!

Also in the evening there might be music, either offered by musicians resident on the week, or by MacLaren himself, perhaps accompanied by Dorine van Oyen, the young daughter of the leaders of the Dutch School, who now attended on him. Mozart's piano sonatas were a favourite choice. This was received with delight by the tired, but enlivened, groups, although on one occasion an exhausted tutor fell asleep, with a very loud clump as he hit the floor.

The whole programme may have seemed harsh. In practice for most students it was a mixture of welcome discipline, unaccustomed study and physical work, spiritual rest or even enlightenment, and moments of great delight, near despair and sheer fun. The response was immensely varied. At best some found lasting peace and contentment and measure for a lifetime. For many the study of texts like the Upanishads, the Bible or Plato became a daily practice. Others were shaken, physically, mentally or emotionally, out of their habitual slumber. Some were forced to face the reality of situations that they had concealed from themselves for a long time. A few simply left, some with attitudes of inadequacy or of criticism of the School.

There were many minor – and perhaps some major – tragedies and comedies of the Stanhill years. People left at the end of a week with cuts and bruises, occasionally something worse. One or two women in the last weeks of pregnancy were rushed to maternity wards. People lost their jobs by insisting that they had a week off from work. Local residents at the village of Charlwood and drivers delivering supplies to Stanhill sometimes had some strange impressions. For example, they might see a group of students standing in a circle with their eyes shut for a couple of minutes, pausing after a work session in the grounds. Men would be seen climbing trees and lopping off branches, or tiling roofs, or painting window frames from high ladders, all without much apparent safety gear. Teams would be scything long grass like medieval peasants, filling holes in the drive like convicts, or pushing large wheelbarrows loaded with wet clay like highway labourers.

One day a group of four men in muddy working clothes were repairing the path near the entrance gate. A rather posh lady walked past, and asked them, in a somewhat superior tone of voice, how they were getting on. Whereupon the team leader solemnly introduced himself and the other three, one by one, as doctor so-and-so. All four were Ph.Ds.

There were stories, too, of memorable mishaps: of the man who fried dozens of eggs for breakfast in pans of washing up liquid; of students, usually women, who left baths running and forgot them, so that huge floods descended through the ceiling; of a man who sawed through a main electric cable when repairing a floor board; of a lunch that was one and a half hours late because the man in charge had only ever cooked eggs and beans before; of a tutor who walked out in the middle of a week, never to return. Yet most students could recall joyful moments, when a revelation came to them in a meeting, when their group was no longer a collection of individuals but of one mind and one spirit, when a fellow student became a friend for life. Later it all became easier. Those who lived through the whole episode near the beginning even suffered a little from pride, from feeling that they were an elite, the pioneers of a movement for the sake of humanity itself.

Doubtless MacLaren had shown too much zeal in his pursuit of the practice of measure. He himself practised what he preached, certainly in diet, although he persisted in his habit of very late nights, which he often spent in lengthy discussions with tutors. Later on the measure programme was modified, mainly by ending fasting and re-introducing cooked vegetables, rice, salad and some other vegetarian products, and by the more comfortable sleeping arrangements. His adherence to the general principle of measure, however, was unshaken. Recognition of it as an indication of natural law that could be found in every corner of life was a major step forward for the School. Perhaps more than any other aspect of the its teaching, except of course for the cardinal message that the Self is Absolute – *Aham Brahmasmi* – it brought many students one stage closer to freeing themselves from the illusion that the pleasures and pains of this earthly life are real. One student said that going back to London on Monday morning was like 'coming back to fairyland.'

Stanhill Court was only one of the School's growing collection of properties. Sarum Chase in Hampstead soon became an important venue for evening and weekend classes. Further buildings were bought as freeholds or leased: St Oswald's Studios in Fulham for the artists, a house in Fulham (given by a student) as a home for the aging Andrew MacLaren, two houses adjacent to the existing one in Queen's Gate, Brinscall Hall in Lancashire, which was a country house for the use of students in the north of England, and, most notably, Waterperry House in Oxfordshire. Meanwhile, the School reluctantly vacated Suffolk Street, its traditional home much beloved by older students, when the lease expired.

Waterperry House had a remarkable history. The grounds contain the church of St Mary the Virgin, which boasts a Saxon chancel arch, a thirteenth-century bell and a carved effigy of a medieval knight. The estate was originally granted by William the Conqueror to one of his leading supporters, Robert d'Ouilly. It once covered two thousand acres. During the centuries of religious conflict, the house became 'a rallying point of Catholicism in the Oxfordshire area',[4] with a priest's hole and a system of tunnels. The front of the house was rebuilt in 1713 in an unadorned Queen Anne style. In modern times the estate became a horticultural school for ladies, and main-tained renowned gardens and orchards. Although not the most expensive of the School properties, Waterperry had the greatest potential. The horticultural school was at the time of purchase failing financially, despite a fine tradition of teaching and cultivation. The site then covered eighty acres alongside the meandering River Thame.

Bernard Saunders was presented with a new challenge beyond his work with the art group. As Steward of Waterperry, he proceeded to transform it gradually into a unique combination of successful business and principal site for School activities, including those originating at Stanhill Court. On the business side it was done by closing down loss-making products, like vegetables, and expanding profitable ones; for example, one thousand new apple trees were planted. The gardens were slowly developed with an eye to artistic landscaping. Later the tea-shop was modernised, and a gift shop and an agricultural museum were opened. In 1976 an annual arts festival, called 'Art in Action', became Bernard Saunders' most imaginative contribution to Waterperry's development and reputation.

Outside London, School branches were still springing up. Courses began in this period in Watford, Croydon, Brighton, Guildford,

---

4 See Michael Shepherd, *Waterperry House and Grounds*, School of Economic Science, 2009, p.21.

Colchester, Chelmsford, Edinburgh, St Albans, Maidstone, Canterbury and Oxford. In Schools abroad not everything ran smoothly.
Wellington and Christchurch broke off relations with London. The
School in Malta was persecuted by the Catholic Archbishop, who was
ninety, and seemingly felt that his long patriarchal dominion over the
island was at risk. Members were threatened with losing their jobs,
and only a brave remnant kept Advaita Vedanta alive there. In Dublin
there was a dispute over the leadership and a split in the ranks. Leon
MacLaren flew to these trouble spots, like a kind of spiritual Henry
Kissinger, often with the difficult task of adjudicating between a
School leader and its most senior students. Sometimes he must have
wished that he were serving on a Commonwealth Court of Appeal
instead! Elsewhere there was progress. New Schools opened in
Cyprus and Toronto. Conferences of School leaders from around
the world were held in London, where briefly they became students,
and imbibed new ideas and practices in intensive sessions under the
leader of them all.

A notable event in the life of the School at this time was the
production of a play, called *Leonardo*, at Stanhill Court in 1975. This
was the climax of an arduous but inspired effort to build a theatre in
the grounds. Teams would come down at weekends to supplement
work done on residential courses. Under the direction of a landscape
gardener, clay was dug out, stones cut by students who studied
masonry for the purpose, and a fine open stage built amongst the
trees. *Leonardo*, written by a retired actor, Frank Carpenter, and
directed by another who was appearing at the time in a weekly TV
drama, employed a few other professionals who were students, and
others whose only drama training was work in rhetoric groups run
by Shelia Rosenberg. Under her guidance they all became one company. The play threaded its way through Leonardo da Vinci's
immensely varied life, from his early days as a painter in Loronzo de'
Medici's Florence, his service first under Ludovico Sforza and then
under Cesare Borgia as armourer, engineer, architect and artist, his
return to Florence, and his death at the castle of Le Cloux in France.
In the minds of actors and audiences *Leonardo* portrayed a man
deeply involved in the creative activity of a renaissance. There was
more than a hint that the School itself might have a role to play in
another such epoch-making event.

Other major developments at this time were the publication of
the first volume of Marsilio Ficino's letters in an English translation,

some public lectures on Economics, and the foundation of St James and St Vedast Schools for children. Two long-standing members received public accolades. Kenneth Jupp, once the Principal, was appointed a judge in the Queen's Bench Division, which effectively disqualified him from holding further office in the School; and Roger Pincham resigned as School Treasurer after twelve years in the post, on being made Chairman of the Liberal Party. He had only just failed to become Liberal Member of Parliament for Leominster in the early 1970s.

In 1975 Andrew MacLaren died at the age of 91. Some years before Leon said what would have been a fitting tribute on his death: that his father had given him three valuable things – the teaching of Henry George, a faith in natural law and a contempt for experts! At the funeral a School choir sang a Mass written by a student, Tony Russell, who had died earlier. Russell had been a professional saxophonist, playing jazz and popular music. At an early age he caught leukaemia. Kept alive by blood transfusions and regular meetings with Leon MacLaren, he began to write a Mass, which he completed with great difficulty just before he died – when MacLaren was on a trip abroad. The performance honoured both the deceased.

Andrew, the 'amiable fanatic' as he was called in Parliament, was buried at Fort Augustus Abbey, Invernesshire, in the monks' grave-yard. For all his disregard of organised religion, he never forgot what a monk had told him when he ran away there at the age of about fifteen: 'Remember that your talents are the gift of God.' Certainly in his life-long advocacy of free land, he had remembered the greater gift that God had made to mankind. The School contributed a window depicting Melchizedek to the Abbey, made by Moira Forsyth, an expert in stained glass, who had cared for Andrew for many years.

CHAPTER TWELVE

The Art
of Philosophy

B EHIND the large entrance hall of Waterperry House in Oxfordshire is a smaller hall, open to daylight from a cupola two storeys above and adorned with colourful frescoes. This is the joint work of architects and artists in the School over a prolonged period, and is the most elaborate effort so far made to express the Philosophy of the School through art. A great deal of reflection, research, experiment and hard work preceded the final production of the paintings. The space itself had been a group of small rooms, linked by narrow corridors and in a poor state of repair. Not only was it cleared out, but the walls and ceiling were rebuilt in accordance with precise proportions based upon the module, or what Vitruvius called the 'standard of symmetry'.

The frescoes themselves were a group project by School artists, the outcome of many years working together under the leadership of Bernard Saunders, originally a wood carver but later occupied with running Waterperry House and the Horticultural School. An art group was formed in the early 1960s, and soon attracted a considerable number – up to seventy – artists in many fields, including amateurs and art teachers.

Leon MacLaren was interested mainly in a smaller group of professionals. His instructions were brief, such as, 'Draw what you see,' or, 'No one can paint anything they do not love.' 'What you see' did not mean a kind of photographic reproduction, but rather what is seen beyond or through ordinary vision, with the eye of the mind. He pursued this further in a question to the Shankaracharya about portrait painting. The answer confirmed that the inner nature of the subject, the subtle form or character, needs to be expressed,

116

something that in the Indian tradition is shown by symbolism. A simple example of this occurred when one artist, having seen a man 'as large as a house', scaled him down in the painting. 'No,' said MacLaren, 'paint him as you saw him.'

The Shankaracharya added that a feeling of unity with the subject is a prerequisite of this 'inner' seeing. Likewise, love for the object painted can only arise when the beauty seen is recognised as one's own, the beauty of the Self. If beauty is only seen in the physical object or form, then it does not connect with deeper levels of mind and spirit. One artist found similar inspiration in a conversation recorded between a painter and a *guru*:

> 'When you paint, what do you think about?' 'When I paint there is only the painting and myself,' replied the painter. 'What are you doing there?' asked the *guru*.

MacLaren added a further principle, based upon his firm belief that everything begins in the Word. A brief sentence from a sacred or philosophical text was chosen, with the intention that a work of art should illuminate it. The artist then reflected upon the words, studied them in depth with the aid of commentaries and dictionaries, and asked for the views of others on whether his or her portrayal truly expressed the text. This was the only question allowed. Often what the artist liked best about the painting had to be sacrificed! Some outstanding paintings or sculptures were completed in this way: the first day of creation, Christ's temptation by the devil, Krishna raising up Arjuna, the goddess Ganga, and a series of allegories by Ficino were amongst the subjects portrayed.

A particularly interesting example was a painting of Christ's parable of the wheat and the tares. The artist took the early designs to MacLaren. He put it on one side, and read aloud the text from St Matthew, asking questions as he went, such as, 'Who were the men who slept whilst the devil came with the tares?' The artist had no idea. They were the men who guarded the field, said MacLaren. The field is the world; its guardians are law, education and religion. Paint them! Why have you painted the devil as ugly? He should look attractive, like people seen in half light. So the artist went away and painted a lawyer, a teacher and a bishop, with a handsome devil sowing the tares! From this episode he learnt much about how to read a text, and how to illustrate it with symbolism.

When the same artist was unable to continue with a particularly large painting because there was an area in it that he did not know how to fill, Bernard Saunders gave him another principle from the Shankaracharya. He was to paint first the areas that he did know about. Having completed these, he found that he then knew how to deal with the difficult space. Saunders' authority in the art group has remained a key factor throughout

Demanding working practices were also introduced. Artists were trained to give their full attention by practising drawing straight lines and circles in the manner of calligraphers. They have made copies of famous works from several traditions, including reproductions of paintings from the National Gallery by masters of the medieval or Renaissance periods. The group collectively made Platonic solids, models of stained-glass windows from Chartres cathedral – having visited Chartres together – and of Roman mosaics. One special project was to illustrate for St Augustine's Church in Kensington the passage in *Isaiah*[1] about truth fallen in the street. Another was to carve a mosaic pavement for the garden of Chepstow Villas. Leonardo da Vinci's notebooks were a further source of group exercises.

Leon MacLaren had expressed a particular interest in sculpture, especially that of the Florentine sculptor, Donatello. There are a few highly skilled professional sculptors in the School who have applied the above principles to their work. Pencil sketches, followed by maquettes in clay or wax, have preceded final pieces expressing words of scripture or wisdom. MacLaren was concerned also with the requirements of the specific site for the sculpture, for example of scale and materials. Commissions were completed for School houses, notably a bronze high relief for the reception area in New York, called 'Philosophy' and based upon words of Marsilio Ficino. Copies of this in marble resin are now installed in several School houses and in St James' Girls School.

As leader of the group Saunders has adhered constantly to the principle that art should be the handmaid of Philosophy, seeking explicitly or implicitly to embody some aspect of this through content or method. Yet he retains a catholic view of art forms. Romanesque church architecture and sculpture and the painting of Fra Angelico, as in San Marco in Florence, particularly appeal to him, and perhaps inevitably Indian art has become of special interest.

1 *Isaiah*, 59:14.

He also arranged that some remarkably expressive carvings from the Shona tradition of Zimbabwe were exhibited for a time in the gardens at Waterperry. A core group of four artists has strongly supported Saunders, particularly in their readiness to experiment in techniques, and even to make career sacrifices in order to find the time for School projects.

A particularly rewarding practice appeared when someone came across a technique recommended by the teacher of the French sculptor Rodin. It was soon endorsed by Leon MacLaren. This consisted of 'one glance portraits', whereby 'draw what you see' became the only real possibility. The sequence was a single observation of the subject, a reflection in the mind of what had been seen, strict adherence to this when drawing, and considerable technical discipline to express it. The results were remarkable portrayals, especially of people, showing inner qualities of great depth even in pictures of rudimentary detail. One, for example, showing a pianist, seems to give an almost tangible character to the attention being directed to the music. Others show essential features often overlooked through familiarity. MacLaren appears in some, in a variety of moods – pensive, judicial, friendly or jovial. A sculptor, using 'one glance', carved a figure called 'Rosemary' in alabaster.

There were some amusing episodes. An artist drew a 'one glance' face. When asked what he had seen, he said it was a man facing him. But he had drawn a profile. He admitted that this was because it was easier to draw! Another drew a head dark with shading. Habit had taken over, for he had seen radiant light in the face, and redrew it with the shading around the face instead.

Some years later this ability to know by direct observation in a matter of seconds was recognised in a best-selling book, *Blink*, by the American writer Malcolm Gladwell:

> The power of knowing, in that first two seconds, is not a gift given magically to a fortunate few. It is an ability that we can all cultivate for ourselves … the task of making sense of ourselves and our behaviour requires that we acknowledge there can be as much value in the blink of an eye as in months of rational analysis.[2]

The work of the art group was given considerable stimulus by the acquisition by the School of Augustine studios, followed later by

Malcolm Gladwell, *Blink*, Allen Lane, 2005, pp.16-17.

St Oswald's studios in Fulham, where Andrew MacLaren, himself a skilled painter and cartoonist, lived for many years. A considerable team of professional specialists used St Oswald's. At one time there were painters, sculptors, art teachers, a book designer, a silversmith and a clothes designer working there. The studios have offered art classes to the public, and have also developed a training course for young sculptors. Exhibitions are occasionally held there.

What may turn out in the long run to be the most significant aspect of the work of artists in the School, however, is the annual event that began in 1977, namely 'Art in Action'. This was another brainchild of Saunders. Essentially it began with the idea of demonstrating the principles of School work by allowing artists and craftsmen to be observed in the act of creating their products. At the same time they would be available to answer questions and to discuss what they were doing. A further principle that Saunders has stressed is that the artist seeks to magnify what is beautiful, especially beauty in the being of a person. About 40 artists were present on the first occasion. Currently there are up to 300, with about 25,000 visitors attending over four days. The timing was changed to July after a disastrous event at Easter, when the high water table and torrential rain caused the car park and other areas to flood. The best demonstrators of School principles on that occasion were the heroic car park attendants!

Artists and craftsmen from the School and outside were invited to demonstrate. The latter much appreciate the service, including a demonstrators' dinner, offered them by the host of helpers from London and other Schools. Painting in oils and watercolours, sculpture, wood-carving, pottery, glass-blowing, lace-making, metalwork, furniture, jewellery, printing, calligraphy and many other arts and crafts are represented. The aim from the beginning has been to maintain the highest possible standards in every field. As a by-product some demonstrators have received valuable commissions. Classes are offered in some subjects. A craft tent sells gifts. Concerts take place in the grounds and in the house, where guided tours of the frescoes are also available. A large number of refreshment facilities are on offer, from tea points to an up-market restaurant. Pancakes and ice-creams are especially popular. Many of these services are provided by School members, although large-scale professional catering has taken a load off the volunteers.

A great deal of preparation is required for weeks beforehand, including work on power and water supplies, signs, car parks, furniture and so on. All this provides 'a great opportunity' – as the phrase goes in the School – for dedicated service. Each morning Saunders and his successor at Art in Action, Jeremy Sinclair, have reminded the several hundred people who turn up for work over the four days of a few simple principles, such as attending fully to whatever presents itself. Meeting the public in this way is a valuable dimension of the work. For some while there was a tendency to draw a sharp line between the School and those outside it. Art in Action has played a major part in breaking down this 'middle wall of partition between us'. Its success in this regard has been amply shown by the letters of approval sent in by visitors. There have been other benefits. One young contributor to Art in Action has started an Art Academy in London.

Since Jeremy Sinclair took over the running of Art in Action there have been some significant changes. He has introduced new ideas into the layout of the site, and tried to make the advertising itself more artistic. Younger artists especially have been encouraged to exhibit. Amongst the new sections have been Abrahamic, International and Mexican Arts, a drawing display to emphasise this basic discipline of art, and a 'Best of the Best' marquee, where exhibits have been chosen by the demonstrators themselves. They may range from small pieces of jewellery to a large display of wrought iron work. Practical classes have been expanded, with teachers from leading Art Schools. The policy is to vary sections somewhat from year to year. Lectures are held daily in the house, and the Waterperry church now holds services and periods of quietness as part of the whole event. A major addition is the use of the new open-air theatre for the performing arts. This has the character of a classical Greek theatre, built into a natural ampitheatre in the gardens, and is now used also for Shakespearean productions by visiting companies during the Summer. Non-School artists and their assistants have always been an integral part of Art in Action, but now helpers from outside the School have been invited also, with the aim of spreading the idea of service without reward.

As a single work of art the frescoes at Waterperry House remain a unique contribution by the art group to the world of contemporary art. Following the principle of beginning with a sacred text, they are an attempt to illustrate three statements from the *Brihadaranyaka Upanishad*:

> This [Self] was indeed *Brahman* in the beginning.
> It knew only Itself as 'I am *Brahman*'.
> Therefore It became all.

These are taken to refer to Spirit, the whole world of mind and law, and the physical universe respectively, in a relation of causality from *Brahman* to matter. Each is portrayed on one floor of the inner hall.

Before the artists could begin, however, an architects' group had to design the hall and oversee its construction, in accordance with the three statements of the Upanishad. Much work on the principles of architecture had already taken place under the leadership of Richard Watson, who had co-operated with Dr James Armstrong in the development of the geometry of Platonic polyhedrons.

In 1993 Timothy Collier, and later Richard Ibbett, took over the planning of the Waterperry inner hall. Since this is between the Jacobean and Georgian parts of the building, its construction had strong repercussions elsewhere. Major changes had to be made to accommodate it. These ranged from renewing the Georgian roof and part of the Jacobean wing, to building two new sets of bath-rooms and – indirectly – to the need for extra accommodation by converting a barn into a new coach house. The roof work, in particular, employed a very large number of able-bodied men in the School, who attended at weekends over a period of about ten years.

Initially Leon MacLaren took a close interest in the architecture, insisting on the application of the natural octave to the proportions, and at one point demanding that a huge oak beam should replace a steel girder that had already been set in place with some difficulty! During the building, when the hall was filled with acros props to sup-port the ceilings, he termed it the Acropolis. This was not misplaced, in view of the great emphasis given to proportion. The heights of the three floors were related in the harmonic ratio 1:2:infinity, the last being achieved by measuring through the main roof-light to the sky. Each section of the hall was related to the others by means of ratios based on the octave, a system confirmed by no less a method than the playing of a harp in each part. This accorded with the principle of Alberti:

> The same numbers by means of which the agreement of sounds affects our ears with delight are the very same which please our eyes and mind.

The Vedantic conception of nine elements was likewise introduced, notably in the construction of a circular staircase descending in sequences of nine landings.

The module used was established by analysis of the dimensions in the existing house and the proposed new space. What emerged was a module of 24.75 inches. From this all the key elements in the design were dimensioned, using simple whole number musical ratios.

Materials included lime plaster, elm, stainless steel and glass. For the bridge on the first floor, a special low iron type of 'white glass' was required to reduce the colour distortion in the light falling on the paintings below. A heating system had to be carefully designed to minimise the temperature contrasts on the frescoes.

Underlying this endeavour, which was largely directed by Richard Ibbett though representative of the work of the architects' group generally, were the words of the Shankaracharya:

All forms exist in consciousness, just as the building existed in the plan and the plan in the mind of the architect. The essential part of what is known as a building existed before the architect got it and will exist when the building is no more. The idea, the concept, is the knowledge; it is the consciousness which resides in its subtlest form in the creative faculty of the Absolute.

In a sense the inner hall was no more than the culmination of the experience gained in applying principles of proportion and harmony in earlier work for the School. Over the years the architects' group have worked on a large number of other projects. All the buildings have also required considerable maintenance, but in addition major changes have been made, especially at the residential sites of Waterperry and Nanpantan. In particular, a large new extension, called the Elizabethan wing, was constructed at Waterperry under the direction of Richard Watson.

In the inner hall at Waterperry the artists took over when the architects had completed their task. On the top floor the *Brahman*, eternal, infinite and beyond all perception, is indicated by the three primary colours plus white, with no form whatsoever. The first floor walls are painted with several images: a meditating figure, rays of light passing through to the ground below, a group of students listening intently (except for one, diverted by a pretty face) to a tutor, the ages of Man from birth to death, the universe held in hands of love, and water symbolising the one substance. A group of bas-relief panels in marble-resin illustrate the ten *Laws of Manu,* such as patience, forgiveness and self-control, observance of which brings freedom and prosperity to all, regardless of nationality, race or religion. These are formed into a pyramid, using the numbers one to four, fundamental in the Pythagorean concept of cosmic harmony. Each law is shown by picturing the results of its acknowledgment and of its denial.

At ground level, which has a floor of polished marble slabs, the wall area is larger and full of diverse images representing stories told by the Shankaracharya that demonstrate how the teaching of Advaita may be realised in the material world, the realm of *maya* or illusion. The largest, which actually extends upwards to the floors above, is a great tree of green and gold leaves, in which perch two birds, one – easy to spot – eats the rich berries, the other – subtly hidden amidst the foliage – sits at rest. They are the birds of the *Mundaka Upanishad* (3.1.i), who represent the self that busily grasps the objects of desire, and the Self that sits for ever at rest as the witness of all. Another large fresco shows the story of ten men crossing the river. Only nine men are portrayed, for the tenth is the observer, looking at the scene, and perhaps forgetting him/herself. Most noticeable on the side walls are a display of many animals – tigers, antelopes, the elephant offering a flower to *Brahman,* the lion cub amongst sheep recognising a lion's roar, the donkey reviving as St Eknath pours the sacred water down its throat. Beside these an old man dances with joy at the news that the Lord will visit him, albeit in more years than the thousands of leaves on the tree that stands beside him. On the end wall a collection of water pitchers each reflect the Sun, indicating that every creature reflects the one *Atman.*

Also on the ground floor stands a remarkable limestone column, consisting of four forms of creatures, classified according to the Shankaracharya as filth-born, soil-born, egg-born and womb-born in ascending order, culminating in Man as the highest member of the final class.

The frescoes on the ground floor are all depicted in brilliant colours derived from the limited number of pigments, such as natural earth red, which can be used in fresco. Bright colour perhaps compensates for the relatively sparse use of perspective. As with medieval or Byzantine art, the images are drawn with more attention to their significance in the context than to physical realism. This gives them a somewhat naïve but direct and forceful effect. There is also a touch of irony. For example, the tutor in the scene of the students listening has his back to the viewer, rather like an MI5 agent being interviewed on television. School tutors have always had a certain measure of anonymity, intended to reduce the influence of the ego.

Technically the frescoes were a breakthrough for the art group. A collective effort was needed as never before. Severe demands of timing were made, mainly because of the precise sequence of stages from plastering of surfaces to the final brushwork, and because frescoes involve painting directly on to wet plaster. Two layers of plaster were put on by professional plasterers; the third by School artists. This dried in about eight to twelve hours, so that painting time was strictly limited. Occasionally it was even done at night. Equally demanding was the fact that the colours gradually get lighter in tone for up to six months after application. Tempera, used partly for finishing the figures, does the reverse. Hence much experimentation and very careful judgment were required.

The wall first had to be wetted for three to four hours, with a system of guttering to prevent flooding, before the final plaster layer was applied. The designs were drawn on paper, then 'pounced' by pricking the outlines, so that the resulting cartoon could be placed on the soft plaster and rubbed over with pigment, giving a precise form on the wall. Colours were then applied, with no binding medium, as they were absorbed into the plaster. Mistakes had to be chipped out when the plaster was hard.

Perhaps more of a trial than the technical problems was the basic method of subjecting every design and idea to the views of one's fellows. Artistic pride, sense of originality and simple egotism all had to give way before the judgment of peers. Sometimes an artist would be taken off a section of the frescoes, so that someone else could finish it. Attachment to 'my work' was loosened. Much was learnt about the philosophical principle of giving up the private ownership of the mind. It was a lesson accentuated here, yet common to every activity within the School, from painting a fresco to studying the Upanishads or doing the washing–up.

The art group seems to have aged. There is no substantial new generation of artists to continue with the principles learnt. But this may be merely a pause for breath after many years of work on the frescoes. Shortly before Leon MacLaren died, he told the artists that he wanted to devote some of the energy left to him to fostering the work of the group. Saunders also has said that the art group demonstrates an inner stillness as great as anywhere in the School. These are grounds for hope that the work will bear yet greater fruit.

An art form not greatly acknowledged today has developed in the School alongside the work of the art group. This is calligraphy, which Leon MacLaren introduced in the 1960s for the practical reason of getting rid of a mechanical approach to the administrative work in the School. If records were to be kept, lists prepared and so on, then they too should be done with care and a touch of beauty. His father had been interested in calligraphy, so Leon was quick to introduce the use of proper pen nibs, boards at 20 degrees from the vertical and the mahl stick, which avoids any handling of paper. Students were instructed to sit with a straight back, hold the writing arm horizontal, and above all to let the attention rest on the point where the nib touches the paper. Practice always began with straight lines and circles, the latter symbolising the undivided unity of God.

Interest in this fine art grew. People went to the British Museum to study medieval and Renaissance manuscripts. A script was selected as a template for the alphabet. The Sanskrit alphabet was added to the material copied. Illumination was introduced, using water-colours and gold leaf. Texts from Plato, Ficino, Vedic literature and British poets have been prepared.

A regular Sunday morning class, led by Jill Basham, met at Sarum Chase. Then classes spread throughout the School, until a Sound and Calligraphy course became a standard element in a student's progress. St James' Schools adapted the subject to the development of good handwriting, although they soon encountered difficulties getting children to use boards as a regular practice. MacLaren, of course, did not lose sight of the spiritual aim of all this. Behind writing was the Word. With hand, heart and mind connected, the presence of this might be felt in the touch of pen on paper. It was a magnificent exercise in stillness and the power of attention.

A few enthusiasts began to use calligraphy in their professional work as artists, publishers and so on. MacLaren had referred to the value of spreading good writing into society, where it was being seriously neglected, particular with the growth of mechanisation in areas previously occupied by craftsmen and artists. A recent step has been the introduction of public classes in calligraphy on Saturday mornings at Mandeville Place.

CHAPTER THIRTEEN

The Right
Promethean Fire

A YOUNG lady of 28, Sheila Rosenberg, had joined the School in 1953 and was to devote the rest of her life to it. She was then an enthusiastic Young Liberal and a history teacher with a degree from King's College, London. Her education and interests were to play a major part in the development of cultural studies within the School, but always in the context of her recognition that the truth comes first. It was through the Liberal Party that she had met Leon MacLaren, when a party member invited her to attend one of his lectures. She joined a Philosophy class, and soon became a tutor.

Sheila Rosenberg's sharp intelligence, learning and obvious devotion to what the School taught, both in Economics and Philosophy, and her whole bearing as a lady of fine character and demeanour ensured that she would become a rather special tutor to the ladies in the School. As one female admirer wrote some years later:

> Astonishingly beautiful right up until the time of her death, with those fine high cheek-bones, unforgettably bright eyes and snowy hair pinned in a graceful chignon, she was always supremely, effortlessly elegant. When she came into a room, every eye turned to her, every back straightened a little. Although this would have been far from her intention, you could not help feeling that, beside her, other women seemed like clodhopping bumpkins.[1]

Leon MacLaren had strong views about the nature and role of women. Whilst he certainly recognised their emotional power, he was quick to emphasise the need for this to be controlled by reason, if

---

1 *Sheila Rosenberg: A Renaissance Lady*, edited by Joan Crammond, Godstow Press, 2004, pp.144-5.

necessary by that of a man. He clearly mistrusted a woman's ability to guard against her own emotional instability unaided. In Sheila Rosenberg he found a woman who was prepared to accept such a view, and to implement it on behalf of the School. She was intensely loyal, self-disciplined and willing to take the responsibility.

Before long she was in charge of Ladies-at-Home groups that met regularly at people's homes and built up a team of tutors who, under her watchful supervision, used material that she wrote. Such groups even sprang up in overseas Schools, and were similarly mentored. A member of a group in Belgium summed them up:

> 'Ladies-at-Home groups' has a rather genteel ring to it today. They were anything but. We frequently left with our ideas and feelings 'all shook up', but also with a sense of enlightenment, stimulation and profound nourishment… We were quite likely to begin the morning reading the story of Ruth and Naomi, reflecting on motherhood in all its forms, sound an invocation from the Upanishads and top it off with the latest piece from *The Times* on the increase of the rat population in our cities and what were we going to do about it?[2]

At a time when feminist movements were in full flood, Sheila Rosenberg did not hesitate to speak about the School's view of the nature of women and their proper role in society. Beyond both nature and society, of course, she realised that men and women are literally one and the same. And she always insisted on this. 'You are constituted of knowledge, happiness and consciousness. I hope you don't doubt that,' she told an audience of women; but she insisted, too, on the natural differences between the sexes, and despised the kind of growing attitude in society that would identify them. Women, she taught, refer back to the *citta*, the emotional centre, and tend to neglect the *buddhi* or intellect, not exclusively by any means, but in contradistinction to the male tendency to do the reverse. *Citta* is the powerhouse, the source of feeling, attitudes and motives. Uncontrolled, it can cause emotional upsets, domination by what one likes or dislikes, and ultimately a life of unreason. Hence women often need help to let *buddhi* control the *citta*, and may turn to men for such direction. This is the root of the idea that men should take charge or govern; that the father is head of the family. Yet lest men should think that this makes them the superior sex, they should remember that, as the Shankaracharya had said, though men are

2 *Ibid.*, pp.141-2.

forceful, the women are the very embodiment of the force itself. One of Sheila's favourite quotations came from *Love's Labour's Lost*:

> From women's eyes, this doctrine I derive:
> They sparkle still the right Promethean fire;
> They are the books, the arts, the academes,
> That show, contain, and nourish all the world;
> Else none at all in aught proves excellent.[3]

As for feminism, she saw it as always demanding rights, when what society needs from both women and men is a full acknowledgment of duties.

How then did the School judge the woman's role in society? Naturally, it was suggested, women are not ambitious. They do not usually seek fame or public success. If they teach, or practise music or other arts and crafts, they do so as service, as devotees, for intrinsic delight, often at home or otherwise discreetly. They are not competitive like men, whose nature leads them to take their professional work seriously. For men it is a matter of earning a living, or protecting the family from the worldly hazards of poverty, abuse or crime, whilst for women their work is to measure out the needs and resources of the home, to nourish and care for the family or the community or – for great women – for the world.

Occasionally Sheila Rosenberg gave way to an ironic impulse towards men's supposed superiority, as when she reminded Philosophy students of the feminine tutelage of even the greatest philosophers:

> I will just mention in passing, in case anyone here is worried about the idea, that both Socrates and Pythagoras admitted to having had lady teachers. If you read Plato's *Symposium*, there is the discourse of Socrates' teacher, Diotima, and Pythagoras had this lady Themistoclea for his teacher.[4]

From her wide knowledge of history, Sheila could usually illustrate the principles that she taught. Catherine of Siena, for example, had helped to save Europe from the disastrous 'Babylonish Captivity' of the Pope, who had fled Rome for the security of Avignon under the protection of the king of France. Catherine's remonstrances persuaded him to return to his proper seat of authority. Was this not a man's work, to intervene in the power politics of medieval

---

3 Act IV, Scene iii.
4 *Sheila Rosenberg: A Renaissance Lady*, p.303.

Church and State? Maybe, but women act when men cannot or will not do their duty. The Pope was negligent, so Catherine took it upon herself to recall him to his task. So, too, did Sheila view the political scene in Britain in the 1980s, when Margaret Thatcher filled the office of Prime Minister with a seemingly masculine degree of power and authority. Where were the men able and willing to run the country? Sheila could be very abrupt. There weren't any, she thought, so a woman played the part.

Women change the atmosphere. Sheila's own home at Brook Green, Hammersmith exemplified this. Inside it was a model of brightness, elegance and cleanliness, despite the presence of a dog and frequent visitors. All were struck by the good order – measure – and many took away with them an impression that would influence their own homes. In some cases Sheila visited them, and advised the removal of what she regarded as unnecessary bric-à-brac! For a degree of severity accompanied her exemplary life. She could be acerbic on occasions and often ironic. But those on the receiving end usually recognised the love that underlay such admonitions, and few disputed that she was right in her censure when it occurred.

In her personal life she fully demonstrated that most women need to be both busy and still; that they can find stillness in the very tasks with which their lives are inevitably crowded – looking after husbands, children or the elderly, maintaining the house, earning money, practising an art or craft and studying. This last was not to be ignored. A keen student all her life, Sheila encouraged all the women she tutored to give time to a serious study, like language, divinity, history or music. Nor was her advice restricted to her own students. She played a major role in motivating teachers in the School, especially those at St James and St Vedast Schools (see Chapter 20) to study their subjects assiduously. Without such study they would never be real teachers. An example of her insight into this was her advice to a history teacher: choose a key event in the period to be studied and read about it in as much depth as possible. The teacher chose the murder of Thomas a Becket, and after a few days of reading found himself delving into the whole issue of the investiture dispute in Europe and its antecedents and consequences in medieval history, as well as the rich complexity of the reign of Henry II of England.

No doubt one element in this advocacy of study was Sheila Rosenberg's lifelong love of books. Indeed she had turned to journalism in the 1960s, and ended up as literary editor of *The Times Educational Supplement*. Above all other literature, she loved Shakespeare. Her talks and conversation were full of allusions to the plays and poetry. These were not, however, literary in the sense of art for art's sake. The references were invariably linked to the Philosophy teaching that was her primary loyalty. For example, she said that Shakespeare 'sees man as having two selves in a manner of speaking...the universal Self, the One, the Absolute ... and the ego.' A sonnet demonstrated this:

> But when my glass shows me myself indeed,
> Beated and chopp'd with tann'd antiquity,
> Mine own self-love quite contrary I read;
> Self so self-loving were iniquity.
>   'Tis thee, myself, – that for myself I praise,
>   Painting my age with beauty of thy days.[5]

The glass shows the multi-faceted ego; but 'thee, myself' is the One. And when Sheila described the horrors of *Titus Andronicus*, she recalled that Shakespeare never omits a final unity:

> O! let me teach you how to knit again
> This scatter'd corn into one mutual sheaf,
> These broken limbs again into one body.[6]

Her perception of Shakespeare's own philosophical awareness was clearly stated, when she said that in creating others' characters he forgot himself, and that his mind appears to us through his works in isolation from his own person. He suppresses individual consciousness in order to bring before us the broad features of universal humanity. Once again a sonnet brought the point home:

> What is your substance, whereof are you made
> That millions of strange shadows on you tend?
> Since every one hath, every one, one shade
> And you, not one, can every shadow lend...[7]

Yet another activity, related to literature, that Sheila promoted within the School was rhetoric. Appointed by MacLaren to run

5 Sonnet LXII.
6 Act 5, Scene 3.
7 Sonnet LIII.

rhetoric groups, she chose tutors who were 'people who would not speak to teach people who could not speak'. As one of them said, her aim was very simple: to allow the truth to be spoken in all circumstances with simplicity and clarity. To achieve this, however, she went to extraordinary lengths. Beginning with pure sound, practised by means of the Sanskrit alphabet, rhetoricians progressed to the practice of listening, to figures of speech, grammar, debate and finally to drama. It was under her aegis that some played parts in the production of *Leonardo* at Stanhill Court.

For the study of drama even Shakespeare was not enough. She investigated the Sanskrit classic on dance and drama, the *Natyasastra*. Further studies included the answers concerning language of the Shankaracharya, especially the parts dealing with four levels of language from *para* to *vaikhari* and writers besides Shakespeare – Chaucer, Traherne, Gibbon, Blackstone and many others.

Fine speech was continually emphasised beyond the rhetoric groups. She realised the real philosophical significance of speech as the ultimate creative force, as stated in the *Gospel of St John*. This was in no way just a theory. In her own clear articulation, careful choice of words and meticulous grammar, and in the demand she made upon students, especially the ladies, for this standard of excellence, she practised the principles that the world is created by sound and the world of mankind by human speech. Around her she witnessed the degeneration of the English language – in schools, universities, journalism and everyday life – and she strove ardently to act against the flow. Her legacy includes much of the speech emanating from senior members of the School around the world.

Sheila Rosenberg was not a dry pedant. Her irony and sense of humour ranged from literary jokes almost to ribaldry. This is how she replied to a letter from a student in South Africa:

> How impressive to share Mozart's birthday! On your dating a letter with it, I am reminded of a youthful tendency to head letters with festive datings like 'Feast of Our Lady of Lourdes' or 'St James the Less' etc. In reply to one such pious beginning, a Dominican with whom I communicated headed a letter, 'Octave of the Dotage of Pythagoras'.[8]

And in a talk on the Benedictine movement she said:

8 *Sheila Rosenberg: A Renaissance Lady*, p.184.

[In the Rule] special care is to be taken of the very old and very young monks, and there is even a chapter – which I particularly recommend to members of this School – entitled 'If a brother be commanded to do impossibilities.'[9]

Once when she was taking her beloved little wheaten cairn terrier for an early morning walk on Brook Green, she was accosted by a man who threatened to make love to her. Caustically she replied that it really was too early for that sort of thing!

Sheila's adherence to the School's teaching was shown by numerous lectures and untold hours of tutoring. One brief example reveals her clarity of mind on the Vedic system:

What that part of the mind, which we call *manas* [discursive mind], can tell you is anything that you have already experienced or learnt or observed, in this lifetime. It can trot out recollections, reconstructions, habitual values, codes and standards, opinions and even beliefs – and does so, at a great rate, when one sits down to reflect. One leaves all that to drop away, because it is limited; nor, usually, is it very interesting.

Then, when all that activity ceases, the *buddhi* [discriminative mind] may go into action... Its level of knowledge is necessarily more profound than that of *manas* because its function is to point the way to unity. It is only interested in questions that can be related to unity – relative or Absolute... To use *buddhi*, one has to abandon the idea that reflection and thought are active affairs. Real reflection, real thought can only be done when the *manas* is absolutely still, and not making all sorts of suggestions. That is why reflection is a very patient business.[10]

The School's Economics teaching had never been forgotten since Sheila's Young Liberal days. It reappeared when she quoted John of Gaunt's speech in *Richard II*, which referred to the landlordism rife in England at the time:

England bound in with the triumphant sea...
... is now bound in with shame,
With inky blots and rotten parchment bonds:
That England, that was wont to conquer others
Hath made a shameful conquest of itself.'[11]

9 *Ibid.*, p.66
10 *Ibid.*, pp.178-9.
11 Act II, Scene I.

In a more prosaic form it appeared, too, in her lecture called 'Western Culture and the Veda':

> For the School, of course, we are very interested in the Veda relating to land. To just take another statement at random, the Veda say the land is of *Brahman*. Of course the whole earth was conceived inside the *Brahman*. It belongs to Him and can never be sold or given just like that. It does not count as wealth but it is to be used and, because the community who use it make it valuable, then its fruits should go to the community. This is echoed in the Old Testament: 'The land is mine saith the Lord.' Quite unequivocal! And there, of course, they get over the problems, or did get over the problems, by having a jubilee year every fifty years to redistribute the land among the clan or tribe.[12]

Sheila Rosenberg's working life in the School embraced nearly every aspect of its activities. She was responsible, for example, for keeping in touch with overseas Schools, of which there were a growing number around the world. This included ensuring that they had the right Philosophy material – no mean task. When St James and St Vedast Schools were founded in the 1970s, she became a key figure as Chair of the Management Committee. In that post her academic qualifications and experience were invaluable, and the head teachers relied greatly on her judgment and keen interest in education.

One development perhaps marred her otherwise immaculate relationship with everything that the School stood for. This was the arrival of Dorine van Oyen in 1973. Until this time, Leon MacLaren had relied heavily upon Sheila for personal support in his domestic arrangements, when he was ill and in numerous administrative matters. She was ready to assist him in any way at any time. Dorine, twenty-three years her junior, and similarly devoted to serving the man they both recognised as a master teacher, more or less displaced her in this capacity. She was a remarkably talented young lady, fluent in English, a fine musician, self-confident and thoroughly educated in the ways of the School from an early age. Her parents had run the Amsterdam School for many years, and had a special relationship with Leon MacLaren. Whilst carrying out her new duties in England, Dorine later even managed to gain a doctorate from Leicester University for a thesis on *The Cloud of Unknowing*.

12 *Sheila Rosenberg: A Renaissance Lady*, pp.296-7.

Typically, MacLaren gave little notice, or even recognition, of any change. One day Sheila was there to attend to him; the next it was Dorine. He clearly expected Sheila to be indifferent to such worldly matters! But even she could not reach such heights of non-attachment after years of devoted service. From 1969 she had worked full-time for the School, and for years before that every moment outside the offices of *The Times* was likely to be filled with work for and with Leon MacLaren. Doubtless she showed no resentment, but between her and Dorine there remained a coolness that contrasted with the open warm-heartedness that they both presented to others. On the other hand, the new set-up enabled her to devote yet more time and energy to her studies, to the provision of material and to a hundred and one other duties. On one level she must have been relieved, for MacLaren was undoubtedly a hard taskmaster.

In 1992 Sheila Rosenberg also gave up direct leadership of the Ladies Groups in favour of a young man, David Boddy, whose authority stemmed from a comment by the Shankaracharya that women may need a man to direct them, in view of their emotional unsteadiness. This role, of course, is often filled by a father or husband, but, within the context of the School, MacLaren saw the need for such a position. In fact, Sheila was aging and would be mortally ill before too long. Most of the ladies accepted the change, though a few departed. David Boddy became a respected counsellor. Having worked for Margaret Thatcher (see page 215), he was probably well acquainted with feminine force and the accompanying emotional turbulence!

On the afternoon before she died, at Waterperry in 1994, Sheila woke up and asked for a cup of tea. 'How strange', she said, 'that, in passing from one embodiment to another, one should still have a desire for a cup of tea!' The final comment on her death, however must come from one of her favourite sonnets, beside which she wrote in her notebook: 'Why so much attention to the fading mansion of the body?'

> Then, soul, live thou upon thy servant's loss,
> And let that pine to aggravate thy store;
> Buy terms divine in selling hours of dross;
> Within be fed, without be rich no more:
> So shalt you feed on Death, that feeds on men,
> And Death once dead, there's no more dying then.[13]

13 Sonnet CXLVI.

Although they had not been the best of friends, Sheila Rosenberg and Dorine van Oyen served Leon MacLaren, and through him the School, with equal devotion. In them both a Promethean fire burnt with the same intensity. Dorine tutored the senior ladies in the UK and on the world tour every Summer, when she was a leading member of the entourage. She had a creative, imaginative mind, which MacLaren found stimulating and entertaining. Some of his innovative ideas probably owed much to their conversations. Her musical ability as a performer matched his own, and he was perhaps never happier than when playing Mozart duets with her at the piano. The translation of Hermes Trismegistus from the Greek (see page 184) was just one proof of her intellectual capacity. Yet Dorine's greatest contribution to the work of the School was her unswerving care for the person of Leon MacLaren. His needs were met for years without demur, even when on some occasions he was ungrateful and cantankerous. During his final illness, she showed remarkable steadiness and good sense, belying paradoxically his reservations about the trustworthiness of women.

CHAPTER FOURTEEN

How May a Nation Change its Mind?

P ERHAPS stimulated by the feeble state of the British economy
in the nineteen sixties, when Harold MacMillan had pro-
claimed that we had never had it so good, and Harold Wilson
had devalued the pound, the School produced an extremely
thorough and penetrating Economic course that ran through nine
terms. It arose out of discussions between Leon MacLaren and Peter
Green, now well established as Principal and also Head of Economics. Adhering closely to the principles inherited from Henry
George and the two MacLarens regarding natural law, the importance of land, and the law of rent, it also developed other aspects,
often with striking originality.

Throughout the course students were reminded frequently of the
well-tried material, especially of the 'island' diagram, that showed
the primary division of wealth between wages and economic rent.
This was now analysed, however, on the lines explored by Leon
MacLaren in *Nature of Society* and elsewhere, so that the precise role
of secondary claims on wealth by landlords, moneylenders and tax
collectors could be explained. What became clearer, especially, was
how all this was related to society as a whole, including the State, the
law, institutions and customs.

A new prominence was given to the point of interaction between
land and labour. This was still illustrated as the place of their conver-
gence at the top of a triangle containing the man-made world, but it
was explored in greater depth. Whilst the two primary factors of
production are visible and tangible, this point is elusive. Its effects are
far-reaching yet subtle. Through this point act the forces that change
cultures and nations. Medieval ideas produced feudal land tenure,
great churches and religious art; Renaissance ideas have produced

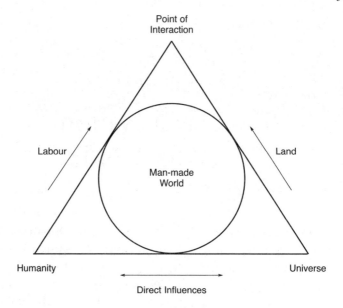

The Primary Factors

private ownership of land, modern science and democracy. The city of Berlin was given as a striking example of the influence exerted at this point. Each side of the Berlin wall in the 1960s was significantly different – capitalism to the West, communism to the East. Profit and neon lights on one side; workers' tenements and Socialist realism on the other. Yet the land and labour differed little. The contrast flowed from the ideas that governed each community.

The point of interaction affects how land and labour meet. At one time they combine under the condition of feudal tenure, at another under that of private ownership. The former makes for barons, knights, and serfs tied to the land, all serving under the ultimate overlordship of the king. The latter allows tenants to take part of the rent in the form of profits after paying the landlords' share, and as entrepreneurs to employ labour that has been forced off the land by enclosure. In both cases the earnings of labour – as serfs or as factory workers – is less than the full wages at the margin of production. Only the idea of free land and free labour, operative at the point of interaction, would ensure that the labourer received his due reward.

Why do men work, and what weakens their will to work? These questions were raised several times. It is natural for men to work, it was suggested, using their talents in work of their own choice. When such freedom is inhibited, work becomes arduous and merely a means to earn a living. Specialisation is society's way of enabling each to use his distinctive talents to the full. Now, however, it has been perverted into narrow tasks on a production line or in a super-market. Minimal wages further weaken the will to work. So, too, does the opportunity given by the capitalist system to live off the earnings of others, through capturing the economic rent in the form of landlords' claim or interest. A symptom of this debasement of work is the tendency of people to develop hobbies that reflect the absence of satisfaction in an office or factory. Only then may their enthusiasm reveal itself. Students were encouraged to see all this for themselves in their own workplace and home.

Production was described as cyclical, beginning with natural resources and proceeding through the stages of access, raw materials, tools, direction, sellers and consumers to the final disposal of waste to nature. A telling example of how only those materials that human discovery and knowledge make available for use are really natural resources was the case of atomic energy. Atoms have always been present, but only quite recent scientific research has enabled atomic energy to be practical. Once more the system of land tenure makes its appearance in the question of access to natural resources and the provision of a location for production. Texas oil millionaires and Arab sheiks were cited as examples of those who control access to valuable land. In Alberta, Canada, by contrast mineral rights are vested in the State government, so that oil royalties provide for roads, schools and hospitals. Tools include many forms of capital, such as machinery, equipment and vehicles. Direction is the function of management, especially at the level of organising the factors of production.

Such cases in the oil industry remind us that the division of wealth depends upon law and custom. Rent can only be received if there is some title to the land. Between 1760 and 1844 there were 3,883 Enclosure Acts passed in the British Parliament. Over five and a half million acres were enclosed for the benefit of privileged individuals. Since then the community has constantly assented to these landowners – and others, of course – being relieved of the economic duty of paying rent for land occupied.

A major new topic was introduced, namely the natural hierarchy that exists in humanity, whatever the particular form of culture,

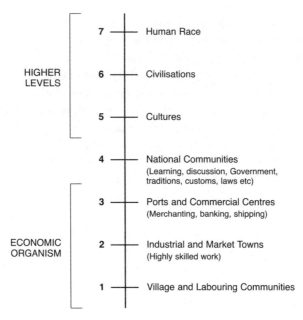

The Natural Hierarchy

society and government. At the base are village and labouring communities, often dependent upon one particular industry, like farming or mining. Above them are industrial and market towns, where more skilled work is prevalent, such as the towns that serve an agricultural area or those manufacturing towns that grew up in the industrial revolution. Third are the great ports and commercial centres that house shipping firms, banks and merchants, such as Southampton, Bristol or Liverpool. These three levels collectively constitute the economy, the powerhouse of a nation, where production is the chief concern. Above these is the level of national communities. Here government bodies, like Parliament, universities, law courts and churches exert authority over the nation, centred in the capital city. Their chief means of influence is language. By speech and writing, their laws, learning, judgments and sermons are diffused throughout the realm. These are obvious, familiar institutions, seen by many as the highest elements in human communities.

At a higher level, however, more subtle and more powerful forces are at work. Firstly, at level five in the hierarchy, are cultures, which are extensive in time and space. They may last for several hundred years, like the medieval culture of Europe or the scientific culture that has prevailed since the Florentine Renaissance. These reach far beyond one nation, prevailing over differences of language, custom and religion. Scientists today, for example, meet and exchange research without regard for national boundaries, except where questions of national security may arise. Even cultures, however, are contained within the greater unity of a civilisation, the most comprehensive order of human organisation. A civilisation is united around one great teaching of religion or philosophy – Christianity, Islam, Greek Philosophy or Vedanta. It may last for thousands of years, and reach around the globe. Within a civilisation both cultures and nations rise and fall. When it dies, a whole epoch seems to come to an end, as Edward Gibbon so eloquently portrayed in his great history of the fall of the Roman Empire.

And yet what continues when a civilisation collapses? The human race itself carries on, however broken and demoralised the vast majority of people may be. For the human race is itself the apex of this hierarchy, which diminishes in number as it grows in knowledge and power from the base to the top. Humanity is one. All men and woman are essentially united in their common nature, above all in *Atman* that abides in the heart of everyone. This fundamental principle was expressed in the Economics material by the term 'Goodness', used with Platonic overtones. Goodness, it was said, is what enables anything to exist. Just as the human race is present at all levels of the hierarchy from the humble village to the greatest amongst humanity, so goodness is found at every stage, for without some aspect of it the culture, nation, town or whatever would perish.

Men at each level both reflect and determine the qualities there. The master teachers of humanity – Christ, Krishna or the unknown authors of the Veda – stand at the top, sustaining the whole human race with their words, which live on through millennia after they have passed away. From the commandment to love one's neighbour as oneself, or from a *mahavakya* (great sentence) of the Upanishads, a civilisation is born, resounding with the spoken words of the master. What maintains a civilisation are the men of justice who revive it with such teaching as the ten commandments or the laws of Solon. For justice is the prime quality of the level of civilisation. When justice is fallen in the street a civilisation is in danger of destruction. Likewise, cultures depend upon men of understanding who know the natural laws that govern societies. They may create the

Philosophy or art or science that is the hallmark of a new culture, or they may revive one that is outworn. Marsilio Ficino in fifteenth-century Florence established a Platonic Academy that blew upon the embers of the dying medieval culture of Italy. So, too, did Shakespeare revive the English language to such effect that it has become almost the *lingua franca* of the modern world.

The respected public leaders of society act at level four. Any aspirations they may have, however, to be the ultimate arbiters of a nation's fate are misplaced. If they do not recognise the superior authority of the higher levels, then they will be driven by the theories, opinions and beliefs of those below. Plato's philosopher king, who descends into the cave from the sunlight of reason in order to rule justly, stands at one end of the scale. The demagogue speaking to the low feelings and instincts of the mob is at the other. Today – in the nineteen sixties – we see government moving from oligarchy, the rule of the property-owning few, to democracy, the rule of the *demos* or common people. The saving grace of Britain remains that representative government, as defined by Edmund Burke and John Stuart Mill, has not get given way to the crude democracy that Plato describes.

Men and women at level three and below do not have much power as individuals. Bankers and merchants, for example, operate through markets and firms that set the rules for their decisions and influence. Yet collectively they are of great importance, at their best providing reasoned advice and sound decisions relating to money, credit and trade. The Metal Exchange in the City of London pro-vided a useful example of how a small but vital market may enable supply and demand to balance through a price mechanism and the holding of stocks by traders. 'My word is my bond' is the keynote of this level, for transactions there are impossible if integrity breaks down.

Skill and inventiveness are features of level two. Entrepreneurs, engineers, artists, accountants, all such trained workers, contribute to the development and maintenance of industrial production of every kind. In the industrial revolution they were the key figures, just as today the new experts in pharmaceuticals, telecommunications, computers and so on have become the driving force of the economy. At the level of labouring communities, the significance of the individual is almost lost. Workers in a firm come and go; they may be unemployed; they move from one unskilled occupation to another.

1. Leon MacLaren *(Photo by Frank Monaco)*

2. Andrew McLaren with Stanley Baldwin

3. Henry George

4. No. 11 Suffolk Street
(Painted by Cheryl Howeld)

5. Sri Shantananda Saraswati, Shankaracharya of Jyotir Math

6. P. D. Ouspensky

7. Sri Shantananda Saraswati at a *Puja*

8. Peter and Ruth Green

9. Stanhill Court

10. Sheila Rosenberg *(left)* and Joan Crammond

11. One-glance portrait at Waterperry

12. Art in Action

13. Work on the Waterperry Frescoes

14. Waterperry House

15. Discantus Choir rehearsing in the MacLaren Hall at Mandeville Place

16. Nicholas Debenham

17. Sheila Caldwell

18. Laura Hyde

19. David Boddy

20. St James' Boys School at Twickenham

21. Paul Moss

22. Attention

23. Abhinaya in the gardens at Nanpantan

24. Fresco at Waterperry

25. School House in Croydon

26. School House in Budapest

27. School House in Buenos Aires

28. Group meeting in New York

29. Economics Forum in South Africa

30. Open-air class at St James' School in Trinidad

31. Music at John Scottus School in Dublin

32. Roger Pincham

33. Graham Skelcey

34. Ian Mason

35. Gardens at Sarum Chase

36. School House in Leeds

37. Nanpantan Hall in the winter

38. School House in Wellington, New Zealand

39. School Headquarters, 11 Mandeville Place, London

40. A performance in the theatre at Waterperry

41. Donald Lambie with student

42. Sunset at Waterperry

43. Portrait of Donald Lambie *(Portrait by Charles Hardaker)*

Nevertheless they are the physical power of the whole economy. On them its productivity depends. It they strike, there is no output. They know their weakness as individuals, especially in a land-enclosed economy where wages are forced down to the minimum acceptable, so in modern times they have formed unions to protect themselves against the worst excesses of capitalism. Yet each has within him or her the goodness that exists at all levels, and in the sight of God is equal with the highest. As the material said, Jesus was born in a village and worked as a carpenter.

Law operates at every level of the hierarchy. Goodness or truth is itself one law. Justice is the law of civilisations: every person receives what in reality is due to him, despite what may appear to be injustice. Cultures are subject to natural law, hence their expression in arts and sciences, where a Leonardo or a Newton may demonstrate the natural law of vision or physics. Nations function at the level of man-made laws, those created by a Parliament or by common law judges. Below these the economy comes under statistical laws that govern events *en masse*, such as the laws of supply and demand or of probability, as shown in markets for products, the fixing of wages and such activities as insurance.

Lest the discussion of the hierarchy became too theoretical, the material reverted to the question of how individual sites are chosen by businesses. A striking example was given of the new steelworks at Llanwern in South Wales. The managing director specified the conditions required. They included integration with the existing activity of the company at Ebbw Vale, transport facilities to London and Birmingham, access to coking coal, iron ore, limestone and large quantities of water, proximity to a seaport and finally room for expansion in the future. 'No other site investigated fulfilled all the above requirements', he concluded.

Some examples of the price of land were given, ranging from £75 per acre for a Cheshire stock farm to £13,000 per acre for land with planning permission for houses in Sussex and £10 million per acre for prime sites in the City of London. These prices, it was pointed out, were closely related to the place in the hierarchy of the use of the land. So too the price varied systematically with the location in the UK.

A nice observation by a lady student showed how the Economics teaching needs to be heard and considered before its full import is recognised. She had walked past a building site in central London.

The pavement had been removed, so that she saw the earth beneath. This was land! The pavements were formed on land, the buildings on land, the whole of London on land. So the School was not just talking about pastures green!

A most illuminating comparison of economic freedom with civil freedom followed this examination of the land situation. Three conditions govern the degree of freedom available in any country: civil rights, the level of earnings, and the system of land tenure. The first of these depends upon the observance by the people at large, including all public servants, of three basic duties: not to assault, not to imprison and not to libel or slander. Claims to rights without this observance are useless. Such duties define what one must not do, leaving people open to do whatever else they choose. At the same time, public authorities, the State, the police and so on, need to be limited to what the law allows them to do. This dual provision for citizens and public servants guarantees civil freedom. English common law has enforced these restraints for centuries, and thereby ensured a high degree of freedom.

In the economic sphere English law, like almost all contemporary legal systems, has failed to state or enforce conditions of economic freedom. Justice in the system of land tenure has fallen away from its relatively free state under the Anglo-Saxons to a lamentable condition of absolute private ownership, exemplified by a famous nineteenth-century judgment in the case of Pickles versus the Mayor of Bradford. The court decided that the landowner, Pickles, had the right to divert water flowing over his land, so that a public reservoir on lower ground would remain empty.

Land tenure lies at the root of the economic system, of course, not least in the part it plays in determining the level of earnings. If land is freely available at the margin, earnings are high. If land is all enclosed, then they fall to the least that people will accept. At present it is only too evident, as witnessed by strikes and unemployment, that this is the case now. The measurement of earnings is in real terms what can be bought out of take-home pay, although the 'social wage' of State benefits should be added back. Without State provision for health, education and so on, the least that people are prepared to accept undoubtedly would be higher.

It is clear that the level of economic freedom is generally very low. Civil freedom alone cannot offer what human nature demands, which is not just freedom from assault and so on from one's fellows, but also the freedom to work creatively as one's own master and to earn enough to support a good standard of life. A quote from Henry George made evident this dependence upon both aspects of freedom:

> Place one hundred men on an island from which there is no escape, and whether you make one of these men the absolute owner of the other ninety-nine, or the absolute owner of the soil of the island, will make no difference either to him or to them. In the one case, as the other, the one will be the absolute master of the ninety-nine – his power extending even to life and death, for simply to refuse them permission to live upon the island would be to force them into the sea.[1]

How then are land tenure and the level of earnings to be brought into line with natural justice? As with civil rights, the universal observance of duties is the key. What are fundamental duties in the economic field? They arise, of course, from the nature of Man. The School concluded that there are four incumbent upon the individual, and equivalent ones due from the community itself. The former are to pay the full economic rent, to keep land in good condition, not to interfere with another's quiet enjoyment of land, and to support oneself and one's family if one is able. The community for its part should enforce the full collection of rent, keep unused land in good condition, make unused land available to those who want it, and support those unable to support themselves.

The course went on to note to what extent these are now observed. Most people pay rent for land, but some do not. Only if all pay it, without exception, are the duties fulfilled. At present landowners and some leaseholders retain rent for themselves. The other duties are fulfilled to varying degrees. The last one, for example, has become partly a function of the Welfare State, but such a huge commitment would be unnecessary were the other duties fully observed. These duties have many unnoticed implications. For example, cases of firms telling employees to clear their desks by Monday morning are significant examples of interfering with workers' quiet enjoyment of land. For to whom does it really belong? Increasingly the State makes laws to ameliorate the conditions created by the failure to enforce these economic duties. Such laws even impinge on civil liberty, for civil and economic freedom are

1 Henry George, *Progress and Poverty*.

inextricably linked. No society in recorded history has fully achieved both. Yet they remain as ideals to be sought by those who love freedom.

On the question of value, the course followed closely the analysis given by Leon Maclaren in *Nature of Society*, concerning the subjective nature of value and the dependence of price in an exchange on four values.. It developed, however, the theme of valuing one's contribution to the community, especially that given by work. Students were enjoined to see how their work is part of a greater whole, and is never complete in itself. The value of co-operation and help given to others were also stressed. This can all be seen against the context of the hierarchy of seven levels.

The subject of taxation was introduced with reference to Adam Smith's four canons, viz:

1. The burden of taxation should be spread as fairly as possible having regard to the ability to pay.
2. Taxes should be certain and not arbitrary.
3. Taxes should be levied at the time or in the manner in which it is least inconvenient to the taxpayer.
4. Taxes should be easy and inexpensive to administer, and should not discourage production.

A tax on the economic rent meets all these requirements, unlike the present system in the UK. What would be the effect of a tax on annual land values in place of existing taxes? A tenant could pass the tax on to the landlord, if he were already paying a full market rent. This would enable the tenant to make larger profits and perhaps pay higher wages. When a lease fell in, the landlord could increase the rent accordingly, but then the tax assessment could be raised. Finally the full economic rent could be collected.

Such a tax is in accord with an inherent balance between public expenditure and taxation, for when expenditure improves the economic structure it raises the rent at the same time. This was well expressed by the Liberal Prime Minister, Asquith, in 1923:

> The value of land rises as population grows and national necessities increase, not in proportion to the application of capital and labour, but through the development of the community itself. You have a form of value, therefore, which is conveniently called 'site value', entirely independent of buildings and improvements and of other

things which non-owners and occupiers have done to increase its value – a source of value created by the community, which the community is entitled to appropriate to itself.

Unnecessary or wasteful expenditure would soon become apparent, for it would not have this effect of raising the value of land and hence of the taxation to finance the expense.

The material pointed out that in 1966 legislation enabled local authorities to levy half rates on empty buildings, a measure that was a small step towards a proper tax on annual land values. (This was repealed by the Conservative government of Mrs Thatcher.) Details were also given of how some other countries had adopted forms of site value tax – Denmark, Australia, New Zealand, Canada and the cities of New York and Johannesburg. Brief extracts from the British Finance Act of 1931, which Andrew MacLaren had helped to draft, were also quoted, in order to demonstrate the precision needed for legislation. All these examples helped to show that such a tax must be levied on annual values rather than on capital values, since the latter diminish *pro rata* with the tax.

In *Nature of Society* and in his lectures Leon MacLaren had explained much about the rise of capitalism, and how its institutions and features, like unemployment and trade cycles, distorted the natural working of an economy. This was developed in the material. The modern economy is a consequence of full land enclosure and scientific progress. Wages have fallen as a share of output to the point where there is no prospect of workers providing their own capital equipment. Banks will not provide credit to them. Hence 'investment' is required from people who are receiving a share of the economic rent. A return on this is demanded in the form of interest or dividends. The Stock Exchange has therefore become a market in claims to these returns. Unlike banks and commodity markets, the Stock Exchange would not be necessary in an economy without enclosed land.

What of contemporary economic policy? In the 1960s there was much talk of incomes policies, exchange controls and limitations on bank credit. These were means of limiting inflation and balance of payments deficits. Incomes policy ignored the way in which the level of wages is in fact determined. Exchange controls were direct restrictions on foreign trade; whilst limiting bank credit reduced inflation at the cost of inhibiting production and new investment. Students were, however, encouraged to study economic news and to be prepared to comment on government policy. Understanding natural law would bring these into perspective.

By contrast the material made a short excursion into the more profound question of justice. The fundamental duties of civil and economic life define justice between people in the community. Yet there is a finer meaning to justice, adumbrated in the Emperor Justinian's maxim that justice is the constant will to render every man his due. What is really due to each man and woman? When one looks at the failure over the centuries for justice in the community to be secured, especially in the economic sphere, one is forced to reason that either there is no justice or that it lies deeper. If people have ignored economic duties, as in the case of believing in an absolute right to private property in land, then what is due to them? Do they not in justice reap the consequences of this ignorance? For ignorance is the act of ignoring. From this standpoint everyone receives his or her due – in the economy and in life.

At this point the material drew substantially on the Philosophy teaching. Justice is blind; above it stands only the truth. Those who have a glimpse of justice need not lament the state of mankind, grim though it may appear to be. Instead they may seek the truth, and through that seeking find their own part in the play of creation. Meanwhile the School needs to fulfil its role of studying and teaching Economics.

From the heights of Philosophy to the depths of the British transport system! A brief discussion of railways and roads followed. Everyone complains that nationalised railways always run at a loss, with the government paying out large subsidies. What is not taken into account is the economic rent that every railway system creates. They try to pay their way on passenger fares and freight charges. That is impossible. If they were credited with the rent attributable to them, they would easily be in surplus. The electrification of lines to Southend and Manchester, for example – this was in the 1960s – is benefiting towns on the route. The price of houses has jumped by £1,000 above the national average. In London the new Victoria underground line has a similar effect on land prices. Likewise the new motorways bring prosperity, and increase rents in places like Maidenhead, Reading, Luton and Northampton.

From transport the course moved on to government, level four in the hierarchy of the community. Its principal functions were stated:

To defend the nation from external enemies, and to deal with foreign affairs.

To secure justice by promoting civil and economic freedom, and to maintain law and order.

To establish and protect the currency.

To deal with internal emergencies as they arise.

To make provision for public utilities that cannot be provided by private enterprise.

To raise the necessary revenue to cover the expenditure of government.

Examination of contemporary government departments revealed that a large number existed largely for the relief of poverty. Attempts to redistribute wealth were made by the Ministries of Education, Labour, Health, Pensions and National Insurance, Housing and Local Government, and even the Board of Trade. Were economic duties fulfilled, most of these would become redundant. Their proper functions, if any, could be fulfilled mainly by the Home Office. About 25 per cent of the UK gross national product went to services that could be provided by the individual citizen in an economy where earnings were not forced down below their natural level.

Similarly a vast amount of legislation was passed for the same misguided purpose of correcting the maldistribution of wealth. Recent efforts included Acts for landlords and tenants, housing, public health, factories, bankruptcy, contracts of employment, workmen's compensation, slum clearance, ribbon development, prices and incomes and much else. Such legislation at best mitigates the more flagrant breaches of natural justice, leaving the causes untouched. Meanwhile trade and industry is hampered by the dead weight of controls, restrictions and taxation.

On a higher note, the material drew upon Emerson's writing on the levels of government in Plato – aristocracy, the rule of the best; timocracy, when the first hint of corruption appears; oligarchy, when rulers' chief concern is money; democracy, the uprising of the oppressed people; and finally tyranny, when the despot appears to free the people, only to set up his own despotism. In history and the contemporary world all can be seen.

This brief reference to Plato made an excellent introduction to a lengthier incursion into economic history. The Anglo-Saxon land system was commended. Both folkland and bookland carried duties to serve the king in warfare and to maintain bridges and other public works, for the land was viewed as belonging essentially to the whole people. William the Conqueror claimed the land as king, but feudal duties retained the concept of obligations attached to landholding. In 1236 the famous Statute of Merton introduced the substantial change that made lords of the manor landowners with the right to enclose common land. By Shakespeare's time he could give to John of Gaunt the classic line in *Richard II*: 'Landlord of England art thou now, not king.' Gradually feudal tenure gave way to ownership and the private collection of rent, until mass enclosure movements left the eighteenth-century oligarchy in control of both land and Parliament. By the nineteenth century the stage had been reached of absolute ownership, as confirmed by the case of Pickles and the dry reservoir. Little had changed fundamentally since then. The Law of Property Act of 1925 tried in vain to simplify the sale of land. The budgets of 1909 and 1931 made efforts to introduce some kind of tax on land values, but were opposed by the vested interests of landowners and financiers. Since the Second World War only futile Acts to tax land development increments have been passed. This resume of economic history cannot show how brilliantly it had been researched and expressed in the material. It led to at least one student on the course taking up a serious study of history!

The course turned to the subject of credit and money. Credit was shown to be a necessity for all exchanges, since if neither party gave credit then the transaction could not even begin. A delivery of bricks, for example, requires that either the bricks or the payment are handed over first. Money, however, is also essential as a medium of exchange, for a promise to pay is only generally acceptable if it is made by a bank or institution with a widely known reputation for integrity. A personal I.O.U. is not generally acceptable. Hence in practice money takes the form of debts acknowledged by banks, either the Bank of England or a high street bank. When a cheque is written, a bank debt for that amount is transferred from one account to another.

Shipbuilding supplied a striking example of how credit and money operate. A ship takes some time to build. The shipbuilder has to pay bills for materials, wages etc. So the bank grants him an over-draft. He pays these costs by drawing on the bank, more or less *pro rata* with the progress of work on the ship. When it is finished, he receives payment from the purchaser, and repays the bank out of the proceeds. Thus wealth has been created by the use of credit and money from the bank, and the overdraft has been cancelled, so that there is no net increase in the money supply.

There is no reason why the banks could not finance all production in this way. The whole cycle of production needs credit at every stage, especially where capital goods are produced. As present banks usually limit their credit to short-run uses, leaving long-run projects to be financed by borrowing from money-lenders. This is a consequence of a distribution of wealth that leaves producers with a minimum and landowners and some tenants with the lion's share. Thus almost all firms are in debt to wealthy 'investors'. The lenders, of course, charge interest, and the banks then follow suit and charge interest on their granting of overdrafts. In fact, the banks could simply cover their costs. They have no real grounds for charging interest, since they create the money that they are lending. This distinction between money being lent, for example, by building societies or insurance companies, and money being created by banks is fundamental, yet completely ignored by governments, economists and even the banks themselves. Were it recognised then firms and individuals would be relieved of burdensome excess charges by banks. In addition, the question of for what purpose is money created could be asked. Is it to finance production, or to finance speculation, especially in land? Only the former is productive; the latter merely raises land prices.

This last point led into a discussion of inflation, which at that time in the 1960s was becoming a serious problem. What were its causes? The supporters of incomes policy and other means of restricting wage demands, believed in the theory that wage costs push up prices. But wages are severely limited already when land is fully enclosed. Inflation, on the contrary, is primarily a result of rising land prices, reflected in rents and prices for commercial and housing land. Economic growth pushes up land prices; money created by the banks for land purchases pushes them up much more. Since land is needed by every firm and every household, the effect is diffused throughout the economy. After all, why do workers demand higher money wages? Largely because they have to pay for housing, often with mortgage interest added for good measure. Were the economic rent taxed, land prices would fall. Meanwhile taxing almost everything else, including wages, inflicts costs on the margin of production, so that there is yet more pressure on prices.

There was a brief account of international trade, which condemned tariffs and quotas as misguided attempts to protect home industries and jobs. Once land enclosure has led to unemployment and low wages, such protection looks like a plausible solution. In so far as it does offer protection, it is at the expense of the whole community losing out from the consequent restriction on international specialisation. If nations freely trade, then individuals and firms can produce what they are best at producing.

A nation gets the government it deserves. How then may it change its mind and deserve something better? This question was offered to students to ponder over between weekly classes. No answer was given by the material. There were, however, some clues. How did England come to welcome the civil freedom ensured by the common law? It took several centuries for the work of the common lawyers of Henry II's reign to bear its full fruit. So, too, the appalling conditions of child labour, slum housing, workhouses and the rest in the industrial revolution were ameliorated only when people generally came to demand a more humane economy. Reform of the systems of land tenure and taxation may take generations. The School and those who study in it have the task of keeping the light shining. For when the nation does begin to change its mind, the knowledge needs to be available to offer a wise choice.

Although this three year course did not continue in the same form when Peter Green handed over the Economics department to Roger Pincham, it remained the feedstock for much later material. Under Pincham the course was streamlined, with more emphasis on contemporary economic events and policy. Subsequently John Allen, in his turn, had a strong interest in the history of economic thought. He developed a new course on this that dealt especially with the ideas of the French physiocrats, who had tried in vain to bring about reform in France, rather than a revolution. Turgot and Quesnay featured large in the material. Adam Smith and Ricardo completed the study of the 'classical' economists. Allen regarded Ricardo as the real formulator of the law of economic rent, and encouraged serious research into his writings. All this added a valuable dimension to Economics in the School.

When Ian Mason took over the department, the emphasis changed once more. Efforts were made to bridge the gap that had always existed between what the School taught and how the world viewed the subject. Other like-minded organisations and individual proponents of tax reform were contacted. In the case of the Henry George Foundation, library facilities are now shared, and meetings are held at Mandeville Place. Several conferences have been organised for such interested bodies.

A notable example of the new approach was a conference held in Johannesburg for School members in 2004. Prior to this the theme of world hunger had been addressed, with the publication of a Waterperry Declaration outlining principles and policies to alleviate poverty. In Johannesburg practical experience was gained of the living conditions of people near subsistence level, and also of such new terms as *Ubuntu*, an African name for a universal concept of common humanity. The traditional wisdom that enables people to live without exploiting others or misusing natural resources was a valuable lesson for well-endowed visitors from the UK and other 'more advanced' economies. Justice and equity, the centrepieces of the Economic department, took on a fresh light.

Ian Mason has felt that, after many years of philosophical studies, the School should re-examine Economics from the standpoint of insights gained from these. One aspect of this is the role of the individual in seeking the welfare of society and humanity. Philosophy has taught that personal advancement should give way before service to others, which is the proper field of the study of Economics. A simple principle given by the Shankaracharya could be fundamental here. Work done is righteous, if both the producer and society gain from it. If only the producer gains, then it is unrighteous.

There remains also much study to be done to highlight the fact that human beings cannot make whatever rules they like in disregard of natural law. The importance of land, meaning the whole natural material world, is perhaps the central example of this truth. Hence the School needs to develop the idea of 'Economics with Justice' into a coherent and practical model based on natural law. This could be its vital contribution in an age when Economics has become a confused battleground, delivering immense wealth and technological development alongside devastating poverty and deprivation. The aim is an environment in which all people can come, if they will, to the natural way of living that the Shankaracharya referred to in his very first conversation.

CHAPTER FIFTEEN

Holding
to the Truth

B Y THE 1970s the School was beginning to take an interest in
the education of children. Many students had families. They
were increasingly concerned about falling standards of teaching and discipline in schools, and looked to the principles of Philosophy for guidance in the care of children, both educationally and at
home. There were professional teachers in the School also, who were
dissatisfied, not only with conditions in schools, but with the way
their subjects were taught in universities and in the classroom.
Should grammar be largely neglected? Was numeracy declining? Had
science become materialistic? Every subject had such questions.

Accordingly, on his next visit to India in 1971, Leon MacLaren
was quick to ask the Shankaracharya about character building in
children. The reply gave great emphasis to the age of sixteen. Before
this age a child spends the 'capital', with which he or she is born, in
acquiring knowledge and character. At sixteen the capital is all spent,
so that the adult life thereafter depends almost entirely on this early
upbringing. The child is truly father of the man. Whereas the adult
has discrimination, the child lacks it. Instead he has a powerful
ability to hold or retain what he learns. Therefore the material presented to the child is of prime importance. Teachers should select
this with great care, in the confidence that good material will induce
the child to ignore the bad.

How is the material to be presented to the child? Never impart
knowledge by force was the direction. Use gentle methods and
repeat the instructions several times, but in varied forms and perhaps
by presenting oneself differently as a teacher. Boredom must be
avoided at all costs. The child only learns what interests it. Women,

said the Shankaracharya, are naturally more suited to teach young children, as they know intuitively how to appeal to them.

MacLaren asked about the corruption of children by sexual impulses and by drugs, especially at an age of thirteen or fourteen. That is a problem common to East and West, replied the Shankaracharya. The sexual realm, if experienced too soon, is like a flood that overwhelms the child, and obscures any view of past and future. In modern society the company kept can be most destructive. Children should be sheltered from it. In particular, the influence of drugs must be strictly guarded against. Educating girls is especially important, as if they behave well the boys will follow suit.

At this point he expatiated on the beauty, and indeed the divinity, of young women, who in truth, he said, are goddesses. The tradition in India is to treat them with reverence. Within a family there may be a mother, sisters and daughters, yet there is no carnal desire towards them. All that is different is the name or the idea. In ancient tradition all women under seventeen were addressed as daughter, those up to about thirty as sister, and those above thirty as mother. From these names arises a natural restraint.

When asked about character in adults, the Shankaracharya used the image of a bamboo, which, if supple and tender like the child, can bend to any shape, but if dry and stiff is only moulded with great difficulty. He referred to various types of character found mainly in *tamassic* people and absent in the *sattvic*. There are those who sleep most of the time; those who live in a twilight world between sleep and waking, living in error and confusion; those dominated by fear, who resist any kind of adventure or innovation; those in whom anger burns up energy and destroys the ability for useful work; those who while away their time in idleness and yet like to stay in the fore-front; and finally those who pretend to be asleep in order to avoid work and responsibility. No doubt MacLaren recognised all six types amongst his students!

A story illustrated the last type. A brahmin had a servant who complained of being ill and incapable of any movement. He lay in bed, until the brahmin had carried out all the household duties, including cooking a meal. Whereupon the servant got up, ate a hearty supper and went back to bed.

Did the future of the School then lie only with its children under sixteen? Were the adults condemned as dry bamboos unable to change their ways? The answer had already been given in an earlier conversation. Good company and discrimination, or reason, can overcome the past. *Sanskara*, the result of previous actions in both present and past lives, is not the sole determinant. More was now said on this crucial topic.

The real nature of everyone is *sat – chit – ananda*: being, consciousness and bliss. Overlaying this is the secondary nature – *sanksara*. This is what Jesus meant by 'treasure' in the quotation about which MacLaren had enquired:

> A good man out of the good treasure of his heart bringeth forth that which is good; and an evil man out of the evil treasure of his heart bringeth forth that which is evil.[1]

Beyond the treasure lies the real nature of the *Atman*. Good company and reason serve to dispel the hindrances of *sanskara*. For them to be effective discipline is required, which must reach into every corner of life, and not just be followed when under the immediate influence of a wise man or of the School. One should seek the company of good men, good books and good society. Just as a farmer prepares the ground for sowing, waters the seedlings and clears the weeds away, so good company provides suitable conditions for growth, which occurs naturally if impediments are removed.

Man, unlike all other creatures, has made a promise prior to his birth, a threefold bond between himself and the Absolute: to respect the rules and regulations of the universe, to remember the Creator, and to seek Him throughout life. This promise sets reason to work. It is nourished by efficient and artistic work of any kind, and when sufficiently developed it leads to a realisation that the world is a great drama in which each has a special part to play and enjoy.

There are five levels of reason. Firstly there is that of the individual, whose welfare each person seeks automatically for himself. Beyond this stands the family, for whom one may sacrifice one's personal interest or perhaps do an injustice to others outside the family. Then there is the greater world of the society in which one lives; and the nation, for which some will sacrifice even their lives. Finally there is the universe itself. The greatest men or women make that their family.

The Shankaracharya told the story of a saint, who began life in a poor family, but studied at night and eventually became a professor.

Luke, 6:45.

Under the guidance of a wise man, his reason was awakened. He declared that he would share his salary with others by putting it on a table and telling all in need to help themselves. When his wife complained of being ignored, he just replied that, as part of humanity, she also could help herself. All children became his children, all women his mothers, sisters and daughters.

Reason observes measure. The Shankaracharya gave further observations on this discipline that the School had certainly taken to heart. Whenever there is an aim, he said, there have to be regulations to achieve it. These are the measure. The aim of the Absolute is *ananda* (bliss), so the regulations are built into the whole of creation in order for bliss to be attained. People want pleasure instead, but pleasure and pain go hand in hand. In seeking pleasure people exceed the measure and cause accidents, when their will clashes with what the Absolute has willed, which is measure. All disease is the consequence of mis-measure, perhaps from long ago. Bliss, however, is eternal. In a lifetime one may move towards it, and prepare the way for its achievement in another life.

A man asked his *guru* for advice about the frequency of sexual union with his wife. The *guru* replied that one union a month was equivalent to chastity. The man was dissatisfied. Then one a fortnight is permissible. Again the man would not accept this. One a week was the response. When challenged once more, the *guru* replied, 'Buy yourself a coffin and live how you like!'

When asked about the Veda, the Shankaracharya said that it is wrong to think of them as books. They are as old as mankind, for they are the system of knowledge held in the nature of things and always available to those who seek them. Any knowledge that is ordered, refined and systematic is Veda, compared to worldly knowledge, which is distorted in one way or another. What are called the Veda today are just what sages recorded some six thousand years ago, when consciousness had declined and memory had become weak, so that transmission by the spoken word alone was inadequate.

Further directions were given about the measure of the day. The three hours of rest should be as far as possible at the same time each day. Songs of praise, study of the scriptures or gentle work without any strain create *sattva*. Other activities are *rajassic*. For this reason a pause between activities is useful to enclose them, as it were, between moments of *sattva*. This practice of pausing was to become a valuable feature of students' lives, especially in the conditions of modern city life and the pressures that seem to beset people.

Measure applies in all three worlds: physical, divine and spiritual. What are these worlds, MacLaren enquired, particularly the divine or intermediate one? This question elicited much about the world of mind, where the forces at work can be represented as gods. Mind, said the Shankaracharya, is an interpreter between the spiritual and the physical. On the one hand is the light of the *Atman*, upon which everything depends for its existence; on the other the inanimate world of matter, which is a kind of frozen form of the past – it has already happened. The intermediate world connects the two. For example, when the mind is present the sense organs are connected with spirit; when it is absent they register nothing. He drew upon the simple analogy of a car. The bodywork is the physical, the gearbox conveys the force that moves it, and the ignition is the spark that initiates it all. The conscious Self is the driver, for whom the whole car is an instrument.

Why is this intermediate world called divine? The forces that it contains are unseen, beyond the senses, like gods. At this point MacLaren asked about actions, like writing a letter, when something unknown seems to take over, so that the letter 'writes itself'. This was confirmed as the work of divine forces. They may be godly or demonic. The latter may occur in a person whose indulgence in anger or hatred or lust, for example, allows a destructive force to gather. If this becomes acute, the person may become a kind of demon, a *rakshasa* or *asura*. Such are those who only take, and give nothing. Similarly, people may become godly by living exemplary lives helping others. The gods, as MacLaren said, are a mixed bag!

The Shankaracharya added that imagination gives forms to these godly forces, which are often described in this way in legends and literature. In the finest works of Indian literature, of course, are found such figures as Krishna and Rama, referred to as incarnations or *avatars*. The Shankararcharya spoke of their divine powers and their vanquishing of the greatest *rakshasas*, like Ravana. An incarnation possesses several – all, in the case of Krishna – of the powers or *shakti* of the Absolute. These include glory, law, fame, beauty, knowledge and renunciation. Indeed the Absolute can only be known through these powers, never directly.

The original Shankara was cited as an example of one possessed of *shakti*. He came at a time when India was riven by religious conflict, ignorance and neglect of *dharma* or righteousness. When he died at the age of thirty-two, he had defeated his intellectual opponents in debate, usually winning them over to become his disciples, drawn to himself by love those on the way of devotion, and destroyed or dispersed the brute force of enemies by obtaining the help of royal armies. His teaching and writing had purified the corrupted tradition of the Upanishads and the *Gita*. Finally he had established the four seats of Advaita Vedanta, of which the northern one was now held by this present Shankaracharya.

This introduction to the idea of divine powers and their association with the mental world, which had already been examined in some depth, was to be a key to unlock many doors previously closed to students in the School. If Indian imagination had given rise to a whole pantheon of gods, so too the Greeks and Romans, the Celts and Anglo-Saxons and other western peoples had created their gods to fill the space where mental forces operate. Was not Mercury the messenger whose very function was to interpret God to Man, as presented in Botticelli's *Primavera*? The literature and art of Western culture could be seen afresh, and given a practical meaning that rescued it from the oblivion of history. Many were stimulated to look again at ancient and medieval literature, at theology, at myth, legend and fairy tales. Those studying Marsilio Ficino's letters were given further impetus to delve into the mysteries of his thought.

Another way of looking at divine powers was given when the Shankaracharya spoke of *punya* (good) and *papa* (bad). These, he said, are substances produced by good or bad actions. Good actions are natural, easy, harmonious, in accordance with reason and feeling; bad actions take place in the dark, opposed by heart and mind, often fearful.

An unusual story showed divine forces at work in this regard. A poor cobbler used to go each year to a festival at Allahabad on the banks of the Ganges, where pilgrims bathed, practised austerities, listened to the wise and gave to the poor. For one month the cobbler mended the shoes of pilgrims for no charge, as his way of gaining *punya*. One day a brahmin had his shoes repaired and insisted on paying. The cobbler would only agree to an offering of money being made to the Ganges. Just as the brahmin made the offering a golden bracelet emerged from the water with the spoken words that it should be given to the cobbler. The brahmin had doubts. So he kept the bracelet. Soon afterwards his house was burgled and the bracelet stolen. It was, however, recovered and became the property of the king. His queen, delighted with its beauty, asked for a matching one. The thieves directed the police to the brahmin, who was ordered to produce a second bracelet or he would be punished with death. Horrified, he sought out the cobbler and told him of his deceit and the consequence. The cobbler prayed to the Ganges that, if his store of *punya* was adequate, could a second golden bracelet be given. The goddess of the Ganges answered his prayer, and the life of the brahmin was saved. Ever afterwards he lived righteously. Clearly the forces at work were beyond the range of the material world. Good and bad actions produce effects in the world of divine forces, the mental world.

When MacLaren asked about a third point, he was told that good and bad are chosen according to *sanskara*, but that if a person is detached, beyond good and bad, the real call of the *Atman* may be heard, and work is then done for its own sake. MacLaren recognised this as the proper method of work in the School, where something is done just because it needs to be, so that the action has a kind of neutral quality in which desire plays no part.

This was developed further when the Shankaracharya spoke of the three ways of action, devotion and knowledge, each of which can be followed without desire. There was a clear connection here with the Fourth Way of Ouspensky. Although each person was naturally suited to one of the three ways, to follow it without desire brings it to fulfilment by tempering it with the other two ways. Thus a man of action, who otherwise seeks success for himself – a seat in heaven or worldly riches, fame etc – may turn to artistic works by bringing knowledge and devotion to his activities. So, too, a man of knowledge may develop reason as an instrument for speaking or writing, when it is accompanied by devoted action. And those intent on devotion or love would find it transformed into love of the Absolute alone by the introduction of refined actions guided by reason. Action, knowledge and devotion, each without desire, gave a new and deeper meaning to the Fourth Way.

The Shankarachary assigned a special place to devotion in the work of the School. Whereas action and knowledge require time to come to maturity, devotion brings an immediate connection with the Absolute. The world and the Absolute become one for the devotee. Hence the School may work under a spirit of devotion at all times. This advice confirmed the importance that had been placed on service to the School since its inception. From the first cups of tea served to Economics students in the war years to the teams that now daily supported the classes and maintained the buildings in London and the branches a spirit of service had been the foundation of the continuing search for the truth.

MacLaren returned to the subject of the three worlds by asking about the nature of the spiritual world. The answer was surprising: the spiritual or causal body is dark. The light of the *Atman* has to pass through it like a beam in the darkness, but impurities obscure the light with colour, dirt or form of some kind. These impurities are what prevent immediate access to the spiritual world. Work is needed to remove them. Those troubled by *vikshepa*, or mental agitation, especially need to become still, to let movements in the mind be, as it were, precipitated. This instruction was to be repeated in other ways, and to become central to the School's teaching. The work was not to build or develop a new man, but to remove impurities or obstacles, so that the real man, who is and always has been the *Atman*, the one Self, should be realised. Nothing need be added.

The Shankaracharya introduced the concepts of *pravritti* and *nivritti*. These Sanskrit words mean 'activity', or 'active life', and 'cessation', or 'a life of contemplation'. He related these to the two directions on the circle of nine points. From one to nine the move-ment is creative, as nature at two develops coarser forms, until finally it reaches earth at nine, where all the elements are found fully manifested. This is the way of *pravritti*, whereby man as an embod-ied creature is the microcosm of the universe, and acts under the impulse of desire. *Nivritti* is the reverse movement, in which activity ceases and a return is made to the one substance that never moves.

This duality is seen everywhere, said the Shankaracharya; in day and night, action and cessation, work and rest, life and death. *Pravritti* is the way of the world; *nivritti* is the way of the wise. In meditation, in pausing between actions, in finding the measure in activities, we may follow the path of *nivritti*, even in the midst of a world ruled by the outward movement of desire, of *pravritti*.

The conversation returned to the subject of *citta*, the heart. New aspects emerged. Although closely connected with memory, the *citta* itself does not need to hold experiences in the form of an imprint or mark. An experience only makes such a mark on it when there is attachment or desire. In that case it is taken into *sanskara* and con-tinues to exert an influence, but if the *citta* is unaffected by desire, no mark is made, like an impression on water, rather than one made on stone or iron. This is why work is needed to rid the *citta* of marks or impurities created by attachment to experience. *Citta* is inanimate, rather like a cinema screen that just reflects what happens. Memory itself is a form of knowledge, and therefore conscious. Thus the pure *citta* of a wise man may accompany a strong memory. No record on the *citta* is required.

From memory the subject of belief naturally arose. A belief can be removed in two ways, said the Shankaracharya: by replacing it by another belief, or by reason providing the truth. For example, a simple man was told that his wife was greatly troubled because she had become a widow. This upset him too – until be realised the truth of the matter! This kind of belief is an extreme case of 'make believe', the *tamassic* form of belief. It can easily be broken, when its purpose is served. Meanwhile it causes separation. A *rajassic* belief is one intended to produce gain, a belief in what one wants. When it is shown to be ineffective, it is dropped. *Sattvic* belief or faith is substantially different, for it is belief strengthened by reason, or the action of *buddhi*. When it becomes love, it is unbreakable. In times of danger or misfortune, faith in one's true Self cannot be shaken, even if all else fails.

Turning from belief to knowledge, the Shankaracharya distinguished sharply between lower knowledge – mere information – and higher knowledge. The former may be learnt from teachers or books, even from scripture, but has not been experienced. Real knowledge is transformed by experience into being. Words become the man himself. Then what he expresses comes from his substance, from consciousness. Without this, learning, however great, lacks love or compassion. For emotion is the means to higher knowledge.

An analogy made this distinction clear. A pilgrim may study the route to a temple in the Himalayas. He may get acquainted with the distance, the resting places, the dangerous spots and so on, but until he makes the journey itself, moved to overcome fatigue and hardship by a love for the sacred place and what lies there, he will not find the rewards of a true pilgrim – spiritual transformation, humility, joy. Likewise, words must be transcended. The meaning must be realised in action, so that the word gains a brilliance, charged with truth and consciousness. This is the experience of higher knowledge.

MacLaren asked again about *aham*, the 'I am' that is the pure existence of the Self. When it gets identified with anything else at all, it becomes *ahankara* – 'I am something, a thought, feeling, action or whatever.' But pure *aham* is the gathering of the forces of consciousness, the very first entry into the world of space, time and *guna*. *Ahankara*, on the other hand, is like a ghost taking possession of oneself, as was to be explained subsequently at greater length.

If one calls a taxi, the conscious driver answers the call. He is the *aham*; yet all calls are made to the taxi, to the *ahankara*, for the *aham* is beyond name and form, even though it answers the call. Another analogy given was of a sweetmeat seller who was asked at short notice to play the part of the villain, Ravana, in a production of the *Ramayana*. As he sat on his throne in black robes, surrounded by demonic attendants, he was confronted by Hanuman, the monkey servant of Rama, swinging a club in his fury. The sweetmeat seller lost his nerve. He leapt up and rushed off the stage in terror. He was identified with his role in the drama, and forgot who he really was. Thus do we believe in *ahankara* and ignore *aham*.

To reinforce this vital message yet another image was used. In a golden ring the gold is *aham*. The form of the ring is *ahankara*. Only that can be beaten into shape, redesigned or broken. The gold is unchanged under any circumstances. Whatever happens, happens to the ring alone. All qualifications allow of change. Beyond qualifications is the subject. Without them one is forever pure, conscious and free.

In answer to a question about justice, the Shankaracharya told a story. A king went to a holy man for advice about ruling justly. Hold to the truth; that alone is necessary, was the response. In the kingdom there was a rule that at the end of a market day everything unsold was bought by the king. This was done in order to ensure that producers could always sell what they had made. One day a cunning man brought a large quantity of rubbish to the market. None, of course, was sold; but he demanded that the king should buy it all for a high price. The king felt obliged to keep his word and pay. The rubbish was stored in the palace. Next day Lakshmi, the goddess of wealth, came to the king and said that she was leaving the palace, as it was such a dirty place. The king could only assent. Soon after, all the gods and goddesses left as well. Without Lakshmi, wisdom, art, crafts, honour and others were not willing to stay. Finally Narayana, the Absolute, came to the king. 'My wife and all the others have left', he said. 'There is no good company here. I am leaving too.' Whereupon the king replied, 'You cannot go. You are the truth. I am

holding to the truth. You may leave only if I follow untruth.'
Narayana had to stay. After a while Lakshmi came back to her
husband. Then the others followed. The kingdom was restored to its
former glory. The king had first enquired about justice. What he had
learnt was that to find justice one needs to do nothing but to hold to
the truth.

At the conclusion of the 1973 conversations the Shankaracharya
told Leon MacLaren to go back to his country and his students, and
to guide them with knowledge and practice. Enrich the society
and the nation was an instruction that reached out beyond the
School, and yet gave emphasis to its future rule in Britain and
the world.

CHAPTER SIXTEEN

And the Word
was God

PEOPLE walking past some of the School houses on a week-day evening, or perhaps even at about 6.30 in the morning, might sometimes hear what sounds like a singing practice. It is more likely to be a language group practising Sanskrit vowels and consonants. This may seem a curious exercise for students of Philosophy. In fact, it has a direct connection with Leon MacLaren's original insight that confusion of tongues is largely responsible for the present-day ignorance of natural law and related subjects.

Very early on in the conversations with the Shankaracharya the subject of language had made an appearance. The whole creation, he said, arose from one fundamental sound, the word *Om*, called the *pranava* sound. (The root of *pranava* means 'to praise'.) This is the fundamental creative force from which everything in the creation arises. It contains the three letters (a,u and m) that manifest as the three *guna* – *sattva*, *rajas* and *tamas* – to constitute the nature of all that exists in the causal, mental and physical worlds. Thus *Om* is the *Brahman* itself in its creative aspect. It is what St John's Gospel calls the Word, which was in the beginning and was with God and was God.

Advaita Philosophy teaches that from this source in the ultimate one substance of *Om* all things arise as name and form. In essence they are words, springing from the one Word, each word giving a unique form to each thing that it makes. As the *Chandogya Upanishad* puts it:

All transformation has speech as it basis, and it is name only...[1]

---

1 *Chandogya Upanishad*, VI.3.4.

Thus behind the creation, as we experience it through our senses and other means of perception, lies language in its creative mode. That is what the Shankaracharya calls the natural language, of which all human or artificial languages bear the imprint. He gives a beautiful example of how a word underlies the physical world, giving it meaning in a human context. Without the word 'mother' two people may be mere physical bodies in no relationship beyond that of space and time. With the word 'mother' they become mutual objects of love, happiness and care. Humanity, depth and emotion are created by the word. A completely new dimension of life has appeared, as if by magic.

Such a radical ontology was welcomed by Leon MacLaren. He it was who had founded the School in order to overcome the confusion of tongues that he saw plaguing the discussion of Economics. Ever since, he had insisted on the precise use of language, on the avoidance of inaccurate terms and false definitions. Only by such means could people really communicate with one another, and join together in the search for truth in any field, especially in Philosophy. It was not difficult for him to introduce into the School the use of key Sanskrit terms that brought more precision to philosophical thinking.

Nevertheless Maclaren was faced with a hard choice when the Shankaracharya said that Sanskrit was a necessary study, if the School was to progress in Advaita. He viewed it as the purest of all languages, closest to the natural language in that in essence it had not deviated from its original form, owing to the tradition of oral transmission by pundits, who for millennia had preserved it. For a whole year MacLaren pondered this, until he came to the decision to introduce Sanskrit. Classes began in the late 1960s, tutored by students who were just one lesson ahead of those whom they taught.

In general Sanskrit has been learnt slowly within the School, except for a few ardent scholars who have studied with exceptional enthusiasm, some even getting university degrees in the subject. Yet this slowness, in an important sense, has not reduced the value of the study. For MacLaren typically ensured that the work was always pursued in depth and not as a superficial grasping of the subject. The Shankaracharya had said that there were two ways of studying it, one the ancient method of following the master teachers, notably Panini, whose *Astadhyayi* is the classic formulation of Sanskrit grammar, the other the Western method as used today to teach classical and modern languages in universities and schools. What is needed, he went on, is a combination of these that links depth with speed of learning. Sitaram Jaiswal, in the course of interpreting the Shankararya's conversations, had sometimes intervened in them, with some feeling, on questions about Sanskrit, especially concerning how it should be taught. His extensive knowledge has always been available to Sanskrit tutors and students. The School, however, has yet to find the best method of teaching Sanskrit in a Western context, even though much progress has been made.

The connection of language, and in particular of Sanskrit, with Philosophy extends far beyond the basic ideas of the *pranava* sound and of name and form. The laws of grammar and the laws of nature, according to the Shankaracharya, are one and the same. How can this be? What possible relationship, let alone identity, can there be between, say, syntax and mechanics, or between grammatical cases and biological growth? Such questions rest upon an assumption; namely that language, on one hand, and the created world, on the other, are quite distinct entities. They take the world to exist independently of language, and language as a kind of system of labels placed on the world by human beings for their own convenience. Advaita rejects this kind of dualism. Things are name and form only; they are no more than the appearance of words. Hence the laws that govern things are the same laws that govern language i.e. they are grammar.

In what manner has the School adopted this apparently strange doctrine? Three examples might be given of how it has been found in practice to be true. The first is found in a study that has occupied – some might almost say tormented – students for some time, viz. the rules of *sandhi*. This term refers to the modification of sounds at the conjunction of letters, syllables or words. Every language has these modifications in speech. For example, in English 's' followed by 'h' becomes the new sibilant 'sh'. Sanskrit grammar formulates all of them very precisely. Where then is the parallel with the laws of nature? These modifications are themselves natural changes in the world of sound, but furthermore they are reflected, or perhaps more strictly they cause, equivalent changes in the world of things. When two people meet there is a new situation that partakes of the nature of each, yet has a character of its own. When one event follows immediately upon another, the outcome is not simply a mixture of the two. It is more like a chemical compound, where some new aspect has been introduced. Conjunctions of events may be on many scales, from trivial to earthshaking. *Sandhi* accompanies a change from war to peace, from one era to another, from one culture to another.

A second example is simpler. Verbs, as opposed to nouns or any other part of speech, are seen by Sanskrit grammarians as the fundamental elements in a sentence. This indicates that in the world what exists is not so much things as activities or movements. What we experience is made up of facts or what is the case, rather than things that exist in themselves. The things are simply how the activities appear to us when we use words like 'body' or 'table'. Not surprisingly, perhaps, quantum mechanics has come to a similar conclusion!

Thirdly, Sankrit grammar analyses the sentence into eight *vibhakti* or concepts, which correspond approximately to the cases used in Western languages, but have rather different roles. These are *karta*, roughly the subject, more accurately that which has the law of the action within it; *karma*, the object, or that most desired by the subject; *karana*, the instrument, or that which is most propitious for the performance of the action; *sampradana*, the indirect object, or that to which the action is dedicated; *apadana*, from which the action comes, or the unmoving point of its origin; *sambandha*, the genitive, or that which joins two nouns possessively; *adhikarana*, the place or time of the action, or the substratum of the action; *sambodhana*, whom or what is addressed, or what is woken up by being addressed! Of these eight 'cases' two do not relate directly to verbs, namely the *sambandha* and the *sambodhana*.

This far-reaching analysis of a sentence reveals the grammatical laws that govern how the sentence operates. All six that relate directly to verbs must be present, although in practice Sanskrit sentences may omit some, leaving them absent but operative. How does this exemplify the principle that grammar gives the natural laws of the world? The answer is that these concepts also govern actions that take place in the world. If, in the morning, a man digs his garden with a spade, taken from the shed, for the sake of growing vegetables, then seven 'cases' are there in the action. If he addresses the spade – 'O, spade!' – that is eight. If the sentence just says 'The man digs' then six, or seven, are implicit in the action, just as they are implicit in the sentence.

These examples only hint at the full force of the ontology that language and the world are inextricably united. The School has a great deal to learn about this. The Shankaracharya has stated that the Philosophy of language is really a complete system in its own right. Certainly he has made it clear that the development of the School depends upon investigating it alongside, and perhaps paramount to, all the other studies that are ongoing. Without knowledge of Sanskrit the ultimate depths of Advaita cannot be plumbed. Other languages do not have the full range of sounds and grammar for this.

At the same time, he gave consolation to those whose aptitude for Sanskrit study may seem limited. Speech, he said, is only distorted at the level of its final expression with the tongue. At a deeper level, particularly in emotion, the person may be natural and refined. Whilst all should be encouraged to correct bad speech, this may be difficult for adults. It is sufficient to try, if the heart is pure. For children the situation is different. As with a young and flexible bamboo, their growth may be moulded in accordance with the best practice.

The reference to levels of speech was explained much further. Every individual holds four stages of expression of language. At the centre lies *para*, the unmoving creative point from which all sound emerges, motivated by desire. From this a word passes to *pashyanti*, the level where the final sound rests in potential, without differentiation or sequence but containing these in essence, like the yoke of an egg. Next the sound reaches *madhyama*, where different and sequential sounds begin to form and meaning makes it appearance. This is the state that one recognises as having a word or sentence in mind without having fully formulated it. It is 'having something to say'. Finally at *vaikhari* the full expression of words and sentences takes place in the mouth by the movements of air generated by the tongue. A place in the body is associated with each of the four levels: in order from the centre, the navel, the heart, the larynx and the mouth.

This exposition of depths of speech has influenced the School considerably. It gave point to the lengthy practice of sounding, for it promised the development of speech to give greater weight and power to discourse. Much attention has been given to the correct mouth positions, as given by Panini, and to purity in sounding letters. Students have found that their speech in very many contexts has become more effective: in ordinary conversation, in professional work, at public occasions, and, of course, in tutoring in the School. The Shankaracharya has enjoined sweetness and audibility, as well as clarity and precision. The study of Sanskrit, in this respect, has yielded valuable by-products. Perfecting the sounding of the alphabet of 42 letters has been most beneficial. The purer the sound the more powerful the effect and the more confident the speaker. This direction was indicated when MacLaren put Richard Elias in charge of the Sanskrit groups. Although Elias is a fluent speaker of French, he has left the development of grammatical studies to a few industrious scholars, some of whom have an academic training in Sanskrit. Instead he has given much emphasis to correct pronunciation of letters and words, as initiated by MacLaren himself.

The distinction between vowels and consonants has been important from the start. A vowel is 'that which exists by itself', a consonant 'that which shines'. The latter is dependent on the former; consonants cannot be sounded at all on their own. Vowels regulate the creation as measures of the will of *Brahman*, whereas consonants are a part of *prakriti* or nature. Though emanating from *para*, the sixteen vowels are held within *pashyanti*, and constitute the powers, or *shakti*, that control events in the world. What after all is the force behind the acts of people and nations, if not the power of the human voice? One voice may start a war; another may bring the peace that passeth understanding. What indeed is the power of a School of Philosophy, if not the voices of its tutors and students?

A philosophical question that has emerged from insight into levels of speech is how the existence of these within an individual is consistent with the idea that the whole creation begins with the Word. Surely this is not an individual matter? No single person creates the world or speaks things into existence. The Shankaracharya implies that the words that create name and form are universal. The world of mind is one, not many. From the universal *madhyama* they trace their existence back through the causal world of *pashyanti* to *Brahman* itself as *Om*. These levels of language are merely reflected in the individual, just as individuals in reality are no more than reflections, like the Sun that shines in many pots.

Other questions remain, as with all the issues raised by the teaching of the Shankaracharya. He himself has said that his words are seeds that need to be nurtured and to grow, rather than a system of Philosophy to be learnt. One area where his teaching on language has been especially effectual is in the children's schools (see Chapter 20). Sanskrit has had a major place in the curriculum from the start. Junior children practise sounding, and begin to learn words and even some elementary grammar. The seniors study Sanskrit up to GCSE standard, and beyond if they wish. Not all pupils take up the harder aspects of language with enthusiasm, but one boy went so far as to learn his Sanskrit homework backwards when the teacher jokingly asked him to do so! Several pupils have gone on to take degrees in Sanskrit.

The text used by the School for most of its Sanskrit teaching has been the *Laghukaumudi* of Varadaraja. This simplifies the system of Panini, enabling beginners, said the famous scholar, Max Muller, 'to find their way through the labyrinth of native grammar'. The text begins with Panini's renowned formulation, the *Maheshvarani Sutrani* (a *sutra* is an extremely pithy rule), consisting of a special arrangement of the letters of the alphabet, such that groups of them form units used in the exposition of the grammar. With them, for example, *sandhi*, definitions, declensions of nouns and conjugations of verbs can be expounded.

Within the School, study groups have proliferated, with all students at one time taking a basic course in Sound and Calligraphy. This included the practice of using calligraphy pens and boards, and – like the art group – learning to draw straight lines and circles before forming the Sanskrit letters. A basic three-year course in Sanskrit has been developed, which for some is the golden thread of Ariadne. More advanced students research Sanskrit texts, including the Upanishads, with one group translating the *Laws of Manu*. A deep connection has undoubtedly been made with the sacred literature of India. Annnual Sanskrit conferences at Waterperry and Sydney have attracted for many years large numbers from around the world. Jaiswal has given lectures on aspects of both Sanskrit and Indian culture. Contact is also being made with Sanskrit scholars in universities and elsewhere.

CHAPTER SEVENTEEN

Conducting the Band

There is a delightful drawing by his father of Leon when he was five years old, standing on a chair, singing to an imaginary orchestra and waving the big conductor's baton of his grandfather in his little hand; underneath is written: 'Leon conducting the band.'[1]

This image of the young Leon MacLaren could almost be taken as symbolic of his whole life's work in directing the School of Economic Science. It has, however, a much more literal interpretation, for MacLaren was passionately fond of music. He had inherited the taste from both parents. His mother had taught him the piano from the age of three, and his father Andrew was a great lover of Mozart. Leon also taught himself to play the clarinet and saxophone. Some of the older members of the School could remember how he used to play jazz on the piano, but this he eschewed completely when more serious matters took his attention.

A similarly evocative picture has been given by a student in the School, who sang a tenor part in MacLaren's musical setting of the *Eesha Upanishad*. This was the only occasion when he conducted a complete performance of his own work. It was at Sarum Chase, and was preceded by a full rehearsal. At a point in this when the whole ensemble seemed to be getting confused, he stopped what he called the 'cats' concert' and brought the room to a deep silence. 'That stillness is at the heart of everything', he said, 'Do remind yourselves of that.' Then the rehearsal resumed. For the performance itself later that evening, he appeared in a scarlet smoking jacket. This time the piece flowed unreservedly. As the singer remarked, 'A new oneness of spirit had entered.'

1 Dorine Tolley, *The Power Within*, p.185.

A message that MacLaren sent to the music group in 1975 gives an insight into his view of what performing musicians should be about:

> When you sing and play, let each beautiful word tell with all its might, and let it travel as far as it will to pierce the thick veil of sleep covering the world. And let the music carry the sound to the hearts of your audience with true pitch, accurate measure of length and pure intervals. Where notes are phrased, observe the phrase; where they are not phrased, let them stand apart. So combine the precision of detail with complete freedom and fullness of singing and playing and let this be serene, joyous as the sun in its splendour and sweet as the rain falling like grace on earth. Words and music strengthen and heal. This is their nature. Give fully and follow the conductor precisely.

This was given to those performing in MacLaren's composition *In the Beginning*, an oratorio drawing mainly on words from Isaiah and St John. Together with the *Eesha*, the *Hymn of Creation* based on the *Rig Veda*, and some songs written for St James' Schools, it made up his principal compositions. They were difficult pieces to play, even for the few professional musicians amongst the School group. In view of MacLaren's frequent assertion that the truth is always simple, and his dislike of undue complexity, this is puzzling. There were several reasons. Firstly he wanted to challenge the performers, especially the singers. For example, he wrote some very high notes for sopranos, often in sustained phrases, and was relentless in demanding their performance. Then singers and instrumentalists alike found his use of bars off-putting. He would compose without bars, and then mark the bars at intervals of nine notes, giving 9/4 or 9/8 time, instead of the familiar 3/4, 4/4 or 6/8. Also an instrumentalist might have to rest for many bars, and then play a single note perfectly in tune and very quietly. Once he even asked the choir shortly before a performance to sing by heart. 'At least it forced them to look at me', commented the conductor afterwards!

These compositions aimed to fulfil the purpose of music, as MacLaren expressed it in the course he prepared for musicians in the School:

> The original song, the first music, is the heart of the universe. It is pure joy, everlasting praise, naturally, effortlessly, reflecting the radiance of absolute-knowledge-bliss. This is the music of the spheres,

the choir of angels, and the infancy of man. Throughout his life it echoes in his heart. It is the special function of music to purify the heart and re-establish memory of the divine origin.

His devotion to this standard of perfection in musical composition began after the death of Tony Russell. The Mass that the dying saxophonist had composed perhaps awoke a realisation that the School needed to produce fine music to counteract the contemporary decline in musical standards. Seeing no one else at the time who could do this, MacLaren typically set about the task himself.

It proved to be a creative exercise in more ways than one, for in producing pieces like *In the Beginning* MacLaren looked deeply into the foundations of music, and passed his findings on to music students throughout the School in the form of a course that appeared in 1971. The opening words convey the essence of what he had discovered:

> We now begin the serious study of music. Like everything else in the universe, music begins in the Word; that soundless Word, the origin of all sound, in which the universe and everything in it has life and being.

This principle, that the Word comes first before all else, he kept to with unfaltering persistence in every aspect of music studies. For example, holding the word in mind enables a singer to find the right pitch; indeed the word gives tone, length and every other quality of singing. Likewise the word in the form of the name of an instrument determines its construction, materials, shape and so on. Such conviction that the Word precedes all clearly followed upon the teaching received from the Shankaracharya concerning language. An interesting sidelight on this came from a singer who had been trained professionally. She had learnt more from sounding Sanskrit vowels, she said, than from all the lessons of her singing teacher.

Other philosophical principles entered into MacLaren's musical studies. His most frequent advice to the music group was to listen. Often this meant repeating a few notes many, many times, until the listening had become more acute. The sound might then become free of personal impediments and limitations, so that something might be heard beyond the obvious sound, something much finer and full of meaning. MacLaren himself had asked the Shankaracharya about this. When composing from the words of the Bible, he had a sense of something deeper than the sound or meaning of the

English words. To this he could set the music. But what was it? The Shanaracharya had answered that this third element was emotion, and that it should indeed be the touchstone for musical composition. Only precise measures of sound, tone, intervals and so on would convey the emotional import.

In practical terms listening meant hearing the sound of one's own voice or instrument. Musicians, MacLaren asserted, tend to listen to the sound that others make, in order to correct the sound they themselves are making. This leads to confusion; everyone trying to get the right sound from everyone else. One's own voice or instrument holds the truth of the matter. With the listening should go a willingness to give the sound out, and retain nothing for oneself. In such a principle music and Philosophy were at one.

Perhaps MacLaren's most original observation about listening to music was the idea of hearing the silence between the notes. This also cut across the conventional practice of musicians, for their training had taught them usually to minimise the intervals by singing or playing *legato* i.e. running notes together. Now they were being told to hear the silence before each note, each phrase, each movement, and before and after a whole performance. This is what the audience needs, said MacLaren. He had noticed this even in the early Economics classes; that people deeply appreciate a moment of complete rest in silence. Every evening of Philosophy or anything else should have at least one such moment. In music the silence before a note is where the sound originates, it is the creative centre, a point of infinite and eternal stillness. To many students this was a revelation, and a guide to listening to a great musician, like Mozart.

From the Shankaracharya's teaching on the nine elements, MacLaren applied to music the notion that the qualities of space, air, fire, water and earth are present in every note. Hence the performer needs to keep in mind the qualities of audibility in space, firmness in air, clarity in fire, sweetness in water and freshness in earth. Articulation, phrasing, length, tone, pitch, harmony and the rest should all respond to the memory of these natural qualities.

What was given the greatest emphasis in the music course, however, was number. The octave, a concept that had played a major part in Philosophy since the days of Ouspensky's teaching, is based entirely, insisted MacLaren, upon number. Every musician needs to know this, and to become thoroughly familiar with the precise mathematical analysis of the notes of the octave. At the heart of this is ratio. Each note stands in a definite ratio to one, which is itself the original doh. The doh of the octave above is two, since the vibrations that create the sound double in frequency. The half cut between these is sol, which is 3/2. The third cut is mi, 4/3. These are the primary intervals. Within the whole scale, the two points at which Ouspensky found the direction to change are where the following interval is least i.e. at mi and si The whole octave in numbers is:

Doh 1 Re 9/8 Mi 5/4 Fa 4/3 Sol 3/2 La 5/3 Si 15/8 Doh 2

MacLaren spent a great deal of time getting the musicians to become adept at 'hearing' the ratios that correspond to the notes, so that this would become second nature to them. From this would come precision in playing and composing. Without it the octave had no natural basis. He had studied the idea of a natural octave in Pythagoras, Plato, Boethius and Zarlino. Later, it must have given him great satisfaction to find his own researches more or less confirmed in a letter of Marsilio Ficino. For not only are the primary intervals of 1, 2, 3/2 and 4/3 given, but Ficino also dwells upon the creative role of unity and the importance of ratio:

> Hearing indeed longs for unity, since it itself is also one and arises from one, but it desires a unity perfectly blended from the many and composed in the same proportion as that by which it itself is also naturally brought to a unity from the many. Finally, since hearing itself consists of a multitude of natural parts which blend fully together into one form, it readily welcomes a number of notes when they are brought perfectly into one note and into harmony. This occurs particularly when one of the two notes in some way absorbs the other into itself or joins it to itself. This can be achieved solely by virtue of those ratios which we have been discussing.[2]

The music course expresses this clearly:

> When a harmony is struck, there is nothing to do: all the sounds are there already numbered. Number selects them according to desire. What a selector that is! Accurate, precise, immediate. First in harmony is unison, one. Let it be one. For this the sound must just come freely, without any doing, without any restriction.

From this reliance upon unity comes, too, the resolution of dissonance. All that is needed is a move to the nearest unity. For example,

2 *The Letters of Marsilio Ficino*, translated by The School of Economic Science, Shepheard-Walwyn (Publishers) Ltd, Vol. 7, p.85.

the dissonance of the note si, which is 15/8, is resolved by the move to the higher doh at 2.

David Ward, a professor at the Royal College of Music, found the natural octave – which he had met under the name of intonation – something of a revelation when taught by MacLaren. It provided understanding in principle and precision in practice. A tempered piano began to sound out of tune! The pure intervals could be heard clearly, and the modes, which MacLaren used rather than key changes in his compositions, became of greater interest. But not all was plain sailing, even for expert musicians. The natural octave did not eliminate the dissonance of some intervals, such as the fifth between re and la, which Ward describes as 'like the crying of a dog in pain'. The tempered keyboard, which enables key notes to be readily changed, helps to even out the dissonance. In fact, MacLaren himself used a tempered piano when composing! Nor did Ward take easily to playing Mozart and other composers in the natural octave. He tried conducting a group of his own professional music students using the MacLaren principles, but their standard techniques proved too recalcitrant.

When composing for the *Eesha Upanishad*, MacLaren found that he needed a harp player. No one was to hand, so Dorine van Oyen undertook to learn. As she progressed, MacLaren often turned to her playing for rest and delight. A more pragmatic use of the harp was found, when the architects' group were told to listen to its chords in each area of the new development around the artists' hall at Waterperry. Dorine also played piano duets frequently with MacLaren, not only at Stanhill Court, to entertain residential groups.

The music group had begun in 1964. after some informal meetings that included Joan Spencer, a professor and concert violinist. That Summer they spent two weeks at Rustington School, near Littlehampton, under the leadership of a Scottish architect, Ian Duncan. He claimed to have no knowledge of music, which accorded with MacLaren's general rule of placing people who were not conventionally trained at the head of activities. In fact, Duncan clearly had mathematical ability and an intuitive understanding of harmony. His instructions from MacLaren were simple: 'Get them to listen, and study the natural octave.' Duncan's own favourite musical maxim came from Ficino:

> Music was given to us by God to subdue the body, temper the mind and render Him praise.

The group began to meet weekly. At first only Mozart was played, 'until people learn to discriminate', but later Giovanni Gabrieli, Monteverdi, Purcell and Vivaldi were admitted and, more recently, a wider range of composers. A string quartet was formed, led by Joan Spencer, which MacLaren was fond of berating for breaking the rule of not listening to others for the right note. When the music course was written, the whole group were expected to attend it.

MacLaren took a close interest, often conducting the choir and orchestra, which grew to a total of about sixty. After David Ward, a professional pianist and later a professor, joined in 1968, at first as a humble viola player, he was soon asked to conduct as well. He was coached at the piano by MacLaren, who reminded him continually of the importance of touch and of phrasing. Mozart sonatas and duets were the main diet. Ward became a concert pianist, performing at many venues around the world, with a reputation especially for interpreting Mozart. Perhaps his greatest gift, however, has been his genial and expert leadership of the music group, which has combined immense respect for MacLaren's genius with mastery of modern techniques.

Ward remembers playing to MacLaren shortly before he died. It was a slow movement of Mozart on an ordinary upright piano. 'Play that phrase again, feel it under your fingers', repeated MacLaren, until Ward began to have an awareness of touch doing the work – 'not my touch so much as touch simply being allowed to operate through consciousness.'

Duncan recalled some compelling incidents with the music group. When the *Eesha Upanishad* was performed in a marquee at Waterperry for 'Art in Action', a fierce storm threatened to blow it away. St James' army cadets clung on to the guy ropes during the performance. The Indian High Commissioner was amongst the audience. On another occasion the orchestra was practising Mozart's Prague symphony. As usual with MacLaren, they repeatedly practised the opening chord, but every time it was acutely dissonant. Later that day they learnt that the Soviet Union had invaded Prague to suppress the movement for Czech independence. There were moments of drama, too, over the sopranos' excessively high notes. Mary Pickering, who led the choir for a while, was not easily bullied!

A small composers' group was also formed. As with the artists' group, MacLaren stressed the need to study a sacred text and let the music follow the words. In listening to his own work, the composer was enjoined to hear if it really did reflect the inner meaning, the emotion that the Shankaracharya had identified behind the apparent sound. MacLaren was quite brutal with any piece that he felt was covering or distorting the text. Nevertheless, several compositions have been performed in recent years.

When it began, the School choir was known by the name of Non Nobis. It tended to lose members to the youth groups as they expanded. By the early 1990s another group of singers under Bruce Ramell had started rehearsing. They took the name 'Discantus', and gave a first public performance in a church near Audley End. From this were intitiated 'Cathedral Days', when they sang at evensong in cathedrals around the country, including Norwich, Lincoln, Ely, Guildford and Winchester. This development was greatly welcomed by Ramell, who was keen to forge links between the School and the Church. This has done much to heal the rift that opened up in the 1980s (see pages 247). More recently a celebratory twentieth anniversary concert has taken place at St James', Piccadilly, and a performance at Valetta cathedral in Malta. A further successful step was taken when the Sanskrit group asked Discantus to sing at an Oxford college during the Waterperry Sanskrit week. This has now become an annual event, which has won acclaim for the choir. Emphasis remains very much on sacred music, as secular pieces, in Ramell's words, 'often suffer seriously from texts that are either totally trivial or express dubious emotions.' The choir has performed new pieces written by School composers, including Ramell himself.

A quite different form of dance began in the late 1970s, when a lady in the Dutch School, who had been trained in classical Indian *Kathak*, introduced it there. This soon spread to London and then around the world, including the children's schools. Initially called Vedic dance, after its ancient roots, it was renamed with the Sanskrit term *Abhinaya*, meaning 'gesture', which reflects its conveying of meaning to an audience.

Under the direction of Dr Ann David, research has continued into several classical Indian forms of dance. A practical way to discover stillness and grace in movement and gesture has been the aim. MacLaren's interest naturally turned on finding the governing principles. With his guidance programmes have been established to teach both adults and children at weekly and residential classes. International conferences have taken place in the UK, Spain and Canada.

At the same time, much artistic work has been done. In particular, the great myths of Indian scripture have been studied in order to produce new dance choreographies. Contemporary music for such pieces is now being written. Participants in these developments, most of whom are of course women, find it a powerful medium to unlock creativity. Dance also provides a means for many to enter more deeply into the emotional realm, a step which has not previously been prominent in School work, despite the great love that Leon MacLaren had for the finest music.

Amongst his many roles in the School, Bernard White for a while acted as a kind of dancing master! Despite MacLaren questioning 'all this prancing about', balls were held at Waterperry for the youth group and St James' sixth forms over which White presided. He had trained seriously as a ballroom dancer in his youth, even appearing on the original series of 'Come Dancing'. On one occasion he and Sheila Rosenberg were demonstrating the tango, when MacLaren and Dorine suddenly appeared on the floor with a dynamic version that upstaged the other pair! Later Elizabethan court dancing was introduced also, described by White as more dignified and peaceful.

CHAPTER EIGHTEEN

The Ficino
Letters

I N A lecture during the 1960s Leon MacLaren had spoken of the idea of a renaissance. Although the aim of the School would always remain to discover the truth itself, an effect of its work over an extended period could be a renaissance for the whole of society. Naturally such a far-reaching vision had a significant impact on some students, particularly those whose work was creative in some form. The concept of a renaissance became an object of study. MacLaren suggested that, not the last Renaissance, but the one before should be a model. Sheila Rosenberg and others began to explore the Renaissance of the twelfth century, the age of the Platonic Schools in France and of the great Gothic cathedrals.

The direction changed somewhat when a member of the School in Amsterdam produced a letter of Marsilio Ficino, and presented it to MacLaren. It took the form of a dialogue between God and the Soul.[1] He regarded it as evidence of an understanding of the principles of a non-dual Philosophy, and decided that the School should translate all Ficino's letters. Only Italian translations had been made previously, with the exception of a few letters rendered into English by scholars. There were twelve books. At first a senior tutor with no knowledge of Latin was put in charge, but was soon replaced by Clement Salaman, who had an Oxford History degree, and later became a teacher at St James' School for Boys. He has led the translation group with great persistence for forty years, despite a few minor mishaps, such as his once losing a briefcase full of completed letters. Initially he merely asked selected individuals to make

1 *The Letters of Marsilio Ficino*, Vol. 1, 1975, Letter 4.

translations of particular letters. Then a more formal group was set up, though most members had only a rudimentary knowledge of Latin.

Gradually the level of Latin scholarship rose with new entrants and considerable study. Translation groups were organised to work on individual letters, whilst a revision group made final improvements. Specialisation has enabled some students to select and interpret manuscripts, to read works in Italian, and to research into histories and biographies in order to write notes on letters and correspondents. More recently, other translations have been made, including several of Ficino's Commentaries, such as that on the pre-Socratic philosopher, Parmenides.

Marsilio Ficino, born in 1433, was leader of the Platonic Academy in Florence, which was associated with such men as Lorenzo de' Medici, Alberti, Pico della Mirandola, Botticelli, Michelangelo and many more key figures of the Renaissance. Ficino himself was a great scholar, a doctor and later a priest. Chosen by Cosimo de' Medici, the effective ruler of Florence, at the age of six to be the future head of a Platonic School, he began translating Plato into Latin in the late 1450s. In 1462 Cosimo gave a villa at Careggi as the headquarters of the new Academy. Thereafter Ficino was to preside over innumerable meetings at which discussion of the Philosophy of Plato (or Socrates) took pride of place.

A simple explanation of Philosophy given by Ficino witnesses to the affinity of his teaching with that of the School. Both see the subject as a practical matter of the fulfilment of Man:

> Thus philosophy, to express it in a few words, is the ascent of the mind from the lower regions to the highest, and from darkness to light. Its origin is an impulse of the divine mind; its middle steps are the faculties and disciplines which we have described; and its end is the possession of the highest good. Finally, its fruit is the right government of men.[2]

Justice in government had indeed been in the forefront of the School's inception. Even the Economics principles found in the works of Henry George and Andrew MacLaren were not absent from Ficino's thought, for he too realised that real justice depended upon the commonalty of natural resources or land:

2 *The Letters of Marsilio Ficino*, Vol. 3, 1981, Letter 18, p.31.

God ordained all the waters of the world to be in common for creatures of the water, and all the earth for creatures of the earth. Only that unhappy being, man, divided what God had united.[3]

Yet beyond this fundamental principle Ficino was not concerned much with economic issues. His mind was set upon the Philosophy that he saw as part of an unbroken ancient tradition descending from the Egyptians and Persians to Greeks, Jews and Christians, under the twin guises of philosophy and religion. His lifework can be seen as an inspired attempt to unite these within the essence of their original teachings. He had traced back a line of this 'holy tradition' to the Egyptian sage, Hermes Trismegistus, the thrice-great Hermes, whose name was the Greek title given to the Egyptian Thoth, god of writing and learning, messenger god and conveyer of souls. Later, Ficino gave similar status to the Persian sage Zoroaster. From these two, wisdom passed to Moses, thought by Ficino to be a contemporary of Hermes, to Orpheus as the founder of Greek philosophy, and consequently to the two great streams of Judaic and Greek thought. Despite their unity in St John's Gospel and in such Church Fathers as St Augustine, the two elements became separate throughout the middle ages. Thus it was the great task of Ficino to reveal their essential unity. The School, whose own sage, the Shankaracharya, speaks of a single tradition that all great philosophies and religions echo in diverse forms, naturally turned to such an authority as Ficino, and sought to bring his largely forgotten works to light.

In Letter 8 of Volume 7, entitled 'A Confirmation of Christianity through the Wisdom of Socrates', Ficino goes so far as to draw a close parallel between Christ and Socrates. The Greek master put the eternally good before the transient, endured physical hardships, like hunger and exposure, was intent on reverence and love, and devoted himself to purifying the minds of men. He subjected himself to certain danger and death in this service, declaring that he had been sent by God for this sole purpose. Was not Socrates accused of irreligion by those very men to whom he had commended the duty of practising religion? When he could have escaped from prison he refused, in order to give to posterity by an unjust death an example of supreme steadfastness and patience. How close a parallel with Christ, even to the extent of the sharing of wine, and the blessing before his death!

3 *Ibid.*, Volume 1, Letter 73, p.119.

Socrates was, of course, the teacher of Plato. Cosimo de' Medici had been inspired with a love of Plato by the Greek scholar Plethon, who had come to the Council of Florence in 1439 to take part in discussions on Church unity. In 1460, soon after Ficino had begun to translate Plato's Dialogues into Latin, he was interrupted by an urgent demand from Cosimo to work instead upon a newly discovered manuscript attributed to Hermes Trismegistus. This Greek version of Hermes, probably a work of late antiquity from Alexandria, has now been translated into English by Clement Salaman, Dorine van Oyen and William Wharton. Its significance for the teaching of the Philosophy of Advaita is indicated by a brief quotation:

> If you do not make yourself equal to God you cannot understand Him. Like is understood by like. Grow to immeasurable size. Be free from every body, transcend all time. Become eternity and thus you will understand God. Suppose nothing to be impossible for yourself.[4]

This excursus undoubtedly made an indelible mark on Ficino's mind in revealing the profundity of Hermes' teaching. He returned, of course, to translating the Dialogues, but the debt was not forgotten. A letter on the Platonic idea of divine frenzy made this explicit:

> Those philosophers I have just mentioned had learnt from Mercurius Trismegistus, the wisest of all the Egyptians, that God is the supreme source and light within whom shine the models of all things, which they call ideas. Thus, they believed, it followed that the soul, in steadfastly contemplating the eternal mind of God, also beholds with greater clarity the natures of all things. So, according to Plato, the soul saw justice itself, wisdom, harmony, and the marvellous beauty of the divine natures.[5]

With our eyes and ears, Ficino continues, we perceive the reflection of divine beauty and the resonance of divine harmony, so that we remember what we knew when we were 'outside the prison of the body'. The soul is fired by the memory, and purges itself of contact with the body to become possessed of divine frenzy.

Platonic remembering is a feature of Ficino's writing. In his correspondence with the remarkable young scholar, Pico della

---

4 *The Way of Hermes*, Duckworth, 1999, p.57.
5 *The Letters of Marsilio Ficino*, Vol. 1, Letter 7, p.43.

Mirandola, whose nine hundred propositions from a huge range of philosophical and religious sources were to be debated in Rome, he wrote that to produce so much with such ease at so tender an age was a mark of remembering, rather than of learning. So such a man as Pico would be 'a friend in eternal memory.'

In a letter to the Archbishop of Amalfi, Ficino states explicitly why he was so devoted to making the works of Plato more widely available. He wishes to 'reveal the Platonic teaching, which is in complete accord with divine law.' It has been decreed by divine providence, he goes on, that subtle minds that find it difficult to accept the sole authority of divine law may yield instead to the reasoning of Plato, which fully agrees with religion. Such a motive could be said to inspire also the School translators.

Ficino's central theme remained the return to oneself, to the one reality in which all are united. One letter prefigures the frequent use in the School of the idea that you cannot be that which you observe:

> I have often looked for myself, Giovanni. First I have touched my chest with my hands, then I have often gazed at this face in the mirror, but I could never say that I have touched myself with the one or seen myself in the other. For, when I seek myself, I am certainly not looking for another but for him who seeks. Indeed, it is exactly the same Marsilio that is both seeker and sought.[6]

With two analogies in a letter entitled 'Knowledge and Reverence of Oneself are best of all',[7] he reminds his reader that the Self is never to be confused with the body. A bird, flying above the earth and looking down, may mistake its shadow passing over the ground for itself. Likewise a boy, leaning over a well, may imagine himself to be at the bottom when he sees a shadow or reflection on the water. 'You believe yourself to be in the abyss of this world simply because you do not discern yourself flying above the heavens.'

In another passage that echoes the words of Christ, Ficino has god speaking to the soul:

> Indeed, I am both with you and within you. I am indeed with you, because I am in you; I am in you, because you are in me. If you were not in me you would not be in yourself, indeed you would not be at all.[8]

6 *Ibid.*, Vol. 1, Letter 38, p.78.
7 *Ibid.*, Vol. 1, Letter 110, p.164.
8 *Ibid.*, Vol. 1, Letter 4, p.36.

A passage in a long letter to his friend Lotterio Neroni can be read as an exposition of what the Shankaracharya himself said half a millennium later about the dream of life:

> We would think the actors foolish and pitiful if they were so taken in by the good and bad events on stage that they were at one moment exulting and rejoicing and the next moment weeping, as though these events were real. How much more foolish and pitiful shall we consider all mortals, who, lulled into a deep sleep, take the shadowy images of good and evil for what is truly good and what is truly evil. Although they rejoice falsely and briefly in fleeting things taken as good, what is really to be pitied is that they truly grieve and are long tormented by false and passing evils. And they deserve this, since they are foolish enough to allow themselves to be deceived into thinking that this anxious sojourn of the heavenly and immortal soul in the earthly realm of death is real life…[9]

The notes to this letter give a reference to the *Enneads* of Plotinus, who, following Pythagoras, taught that the body is the tomb of the soul, and that it is reborn when separated from the body at death.

It was natural enough that the correspondence between the teaching of Ficino and that which the School has developed through the study of the Fourth Way, Plato and the Shankaracharya should have led to comparisons between the two institutions, Ficino's Academy and the School in London. Well might the School echo, more prosaically perhaps, the exhortation of Ficino to Bessarion, the Greek master of ancient learning, to engage wholeheartedly in philosophic discussion to purify the mysteries of theology, 'as gold is purified by fire'.[10] The beautiful inscription that ran round the walls of the Academy were indeed literally transcribed one Christmas on the walls of Stanhill Court:

> All things are directed from goodness to goodness. Rejoice in the present; set no value on property, seek no honours. Avoid excess; avoid activity. Rejoice in the present.[11]

A letter to Lorenzo de' Medici contains what could well have been an injunction by Leon MacLaren to all his students, in the urgency and force of its instruction. One's life should be turned right round

9 *Ibid.*, Vol. 5, 1994, Letter 48, pp.77-8.
10 *Ibid.*, Vol. 1, Letter 13, p.53.
11 *Ibid.*, Vol. 1, Letter 5, p.40.

in the opposite direction. What we have mistakenly learned in the past by ignoring our own Self, should be unlearned. What we neglect should be esteemed; what we esteem should be neglected. What we flee from should be borne, and what we pursue, from that we should flee. The smile of fortune should be tears, and the tears of fortune a smile. Then we will not be undone by weakness or desire. We shall be cleansed, and go forth, devoid of dreams, but filled with beauty.

In the courtly language of fifteenth-century Florence, which to modern ears may seem fulsome, Ficino praises that love which is common to the traditions that have found expression in the Academy of Plato, the Christian Church, the Florentine Academy and now in the School of Economic Science:

> Acknowledge, therefore, how great love is: I [Love] have created you through my love; you also, through your love, through love of me, will create yourselves anew in me. Minds, I have made you through love, but through love of God you will one day recreate yourselves as gods. Then shall I say, 'Ye also are gods, and all of you are children of the most High.'[12]

There is a parallel, too, in the political and social conditions which Ficino's Academy and the School have both experienced. War was prevalent in fifteenth-century Italy. Indeed, the militant aspect of Islam was a threat then as now. After their conquest of Constantinople in 1453, the Turks were threatening the Balkans and Hungary, even making a landing in Otranto in 1480. Ficino's letter, 'Exhortation to War against the Barbarians', sent to King Matthias of Hungary at that time, might even find a parallel in modern, if less picturesque, condemnations of Al Quaeda.

A closer threat to the Florentines came from the alliance of Italian States formed by Pope Sixtus IV after the Pazzi conspiracy. The Pazzi family, rivals for power in Florence of the Medici, tried to assassinate Lorenzo in the cathedral in 1478, only succeeding in wounding him and killing his brother Guiliano. After the rounding up and execution of the conspirators, including two of Ficino's correspondents, Francesco Salviati, Archbishop of Pisa, and Jacopo Bracciolini, the humanist and Secretary to Cardinal Riario, a dangerous war broke out, which was only brought to an end by the courage and insight of Lorenzo, who undertook a risky expedition to

12 *Ibid.*, Vol. 6, 1999, Letter 44, p.59.

negotiate with the tyrannical King Ferdinand of Naples. Ficino, for once abandoning his philosophic disregard for politics, had advised both Salviati and Bracciolini to abstain from any rash adventures. He is most unlikely, however, to have known of any plot to murder the Medici. Similarly, Ficino had intervened in the war to the extent of writing to three leading protagonists: the Pope, Lorenzo and the King of Naples. In each case he reminds them, not of the political situation, but of their own nature. He reminds the Pope to fish 'in the deep sea of humanity', like the Apostles. He recalls Lorenzo from an evil mind, like 'a wood dense with tangled thorns', to one 'endued with fine principles ... like a calm and peaceful sea'. And King Ferdinand he advises that 'In peace alone a splendid victory awaits you ... in victory, tranquillity; in tranquillity, a reverence and worship of Minerva'. Peace negotiations were in fact undertaken five months after these letters.[13]

Ficino's relationship to political and other worldly events was never divorced from his study of all things philosophical. He had a strong interest, for example, in astrology. As always, his approach was that of a rational enquirer. Not for him the blind acceptance of fate as apparently decreed by the heavens. Yet nor was he critical of those who looked to the stars for knowledge of events. His view was a subtle balance between these extremes. The stars are signs, not causes, of what occurs on earth:

> The events that are often portended through the assenting move-
> ments of the heavenly spheres are not caused by those bodies in the
> heavens, nor do they occur through their agency. They are caused by
> the divine minds which rule and move those globes and they are
> indicated by the heavenly bodies as if by their own faces.[14]

Man, however was Ficino's first love, after God. Careful scholar-ship was well demonstrated by the translators in their rendering of 'love of Man' for the Latin *humanitas*; and the notes point out that the modern term 'humanities', meaning the study of literature, especially of the classics, is a poor substitute for the original meaning. For *humanitas* as 'love of Man' lay at the heart of the Florentine Renais-sance. This great movement was much more than a revival of clas-sical learning, even though that was an essential prerequisite for much of the art and literature that was created. Nearer the cause of

13 *Ibid.*, Vol. 5.
14 *Ibid.*, Vol. 6, Letter 17, p.27.

the Renaissance was this love of Man, so treasured by Ficino and his Academy. And what this was itself founded upon was the recognition by the leaders of the Renaissance that Man was divine, that essentially Man and God are not separate, but are eternally in unity. This non-dualism, rediscovered from Hermes and Zoroaster, from Plato and the Gospels, was expressed in Ficino's finest writings – in his major works, *The Platonic Theology* and *The Christian Religion* – but also scattered throughout his letters. Nowhere is it better expressed than in a letter to his closest friend, Giovanni Cavalcanti:

> It was not for small things but for great that God created men, who, knowing the great, are not satisfied with small things. Indeed, it was for the limitless alone that He created men, who are the only beings on earth to have re-discovered their infinite nature and who are not fully satisfied by anything limited, however great that thing may be.[15]

These words could be taken as a key to understanding the whole Renaissance, for the search for the infinite within themselves can be seen as the motivation of such creative geniuses as Brunelleschi, Masaccio and Donatello – before Ficino's time – and of his contemporaries, Leonardo, Michelangelo and Botticelli. An example lies in Ficino's description, in a letter to Lorenzo de' Medici the Younger,[16] of human nature as the figure of Venus, whose soul and spirit are love and kinship, for this may have led to Lorenzo's commissioning of Botticelli's painting of Venus in the *Primavera*.

Ficino wrote to the distinguished scientist, Paul of Middleburg, of how there are men of iron, bronze, silver or gold intellect. An age can be golden, he says, if it produces minds of gold in abundance. His own time he regarded as such an age, for it 'has restored to the light the liberal arts that were almost extinct: grammar, poetry, rhetoric, painting, sculpture, architecture, music, and the ancient art of singing to the Orphic lyre.'

The last letter of Volume 5 gives support to this view of Florence's – and Ficino's – place in the Renaissance. Ostensibly it was written in praise of the commentary on Dante's *Divine Comedy*, published by Cristoforo Landino, a member of the Academy. The School translators suggest that Ficino was speaking of something much greater; that he is writing a hymn of praise to the Renaissance itself, as a revival of all the arts of Florence:

15 *Ibid.*, Vol. 4, Letter 6, p.10.
16 *Ibid.*, Vol. 4, Letter 46, p.61.

Look up for a moment, my people, look up at the heavens. Behold now, behold! While our Dante is being crowned here, the dome of mighty Olympus is opening. The flames of the Empyrean heaven, never seen more fully, blaze before us this day in honour of Dante's coronation.

And what do you think this sound is, so fresh and so sweet, that is filling our ears? Undoubtedly, it is the sound of the nine spheres and their muses, a sound heard in no other age and in no other place, now openly celebrating the coronation of Dante.[17]

Within the School one effect, both upon the team of translators and upon readers of *The Lettters*, has certainly been to arouse further interest in the idea of a renaissance. Efforts have been turned to looking closely at Florence and Italy in the fifteenth century. Visits there have multiplied, especially by pupils of St James. The translation group itself have visited Tuscany several times. On one occasion they were perusing the art works in a villa that they thought was connected with Ficino, when an irate owner accosted them as trespassers. They had come to the wrong one! The art group also have studied and painted in Florence. A trilogy of historical novels has been published. All this was deeply influenced by the research into Ficino and his associates. Yet the translators would no doubt give first place in their aspirations to the value of Ficino's letters as pure Philosophy, as a confirmation of the teaching of Advaita.

The Letters have made their mark on contemporary scholarship. They have been welcomed by leading scholars, like Professor Paul Kristeller. Members of the translation group give lectures, attend academic conferences on Ficino, and have broadcast as experts. Others give support to translation groups in the School outside London – in the north of England, New York, Melbourne and Sydney. One member commented that his best reward was to hear reports from people who, in times of bereavement or physical suffering, have found solace and relief in reading some of the letters. For Ficino knew how to heal both souls and bodies.

In the early years, particularly, the indefatigable leader of the whole project, Clement Salaman, consulted Leon MacLaren on the *The Letters*, and was often advised to take account of philosophical reflections that modified the final translations, a task that required both tact and scholarship. MacLaren knew no Latin, and

17 *Ibid.*, Vol. 5, p.xvi.

insisted on a word-by-word translation being presented to him. Yet, in Salaman's view, MacLaren's insight could produce highly original outcomes. Shepheard-Walwyn, the publishers, have also needed a degree of patience to deal with such a diverse group of talented amateurs. Even so, the result has been a unique collection of works in English by the master teacher who stood at the fount of the Florentine Renaissance

CHAPTER NINETEEN

The *Brahman* Exists, the World is Illusion

A DECADE after the conversations between Leon MacLaren and the Shankaracharya had begun, it became clear that many of the basic concepts of the Philosophy of Advaita had been absorbed – if not fully realised – by more senior members of the School. The emphasis changed somewhat to actual steps to be taken towards self-realisation or the full recognition of unity. For example, the 1974 conversation began with a basic distinction between *samashti* (a collective unity) and *vyashti* (an individual). For realisation a movement is required from *vyashti* to *samashti*, but this is a matter of steps, as though from a small circle of existence surrounding the individual person to increasingly larger circles, until the unlimited unity of the *Brahman* becomes a reality. Each circle is really no more than an idea of oneself or of one's world. Movement takes place according to the natural way preferred by each individual, to the predominance in him or her of reason, devotion or action. Reason, however, is the most effective tool for the transcendence of limitations.

What holds a person within a circle is attachment. This itself is no more than a form of love. Attachment carried to extremes becomes delusion, when someone may seek to dominate another, and generates hatred and misery. But the very same substance of love may rise above delusion and attachment and give rise to compassion, mercy, renunciation and other attributes of love unattached. Thus when attachment is released a circle is transcended, and one moves into a larger world.

To illustrate this the Shankaracharya told a story of a young

African man, who travelled from his tribal home to a distant city. Whilst there he happened to buy a small hand mirror, which he kept in a case. When he returned home, his wife was curious to see what was in the case. On looking into the mirror she was horrified to see the face of an attractive young woman. She accused her husband of being unfaithful to her, his wife, and of keeping a picture of his mistress. She demanded a divorce, and the matter went to the elders of the village for judgment. The husband showed the mirror to them, and all, including the wife, came to understand that the mirror merely reflected whatever was presented to it.

What does this story show? The world is a reflection, called *maya*, of the one Self, the *Atman*. When we see the world, we see a reflection of this Self, and nothing that independently exists. The Self is the *samashti*, the unity that underlies everything. The world, and each thing that it contains, is a *vyashti*, something individual but dependent. To transcend the limiting circles is to remove the illusion that what is seen in the mirror is the truth or reality. It is reason that distinguishes between the Self and the non-Self, the *maya*.

Caring only for oneself as *vyashti* is bondage; serving all, the *samashti*, is freedom. A king once held a feast, said the Shankaracharya. It began with the most ignorant people. Each had to put on a bamboo jacket. As a consequence no one could eat, because they could not bend their arms to put food in the mouth. Other people were brought to the feast. None could eat, until finally the wise men came, the brahmins. They, too, wore bamboo jackets, but they fed each other, and taught the ignorant people to do the same. Thus all were happy.

The desire for the truth that motivates the change from *vyashti* to *samashti* is like the river Ganges. It starts from a small source, and soon is confronted by high mountains. To pass them it must accumulate waters to flow between the peaks, through valleys and ravines, over obstacles of many kinds, winding for many miles, but ever onwards. Nothing can stop its course to the sea. So, too, the search for truth can never be stopped. Even the high mountains of old traditions of religions and philosophies, which have become immovable, cannot stand in the way. They may meet the aspirations of many, but they are limited, and leave unanswered the final questions of the truth seeker.

For the School the search for truth had become a matter of following the path of Advaita Vedanta. 'What was the pure concept of Advaita?' asked Leon MacLaren. It is encapsulated in one sentence of Shankara was the reply: 'The *Brahman* exists; the world is illusion; there is no difference between *jiva* [individual soul] and *Brahman*.' The existence of the *Brahman* is absolute, eternal and entirely independent. All else, the world, does exist, but not independently. It exists in space and time, is created, endures for a while, and finally is dissolved. What it depends upon is *Brahman*. The soul, or individual self, is in reality no different from *Brahman*, but it appears differently because it has acquired *upadhi* or qualifications. These place limits upon people. A person is a householder, a craftsman, a doctor or a Bachelor of Science. He believes himself to be these things, rather than the pure *jiva*, which is *Brahman* itself.

Analogies were given – the familiar ones of the ocean and waves, the clay and the pot, the gold and the ring. Ocean, clay and gold are the unchanging, undifferentiated reality, the *Brahman*. Waves, pot and ring are the qualifications, which the undiscerning take to be real, or separate from the underlying reality. These come and go. When they cease to be, there is only the substance, of which they are a mere form. Hence the world and all it contains are an illusion in that sense. All created things are transient. They are the 'cloud-capped towers, the gorgeous palaces'.

The discussions of both *vyashti/samashti* and of Advaita led to a question about whether there are stages on the journey towards the truth. Could practical use be made of knowing these? This provoked a lengthy answer that went through the seven stages that characterise the way of knowledge, the way followed by Shankara himself.

The first stage is a good impulse, a turning towards the truth. This may be induced by a teacher, a school, a book or an incident in one's life. Many students in the School would remember the occasion when some words, or an event, had aroused in them an initial desire for something that reached out beyond their routine life. Others may have experienced such an impulse owing to *sanskara*. They were born with the desire for the truth already implanted in them by their endeavours in an earlier embodiment. They start from where they left off.

Soon the initiate finds himself troubled by doubts and conflicts of interest. Opposing forces press upon him, until reason comes to his aid, and he makes a decision to stand for the truth. This is the second stage. As he progresses further, he learns to avoid what is harmful, to rid himself of unnecessary habit and memories, to cleanse himself from the stain of the world. Such is stage three.

From now onwards his use of energy becomes efficient. *Sattva* grows within him, and he seems to gather light and to bring light to his dealings with others. Fear, the product of darkness, is dispelled. He can move onwards with courage and hope. This fourth stage is the middle one, where the transformation to higher levels begins. For now the vision undergoes a profound change. He no longer sees only what is apparent. Nor is he bound any longer by attachment, for the unreal has lost its hold upon him. What he sees now is always new; it is a brilliant drama unfolding before him moment by moment. This is stage five.

The next stage, the penultimate one, reveals an ability to be aware of both the apparent and the real. The former is as though transparent, allowing the underlying *avyakta*, the matrix that holds all in potential, to be seen. Space, time and *guna* are all present in it, as the basic conditions for the manifestation of the world. It is like seeing the pot and the clay at once, the ring and the gold, or the cloth and the thread. All comes into view as the expression of the *Brahman*. Nothing is negated; rather all is transcended. The student is now like a lover, seeing the beloved wherever he looks. Yet dualism remains. There is still an individual and an Absolute. *Jiva* and *Brahman* appear as if distinct.

The final stage is union, or *turiya*. But there is no stopping, no sense of achievement, no claims of any kind. This is not really a stage or even a state. Of what could it be a state? The unchanging *Brahman* has no states. Yet there is creative power, even though the creation itself is no longer separate from it. *Vyashti* has become *samashti*.

The Shankaracharya's account of the way of knowledge led Leon MacLaren to ask once again about the three ways of knowledge, devotion and action. How, in particular, did one identify people who were suitable for each? The answer was that *sanskara* is the primary factor, but that the School needs to watch for the marks that indicate predilection for one way or another. Keen observation, rationality and the ability to analyse signify a man of knowledge. The way of devotion is shown by a love of service and by energy turned in that direction. Preference for action is revealed by a readiness to work hard, to be efficient, to obey instructions, and to eschew reward. All three ways require use of the subordinate two aspects: the way of action, for example, uses emotional and intellectual forces to support activity. People should discover their own type. A teacher can only help by providing information about the three ways.

What then of the way of devotion? Once more the Shankara-charya prescribed stages or steps on the way. This time there were nine, but, unlike the seven stages on the way of knowledge, each of the nine is capable of bringing a devotee into full union with the Absolute, if it is followed without reserve. The way begins with hearing. Confronted by the immensity and incomprehensible nature of the universe, one looks for solace in some being of great power, and hears of the concept of an Absolute. Attracted by the infinite qualities of goodness, knowledge, beauty and others, the devotee then feels an impulse to sing in praise. Following the poets who have composed in honour of the Lord, he sings to express his love, and to bring himself to a state of peace. To complete the preliminary three steps, the devotee then allows his memories of the Lord and the sound of his own songs of praise to sink deeply into his mind.

The middle three steps are more active, as the devotee moves nearer to the cause of his devotion. Firstly, he learns to serve the Lord, to give himself with humility, now that he can glimpse the grace and mercy of his master. Step five, the central one, sees service transformed into sacrifice. This may involve rituals as pre-scribed by the scriptures, but equally it can be merely the offering of one's work to the Lord by means of an act or words of dedication. Sacrifice is followed by prayers asking for the grace of the Lord. These may be accompanied by holding an image of him in mind.

Now the standpoint of the devotee changes. He approaches the Lord firstly as servant, then as friend, and finally joins him in complete union. These three steps are indicated in the great epic of the *Ramayana*, when Hanuman, the monkey servant of King Rama, says of his relationship to Rama, 'On the level of the body, I am his slave; on the level of the mind, his friend, but in truth I am Rama.' So the way of devotion ends with obedient service to what is recognised as the one conscious being; friendship, based upon the freedom, purity and capability of the mature devotee; and, at the end, union, when the devotee surrenders all to the Lord, includ-ing his individuality.

Each of these nine steps may be sufficient for realisation of the Self. Why is this? Real love is not like worldly love, full of likes and dislikes, changing feelings, even deceit. Love, as Shakespeare likewise affirmed, is immutable, eternal, demanding nothing, offering everything. In love there is no duality, no other party, no personality, no ego. Hence it can be found at any point or at any time. It needs no steps; it is here now.

In a sense the way of action cannot be seen as an independent path to self-realisation. For the Shankaracharya said that in itself it relates only to the physical world, and therefore can only look to refinement of work. To aim at greater skill or efficiency does not raise action above the level of the physical. The one factor that does so is the dedication at the commencement. When it is offered with true emotion or love to society, humanity, or better still to the Absolute, both work and the one who makes the offering are transformed. Actions are affected by *sanskara*, by the *guna* balance and by other circumstances. An individual is governed by these in his choice of action, but to whom or to what he dedicates the action need not be determined in this way. In this alone he or she is free. He may dedicate it to his own gratification, to another, to the world, or to God or the Absolute. Every action is dedicated in some way. When it is constantly offered to the Absolute, then the way of action becomes a path of spiritual development.

An amusing story illustrated this. A great elephant, a chief of the herd and lord of the forest, immensely strong and proud, found himself caught by a crocodile that had grabbed his foot as he stood in a river. Slowly he was dragged down into the water, helpless to escape. In desperation he picked with his trunk a small flower that grew on the bank, and offered it with all his heart to the Absolute. Immediately the crocodile was struck dead and the elephant released. His dedication of the flower, though so humble, had been pure. As with the widow's mite, the value of the offering was nothing besides the purity of heart with which it was given.

A corollary, however, was added to the story of the elephant. While he stood, freed from the deadly attack, he saw the crocodile being taken up to heaven. He appealed to the Absolute. Had not he made the offering, whilst the crocodile was the aggressor? The balance must be restored was the reply. The crocodile had been killed, and must be compensated.

This question of dedication has a strong bearing upon *sanskara*, for action without any desire for a result, with no dedication to one's own pleasure or interests, creates no *sanskara* and leads to freedom. But is there a universal *sanskara*, asked MacLaren. Has the *samashati* a

sanskara, and therefore a *prarabdha* and a *kriyamana* also? The universal *sanskara*, said the Shankaracharya, is always pure. Whilst that of
the individual is a mixture of purity and impurity, leading to good
and bad actions, that of the *samashti* can never be impure. Nor does
it have *prarabdha* and *kriyamana*. Universal *sanskara* is the law, or the
will of the Absolute. This is not subject to *guna*, or to any other
aspect of the creation. On the other hand, the *sanskara* of the
individual is subject to the effect of good or bad company, and also
may be modified by discrimination. Law is above such modification.
When an individual is free from his or her own *sanskara*, he simply
follows the law. Freedom is obedience to the law.

The subject of law recurred in an answer to a question from
MacLaren about sensory appetite getting out of control. He gave
examples of a man who became obsessed with tidying up everything
he could see, and then gloating over the result, and of a musician
who related all sense experiences to the one sense of touch. All
actions should be referred back to their source, which is the
Absolute, replied the Shankaracharya. By means of this referral,
measure is brought into the action, for measure is observance of the
law, the will of the Absolute. Thus misplacements, like those
mentioned of sight and touch, can be corrected. Suppose a man
intends to shoot someone. He loads the gun, takes aim and pulls the
trigger. After that, the action is irreversible – the bullet is on its way.
But referral to the Absolute at the beginning, or even at any stage
before pulling the trigger, would enable the man to refrain from
action. Senses out of control are the speeding bullet. There is
always a moment of non-activity before the action is implemented.
Obviously the practice of pausing before actions is based upon this
principle, for the pause simply acknowledges this moment.

In earlier conversations the Shankaracharya had described life as
a drama, in which one only needed to play one's part nicely. When it
is seen as real, he now said, it becomes a burden. Attachment to any
aspect or part in the play makes that part heavy; it becomes the
burden. In the *Bhagavad Gita*, Krishna says that in truth all actions are
done by the physical and mental organs, whilst the *Atman*, the Self,
merely observes the seeing, hearing, touching, sleeping, eating,
moving and the rest. If one could truly understand this, life would be
light and easy, for the burden of 'doing' would fall away.

Thinking that one is the doer, being attached to a part in the play,
is founded upon a belief in the illusion, that the play is the reality.

The only reality is the *Atman* itself. The play exists, but only in dependence upon the *Atman* that creates it. The traditional analogy of the rope and the snake makes this clear. A rope is mistakenly seen as a snake. There is genuine fear and alarm, until it is correctly seen as a rope. It never was a snake, but it was believed to be one. The world is *maya*, the dream of the Absolute. Those who see it as such can play their parts fully and artistically. Those who believe in its independent reality are burdened with doing, and suffer fear and alarm.

The Shankaracharya introduced a new concept to emphasise this fundamental point about illusion and reality. In reply to a question from MacLaren about the distinction between inner and outer experience, he gave the surprising answer that there is really no such distinction. It arises from *avesha*, being possessed. An individual gets attachments, feels pleasure and pain, and places limits upon himself. Hence he believes in a line between inner and outer experience. None of this is true. He is, as it were, possessed by a ghost. Only reason can exorcise the ghost, by showing him the truth of the matter: that there are no limits. Even pleasure and pain are unreal, for the reality is the bliss of the *Atman*. One may find bliss in pleasure and in pain.

Arjuna, in the *Gita*, was so possessed. Overwhelmed by pity and compassion on seeing his relatives and respected friends confronting him on the battlefield of Kurukshetra, he loses the will to fight, and collapses in despair. By awakening his reason, the Lord Krishna convinces him that he must do his duty as a warrior and fight for justice. The ghost of unreason is dispelled. Arjuna exclaims that he is no longer deluded, and memory of his true Self is regained.

This example of Arjuna led to a question about duty. A common question from students in the School, said MacLaren, is, 'What should I do?' Could something be said about duty and law? Law exists on several levels, said the Shankaracharya. For the individual it appears as what ought to be done. If this is obeyed, the man follows the law, *dharma*, which is both law and righteousness, for it is the will of the Absolute. If the man does just what he feels like doing instead, then he breaks the law, and comes under coarser forms of law. Law is what holds everything. It is like a seed that becomes the cause of action. Knowledge that leads to action is therefore awareness of the law. From this knowledge arises a resolution, which precedes the action itself.

Duties dependent upon law can be on three levels. Firstly an individual has ordinary regular duties of daily life, especially in relation to his home, family and work, but also towards the society and nation. Beyond these are special duties that occur from time to time, and should supersede the ordinary ones. They may involve a journey or other diversions from routine, in which the regular duty may be left or deferred. Thirdly there are duties that are created by new situations of importance, whereby a society might develop culturally or in some other way that heralds a positive step towards a more civilised way of life. These take precedence over all other duties, for they involve a higher level of consciousness for all. Yet it is for the individual to recognise these three levels, and to decide on their relative priorities. Only the man or woman on the spot can be aware of what is necessary, of what the law requires.

What about the cases where someone is aware of an important task to be completed and ignores it – as has happened in the School? That is a matter of *sanskara*, replied the Shankaracharya. The person concerned is compelled by his past to make the denial. He should be helped with gentle advice and love to overcome this. Knowledge would lead him to reconsider and make the right choice, for the law is within him, otherwise he would not recognise the duty in the first place. The teacher may even forestall the arising of the *sanskara*, for it lies dormant until provoked in some way.

Discussion of duty naturally led on to the question of right and wrong. What could be said of this, which the Shankaracharya had earlier described as the greatest duality? The *Gita* was again mentioned. It distinguishes between three states of *buddhi* by which right and wrong are judged. *Sattvic buddhi* knows immediately what is right and acts upon it. Thus it has no problem with duality. So, too, *tamassic buddhi* has no such problem, because its judgment is perverted. What is right is wrong, and vice versa. Its decisions are made in ignorance or darkness. The issue of dualism looms larger for the *rajassic buddhi*, particularly for people engaged in active work in the world, like intellectuals, writers and craftsmen, who know something of the spiritual, but more of the mental and physical. They have doubts about such questions, and need help in letting *buddhi* become still, when doubts can be resolved.

More was said concerning the spiritual realm. There it is a matter of going deeper towards the Self, through the five sheaths of body, breath, mind, intellect and blissfulness. At each stage the coarser is rejected in favour of the finer. This is the proper work of *buddhi*, beyond the duality of good and bad. It leads to rest, where all duality is at an end.

The teaching of Advaita needs time; but this is not time in days or years. It means the number of times that the knowledge has been put into practice. Such practice yields experience, so that real knowledge, as opposed to information, can develop. Then it becomes a part of the being of the aspirant. Someone learning to drive makes mistakes, like putting a foot on the accelerator, instead of the brake, in a critical situation. The mature driver does not do this.

Students need constant reminders, and conditions that force them to use their knowledge or take the consequences. After some years in the School, the Shankaracharya observed, they should be prepared to take on responsibility both within the School and outside. Situations should test their trust, efficiency and intelligence. Problems should be faced and new situation dealt with. For example, the great master of archery, Drona, was teaching a group of warriors. He presented them with a beast tethered to a stake, and told them to shoot it through the mouth. But it was facing away from them. All were perplexed, until Arjuna stepped forward, and drew his bow. Then he whistled. The beast turned its head, and the arrow entered its mouth. Leon MacLaren clearly took note of all this, and was fully prepared to create opportunities for students to show their capacity to take on fresh challenges.

Conversations had taken place in India in 1974, 1976 and 1978. In a final message after the first of these meetings, the Shankaracharya said that the people of this age are not really capable of hard disciplines. Yet truth and bliss are available to those who follow the teaching of the scriptures, and especially through meditation. Four years later he concluded by emphasising that, if further help is needed, he would always be available.

CHAPTER TWENTY

Education:
The New Schools

THE ANSWERS that the Shankaracharya had given earlier to questions about education began to bear fruit in the 1970s. School parents were becoming increasingly concerned about the state of schools generally. Teaching methods, syllabuses and discipline were often regarded as unsatisfactory, even alarming. Some parents looked to more traditional forms of education, but could not afford the types of schools where these might be found. Others saw that even the more prestigious independent schools no longer offered an education that met the spiritual and emotional needs of children. Hence there arose enquiries about whether the School itself might start schools for children, based upon the philosophical principles that it had developed and taught.

The Shankaracharya had given the ages at which children experience significant changes in development. Up to five years they should be treated with love and care, and should learn only by play. From five to ten, whilst still predominantly self-centred, they take a keen interest in new experiences, and need discipline to stop them from pursuing anything that attracts them. They learn easily, and hold what they learn, even though some repetition is required. The simpler the material offered the better. At the age of ten, intelligence, or *buddhi*, begins to operate. Interest widens greatly, so that this is the period, until fifteen, when new subjects are introduced. They learn about the world and what is needed to live a useful life. How they relate to other people, and their responsibilities to them, become important. The congruence of home, school and society makes for harmonious development of the child. Stronger discipline may be needed as their capacity to absorb ideas and influences from society expands. As mentioned earlier (see page 155), between the ages of ten and fifteen the sexual drive can easily dominate all else, and lead to the use of drugs and to promiscuity.

The analogy of a potter was given. One hand moulds the clay from within, with gentle attention to its form; the other holds firmly to the outside of the pot, preventing any undue expansion or irregularity. So, too, the teacher and the parent offer love and care, whilst simultaneously providing discipline to prevent disruptive forces in the growing child from running wild.

At sixteen the child becomes an adult. He is now fully responsible for his own actions. Accordingly, he or she now wants advice, rather than directions and punishment, and should be treated as a friend. By this time his interests should be focussed on the particular subjects that suit his nature and talents. Study of these may lead to his lifetime's work or vocation.

This overall pattern of growth gives the framework for much else. The material used, which is of prime importance in education, should match the stage of development. For example, after ten the subjects introduced embrace literature, history, science and so on. What is essential is that a spiritual content is presented at all stages. This should be done with the use of scriptures: the Bible, the Upanishads and the *Gita*. Above all a connection with the Absolute, or *Brahman*, needs to be made throughout.

Great emphasis was placed by the Shankaracharya on the selection of teachers. Character should be exemplary, since the child observes and emulates this, even more than the precepts or learning of the teacher. Outward behaviour must accord with inner thoughts and emotions. What is thought, said and done should be in unison. No one of immature emotions should be allowed to teach. Moreover, a teacher should be master of his or her subject, so that he or she speaks from genuine understanding, rather than from a superficial grasp of material. These were severe standards, and were to put the management of the new schools to some pains in selecting staff, as the whole project expanded.

There were other more particularised conditions. Meditation was recommended, but only for children of ten years and older. Sanskrit, of which the Shankaracharya had already spoken at length in relation to the School was advocated on the grounds that it is the foundation of other languages, and especially because it offers purity of sound and a perfect grammatical system. It could be taught to children as young as five, by means of the Indian textbook *Laghukaumudi*, which was based on the great grammarian Panini. Finally, the separate teaching of boys and girls was important. The education of girls had a special significance, for if the girls behave well, the boys will follow suit.

St James and St Vedast, the two schools that were founded in the 1970s, evolved out of earlier, somewhat experimental, efforts at education within the School. In the early seventies a group of teachers met every Sunday during terms at Sarum Chase to teach about twenty or thirty children, mainly under twelve, of School parents. Julian Evans, a professional head teacher in the School, took charge of the operation. Subjects ranged from scripture to art and music, with the intention of filling gaps in what the children were learning in their schools. Philosophy was thus a component also. This all proved to be valuable experience.

A second project prepared the way for secondary education. Four young ladies were living at Waterperry House, owing to family circumstances. Three had been sent by their parents in South Africa to be cared for by the School. Leon MacLaren decided that teachers in the School should educate them. Hence several qualified secondary teachers spent one day each at Waterperry. Learning one subject for a whole day was an interesting experiment, but did not find its way into the new schools. Several of the teachers concerned, however, were later recruited. One of the young ladies became a classics teacher at St James.

Yet another educational innovation preceded the actual creation of the two schools. This proved longer lasting and for a while highly influential. MacLaren, who had of course overseen both the other projects, set up a teachers' group, initially in order to support the trade union leader, Tom Chapman, in his efforts to combat disruptive forces in the National Union of Teachers (see pages 104-6).Once formed, this group acquired an impetus of its own. After a short period under a senior School tutor, it came under the leadership of Nicholas Debenham and Sheila Caldwell, soon to be head teachers of St James and St Vedast. With direction and encouragement from MacLaren, and especially from Sheila Rosenberg, the aim moved from trade union affairs towards the study of academic subjects. 'Master a subject' became the keynote. No less than three weeks in the Summer were set aside for study at Stanhill or Sarum Chase, with other weeks at Easter and Christmas. Many teachers became, for the first time, ardent students of a subject, not necessarily the one they had previously followed. There were converts to classics – one maths teacher went off to Oxford to get a classics degree – to history and science. Even Sanskrit attracted a band of dedicated scholars.

MacLaren and Sheila Rosenberg gave advice on principles, like looking for the point in the subject and reading only authoritative texts by master writers, whilst Debenham proved a brilliant director of organised study sessions. He had a particular ability to get to the root of a subject, or at least to induce a specialist teacher to do so. By keeping to the search for this as the essential requirement for any worthwhile subject, he encouraged teachers to look beyond points of detail and classroom difficulties. In the field of languages he played a leading part, especially as he was an assiduous student of Sanskrit himself, but even in areas like history, mathematics or sciences, he could usually elicit from the specialist a reasonable view of the foundations.

Debenham's own education was of high pedigree: Radley and King's College, Cambridge. Two years with a national service commission in the King's African Rifles preceded his going up to King's, where he had won a classics scholarship. Perhaps mistakenly, he chose to read English and Economics. He had also spent a great deal of time on the river, becoming stroke of the college first eight and president of the boat club. A successful career in business followed. His conversion to school teaching took the form of two years as a geography master at Westminster Under School.

Sheila Caldwell played a less conspicuous, but similarly important, part in the teachers' group. She helped with the organisation, and made significant contributions to English and language studies. But perhaps her principal role was to care for the women teachers, especially those – of which there were several – who found the regime a little too much like a boys' public school! Debenham could occasionally be severe, perhaps sometimes mistaking genuine academic or emotional difficulties for prevarication or idleness. Sheila was always there to assist and console. In her own case, there was no lack of both academic ability – she had an English degree from Reading with knowledge of Anglo-Saxon – and of toughness. Oddly enough, she too had rowed at university.

Sessions in the teachers' group were devoted to reading such texts as Plato in the original Greek, Newton's *Principia* (in English!), Gibbon's *Decline and Fall*, Blackstone's *Commentaries on the Laws of*

England, Shakespeare, the King James Bible and Panini's *Ashtadhyayi*. Some felt that they were attending a real university for the first time. Science teachers devised new experiments based on reading, for example, Faraday or Mendeleev – on one notable occasion the chemistry teacher created a magnificent explosion during a meeting in the withdrawing room. They also grappled with the circle of nine points. The nine elements were a serious challenge to the periodic table. Even Charles Darwin was read in depth, with a view to tackling the deep questions of the origin of consciousness – if it has one – and the evolution of humanity – if it occurred. Language teachers struggled with the problem of reconciling various systems of grammar, and in particular assimilating English, Latin and Greek grammars to that of Sanskrit. This proved at the time a bridge too far. Lighter relief came with productions of scenes from Shakespeare, acted with amateur bravado, physical training run by a zealous but entertaining sports master, and concerts in the evenings by some highly competent music teachers. All this was deftly organised within the context of School practices, such as meditation, Philosophy discussions and a measured day.

There were hitches. A few teachers failed to find a subject to study at all. Some felt denied the opportunity to prepare lessons. Debenham frowned on this, as obscuring the proper task of delving deeply into a chosen area. He saw the group as an attempt to restore the self-respect of teachers by means of scholarship, at a time when teacher training in the UK had been attenuated by unnecessary rules and misguided methods of teaching. Following MacLaren, he believed that most of the problems experienced in the classroom originated in a failure by the teacher to acquire a thoroughgoing knowledge of what was being taught. Those who love a subject can always hold the attention of a class. Whatever else was achieved – and there were teachers for whom this renewed study was life-changing – it certainly provided an excellent seed-bed for future teachers, as well as continually reviving scholarship.

The ladies groups of Sheila Rosenberg had turned the minds of many mothers towards the idea of a better education for their children. Nursery groups, using carefully chosen material, looked after the children during the ladies' meetings. All this gave a further impetus to the movement towards new schools. Another key role was played by Bernard White, who has been a most industrious player in the School for over half a century. In the early seventies he was bursar of Waterperry, where he was aware of the education of the young ladies, as well as looking after the fabric of the London houses. It became apparent to him as a tutor that many parents were concerned about the state of schools, and were asking for advice. He noticed that the School houses had spare capacity during the day. With MacLaren's approval, he arranged a meeting at Brook Green, attended by interested parents, Sheila Rosenberg, Richard Watson – an architect and future school governor – the prospective head teachers and himself.

'Start a school that will last five hundred years,' said MacLaren. Enough pupils came forward to make the project practical. An educational trust, called the Independent Educational Association, which was legally quite distinct from the School, was created to manage the schools. Roger Pincham was appointed chairman of the governors. As a stockbroker with City and other connections, and as Treasurer of the School, he was to play an extremely influential role in introducing benefactors and friends, organising fund-raising events – one was held at the Mansion House – and chairing meetings, often when disputes were in danger of spoiling the best-laid plans. He also invited eminent figures, such as an ex-Speaker of the House of Commons, to give annual lectures to the Schools at the Royal Society of Arts.

St James opened at 90 Queensgate in January 1975, with 53 pupils of junior age. The name was chosen by Nicholas Debenham, who subsequently made great use of St James' Epistle, even reflecting later that 'Swift to hear; slow to speak; slow to wrath' should have been the school motto. Besides the head teachers, there were two other members of staff, whilst an unpaid bursar, a secretary and ladies in the kitchen gave support. It was to become a feature of the schools that many mothers would help with such duties in return for free, or discounted, places for their children. Indeed, Bernard White, as bursar, used some ingenious accounting and tax avoidance to enable children to attend without payment of full fees, until the tax authorities closed most of the gaps. Free places for teachers' children compensated greatly for low remuneration.

Teachers were rewarded according to the principle stated by MacLaren that the passing on of knowledge should always be a free gift. Hence for many years there were no structured salaries, only payments to maintain teachers' living standards, in particular to pay their mortgages. Some who had private means were paid nothing

at all. The recruitment of non-School staff, the intervention of the
tax authorities and the rising price of houses eventually made this *ad
hoc* system unsustainable, with the result that the very low initial fees
rose, until they now match those of comparable independent
schools.

Another of MacLaren's innovative ideas was that the same form
teacher should be in place throughout a form's progress from five to
eighteen. This teacher was fully responsible for every aspect of each
child's growth – spiritually, mentally, emotionally and physically – and
in the primary stage up to ten would teach all subjects, except
perhaps art, music and physical training. After ten, specialist teachers
would be employed, but the form teacher retained responsibility,
especially as he or she taught the key subject of Philosophy. Later
on, as the junior and senior schools became more distinct, this
was modified, so that most teachers remained in one or the other
school.

Leon MacLaren, as the founder of the schools, formulated the
main principles, but he took a close interest also in the curriculum.
Together with the head teachers, he turned to Plato, notably to the
Republic and the *Laws,* for guidance. Music for the soul and gymnastic for the body were the outcome. Music in Plato, however, included
literature, language, mathematics, art and all that contributed to harmonious development. Gymnastic covered all physical training,
including the military art, diet and general health. There would be no
reversion to a merely traditional British education. Every subject
would be directly related to the pursuit of truth in oneself, to the
Atman. Thus language was to be taught through the medium of
the great scriptures: the Bible, the Upanishads and the *Gita.* Mathematics would begin with the circle of nine points, with no concession to counting physical objects, like apples and oranges. Music and
song would involve the mastering of the natural, untempered octave,
and practising only songs based upon it, such as those of medieval
times. Art would teach awareness, observation and technique.

MacLaren gave four rules that underpinned all this. The child
should learn the simple principles of spiritual knowledge; knowledge
of the universe; knowledge of Man; and the relation of the individual to these three. Instruction in these, however, was to rest on the
Platonic idea that it would connect with the inner knowledge already
present in every child. He added to these four rules the need to
remind the child of the threefold duty of every human being, as

taught by the Shankaracharya: to remember the Creator, to live according to the fine regulations of the universe, and to find one's way back to God. Accompanying all this would be disciplined practice in spiritual, mental and physical fields. Upon this brief but potent formulation the new schools would proceed.

But there were many other matters to be decided. What would be the school uniform, for example? On MacLaren's prescription that the mark of junior children should be innocence and brightness, and that of seniors uprightness and strength, a School artist came up with the colour blue, lighter for juniors, darker for seniors. Diligent ladies were assigned the tasks of designing uniforms and finding craftsmen to make them of pure cotton or wool. Great efforts were made to perfect these, even though some mothers proved somewhat ungrateful – understandably, when faced with the problem of hand washing!

School lunches were another area of radical innovation. Bread was baked on the premises. All other food was uncooked, fresh and vegetarian. Later this gave way to the need for a hot dish, especially as some children had long journeys home. Each form ate with their form teacher, under a strict rule never to help oneself. A few miscreants would wait until their own plate was empty, and then ostentatiously ask others what they wanted.

Physical training was daily. Athletics and gymnastics became important sports, with frequent success in inter-school competitions. There were winners even at the national level in gymnastics and cross-country running. Swimming played a prominent part, together with the usual rugby, cricket and, less conventionally, girls' lacrosse. Girls were also introduced to horse riding. The art master turned out to be a boxing enthusiast, and trained some formidable fighters. Even fencing later came on offer to the boys from a keen parent.

The relationship between the schools and the parents was not always happy. MacLaren had little respect for modern parents, even those in the School. His meetings with them were somewhat authoritarian, and the head teachers rather followed his example. Some parents objected to what they saw as arbitrary rules. Uniforms created a problem for some. Others thought that the discipline was too severe. In some cases it was; in others the parents were too ready to believe whatever their children told them. A few teachers, some with little professional experience, caused problems in relation to teaching methods or discipline. All such matters came to a head in

the crisis that all the children's schools and the School itself faced in
the 1980s (see Chapter 23).

After almost twenty years of running both junior and senior
St James' Schools, albeit with the sterling help of their deputy heads,
Nicholas Debenham and Sheila Caldwell handed over both junior
schools to Paul Moss in 1993. He resigned from the headship of one
of Thomas's London preparatory schools in order to take up his
new post. On his first day at St James he stood on the pavement to
greet each child, a practice he continued every day subsequently. It
signalled his devotion to the care of young children. Under his
headship numbers grew steadily.

Moss presided over the move of the junior schools to Earsby
Street at Olympia in 2000. For the first year they endured the dust
and confusion of building works, until what he described as the 'air;
light and space' of a renovated school emerged. His wry sense of
humour was typified in an interview with a lady Schools Inspector.
At the end of the meeting he lit a cigarette. She asked him if this was
consistent with the Philosophy of the school. 'Oh, yes,' he replied
airily, 'I drink and chase women as well!' There was a shocked pause,
and then they both burst out laughing. The inspection was entirely
successful.

This outgoing attitude was well suited to the progress of the
schools at that time. He himself became a Schools Inspector, ran
Inset courses and in 2004 was Chairman of the Independent Schools
Association, to which all the St James' Schools belonged. When he
left in 2009 to become Principal of the St James' Junior Schools, with
the task of promoting the family of schools round the world
through the instrumentality of the Education Renaissance Trust, he
said that he had never sought to make a mark on St James, only to
nourish the children there and to try to set an example in the world
of education generally. Teacher training has become a special feature
of his new work. He has many years experience of this, in running
courses sponsored by the Education Renaissance Trust, as well as
by Unicef and other charities. His place was taken at St James' by
Catherine Thomlinson, a former pupil of St Vedast, who had taught
at the schools for many years.

The principle that teachers should study and aim to be masters
of a subject, although important at the primary stage, was most
evidently beneficial in the secondary school. Language, in various
forms, occupied the central place in the curriculum. Under the

general direction of Will Rasmussen, an American classics graduate from Dartmouth College, USA and Oxford, Greek and Latin supplemented the Sanskrit that was taught from the beginning in the junior schools. The original idea of MacLaren was that Sanskrit and Greek would give access to the great spiritual and cultural literature of both traditions, notably to the Upanishads, *Gita* and Plato, but for the best pupils to become university classicists entailed also learning Latin. Three ancient languages put the whole curriculum under some strain, and meant that, whilst a few outstanding pupils became exceptionally well-qualified classicists, others less gifted at languages were struggling. Changes were made later.

Despite these problems there was no dilution in other areas. Three sciences – physics, chemistry and biology – continued throughout under highly qualified science teachers. One produced a fine introductory textbook. The schools turned out a considerable number of science and medical students. Mathematics had a somewhat chequered career, owing to a courageous effort to introduce Vedic methods, based upon a book written by an Indian master of Advaita Vedanta. The system related every operation to the nearest power of ten, and undoubtedly trained the mind to think in terms of unity. Most teachers, themselves brought up on conventional methods, were not adequately versed in the new techniques. Some bright pupils became capable of amazing feats, such as one line division, whilst others failed to know how to divide at all. Common sense prevailed in seeing that the great majority got through to GCSE mathematics with sufficient ability.

History in the schools was given a powerful impetus by a statement from the Shankaracharya in answer to a question from MacLaren. It was, he said, a charting out of the journey of consciousness in search of the glorious aspects of life, especially of conscious efforts to advance civilisation, including overcoming difficulties. Unbiased accounts of lives and events that inspire others to face evil were needed. Elsewhere he remarked that other subjects, like science, should teach about the great men and women who have led the way. Consequently the lives of people like Newton, Faraday, Wren, Mozart and Florence Nightingale entered the syllabus in unexpected places.

In view of Debenham's experience as a geography teacher, there was a rather surprising deficiency in this area. Two years of elementary geographical information was valuable, but thereafter there was a hiatus. The legendary school geography report, that complimented a boy only on his ability to find his way home, perhaps came too near the truth. Some geography, however, was absorbed from school holidays and other trips.

These holidays were recommended by MacLaren in order to show the children in a new environment. They became quite ambitious: juniors reached the summit of Snowdon; seniors went to the USA to play lacrosse and to India to play cricket. Cultural trips abounded. Favourite places were Greece, Florence and Chartres. The Shankara-charya's advice to connect emotionally with sites of spiritual endeavour was taken seriously, and children of all ages were deeply affected by great buildings, art treasures and antiquities. Occasionally there were awkward moments. Some sixth form boys got entangled with American girls in a Greek hotel, which required intervention by the headmaster, who happened to be on that trip. Girls had to be chaperoned carefully in both Greece and Italy. One boy disappeared for a day in Athens, having slipped away to spend all his pocket money on carriage rides around the city.

The art master was not only a boxer, but also organised a cadet force. This was very popular, with regular army camps and manoeuvres. Parachuting became a leading feature – which some sixth form girls also took up – and a connection with the Parachute Regiment established. Over the years several boys chose an army career, usually with entrance to Sandhurst. A boy from the original Sunday school, noted for his blithe disregard of the rules, became an officer in a bomb disposal unit.

MacLaren resisted for some while the idea of introducing modern languages, on the grounds that the language embodies the national culture. He did not want 'l'amour and seven course dinners', and disliked the sound of German and Spanish. Nevertheless the practical advantages of French eventually outweighed his opposition, so that it has been taught very competently up to A-level standard. In the boys' school there were also part-time teachers of German.

Art, music and drama played an essential role. The comprehensive nature of the intake of children – very few applicants were denied entry – meant that there were several of moderate or poor academic ability who were gifted in the creative arts. They were given every encouragement. All the pupils constituted the school choirs. Whole classes performed plays, usually of Shakespeare or of classics like the *Ramayana*. Competitions were won in art, singing, instrumental music and speech. For example, Thomas Cranmer Prayer Book awards were gained for recitation from the 1662 prayer book. There were epic performances, such as *The Odyssey* at a London theatre, where gods and humans vied for attention. Music written by Leon MacLaren was practised, including two songs: 'Holy is Govinda' and 'O, Thou Lord Supreme'. Unfortunately the former was somewhat degraded when it was found that *Govinda* was not only a supposed Sanskrit name for God, but also the name of a local newsagent! Art reached a very high standard through the efforts of several teachers, who were talented artists in their own right.

The crowning gem of these subjects, however, was naturally enough Philosophy. It was, of course, a radical departure to teach the subject at all, let alone to children from five upwards. At first, MacLaren wrote the material. This had a twofold effect. On one hand, it was profound, penetrating and far-reaching. On the other, it was difficult for many children to understand because of the vocabulary and style. He did not believe in making much concession to age. The first material was written for seven year olds, and was used also for the younger ones. It contained Sanskrit words. Teachers were not bold enough to stray from the script. Lessons tended to follow the pattern of adult groups, with reading and discussion.

Children slowly got used to the idea that unity and bliss underlie everything that one sees, hears and touches; that this unity really is oneself; that no one is separate. Gradually the material was simplified, especially when the head teachers revised or rewrote it. There is no doubt that most children at the schools, by the time they left, had an understanding of themselves and of the world that offered the prospect of a good and truthful life. If sixty per cent followed it, said the Shankaracharya, the schools could be counted a success.

Besides this the failures come into perspective. In the boys schools the discipline was too severe in some respects. A few teachers could over-react to bad behaviour; some prefects abused their power over younger boys. In particular, the cane was used rather too frequently, although Debenham, and later Julian Capper as head of St Vedast, were careful to reserve it for very serious offences, such as bullying, lying and disrupting classes. Unfortunately some publicity centred upon caning, so that when the headmasters defended it in public the schools became unfairly noteworthy for its use. In Debenham's later opinion, the real mistake was to adopt a system of

punishment in the 1970s that would have been quite acceptable
in the 1940s. In the girls schools, Sheila Caldwell was capable of
reducing miscreant girls to a state of contrition purely by word
of mouth. What perhaps upset the senior girls more was the enduring issue of full-length skirts worn by the sixth form. This caused
dismay and anger, especially for those travelling by public transport
or attending outside events, like conferences, when others girls were
present. In the 1970s and 1980s long skirts for teenagers aroused
astonishment and even derision. Eventually the schools relented, and
the hemline rose.

One special feature that later attracted some approbrium was
that the seniors were asked if they would join the School. In itself
this was natural enough, in view of the connection, but there was a
tendency to go further than just encouragement. Head teachers and
staff in the early days were heavily committed to the School, and felt
that they were serving the best interests of pupils in getting them to
join. In practice it probably made little difference, as those whom the
School suited stayed and those who were unsuited soon left.

Some parents wanted similar schools to St James for children who
were too old for entry. After MacLaren had firmly vetoed this,
demands continued persistently, and he consented. St Vedast, named
after an early medieval saint, the mentor of Clovis, first king of the
Franks, took pupils of eight to eleven years, and subsequently
only had a secondary intake. It opened in the Autumn of 1975. The
principles were the same as those of St James. Sheila Caldwell became
headmistress of the two schools, although from day to day St Vedast
was largely run by June West, a dedicated teacher with a training in
drama. Nicholas Debenham, after a spell in both posts, handed St
Vedast boys over to Julian Capper, a classicist from Winchester and
Trinity, Cambridge, who gave the school a robust character of its
own, until it fell foul of adverse publicity (see pages 251-3).

The reason for MacLaren's reluctance showed itself in practice,
when discipline problems arose in both St Vedast schools. The
primary education of the pupils had not laid the same foundations
of character and study that were evident in St James. Although many
St Vedast pupils were highly talented, and went on to successful and
worthy careers, there were a minority who caused serious problems.
As a result, discipline was tightened, punishments became more
severe, and all this later fed the appetite of investigative journalists.
Nevertheless the brief life of St Vedast schools promised much, and

most pupils remain outstanding examples of its educational value.

One difficulty common to all the new schools was that of premises. To find suitable ones in central London at affordable prices was almost impossible. On the other hand, a move out of London would have made them inaccessible to many of the School families. Hence the only solution was to use school buildings, as Bernard White had first suggested. This only became a serious problem as the schools expanded. There were quite frequent and somewhat disruptive moves from one house to another. Queen's Gate remained the home of the junior schools for many years, until they went to Earsby Street. The seniors soon moved from Queen's Gate: the girls to Chepstow Villas and the boys to a house in Eccleston Square, near Victoria, previously occupied by Westminster Under School. Then the boys moved to Twickenham, where a convent had previously run a school by the river. This had a very fine view along a curve of the Thames, and was suitable for rowing. The senior girls also found a much larger school building with good potential for development alongside the juniors at Earsby Street. Finally the senior boys acquired a very large site at Ashford, Middlesex, the previous home of St David's Girls School, which should satisfy their requirements for many years to come.

Laura Hyde took over as headmistress from Sheila Caldwell in 1995, after two terms as assistant head. She has described her role as that of an instrument, rather than as an author. Her training as a primary teacher was followed by some years in a church school and in St James, and five years as Leon MacLaren's personal assistant. Without changing the fundamental principles of St James' Senior Girls' School, she has made some radical innovations appropriate to a new phase of development.

In Laura Hyde's view there was an undue intensity in the teaching of Philosophy to the girls, so that some reacted against it. It has now been revised. From a relatively acute concentration on Advaita Vedanta in the form given by the Shankaracharya, it has become broader in content, with material drawn from many authorities but centred on the notion of wisdom. Stories, other resources and more discussion supplement traditional material. She sees this as giving a more comprehensive meaning to the notion of Advaita, whilst retaining the core concept of an essential unity.

The whole spirit of the school, she believes, is to make practical the words of James' Epistle:

Of his own will begat he us with the word of truth, that we should
be a kind of firstfruits of his creatures.[1]

The 'firstfruits' are the girls who leave St James' with an open
heart, compassion and a willingness to meet whatever the world
holds, ready to 'visit the fatherless and widows in their affliction'.
The very first note sung by the school choir at concerts, she has
remarked, characterises this openness of heart. At the same time the
school continues to produce excellent academic results. Entry to
the school is by examination and interview, with a strong emphasis
on a girl's propensity to benefit from and contribute to the ethos of
St James'. Every year group in the girls' school is now a two-form
entry, which indicates the level of growth since the 1970s.

The curriculum has been modified, principally by removing
elements that in modern conditions are more or less impracticable.
Vedic mathematics has been taken out. Sanskrit is taught only to
ex-St James junior pupils, who may choose to continue it at GCSE
level and beyond. Music includes modern works as well as the previously favoured Mozart and early songs.

In 2004 Nicholas Debenham became ill and had to resign. There
was no obvious successor, but into the breach stepped a man with
considerable experience of leadership in politics and business. David
Boddy had risen to be press secretary to Margaret Thatcher during
the election campaigns of 1979 to 1983 and director of press and
public relations for the Conservative Party. He left politics to start
two companies, one specialising in leadership training. By which time
he was deeply involved with education, through becoming a founder
trustee of the Education Renaissance Trust, which trained teachers
on the St James model.

Boddy felt that St James Senior Boys School was in transition
from being seen as an 'experimental' new school to becoming a
successful main stream one with a strong philosophical and spiritual
content. He sees his task as completing this transition. Accordingly
he introduced some changes. The system of meditation for boys was
revised by introducing a 'quiet time', when every boy is expected to
meditate or pray in a manner suited to his particular religious or
spiritual tradition. The only rule is 'Do not disturb the peace of
another.' The school has become more evidently multi-cultural, with
boys from Christian, Jewish, Hindu and Muslim families brought

1 *James*, 1:18.

together under the implicit Advaita teaching that there is one God under many names and that every person is divine. The principle taught is that the essence of every religion is true. Boddy feels that a new language needs to be developed to make this explicit.

Training for leadership has become a chief feature of the school. This is seen as service to the community, taking such forms as setting a standard of excellence in a profession or trade. Appreciation of cultural values plays a major part; hence the St James tradition of cultural visits has been expanded to include regular trips to Pompeii, Greece, Paris, Florence (which includes a leadership programme at Lucca), and an optional sixth form period in South Africa or India. Leadership is encouraged, too, through a school council of two boys elected in each class, which deals with anti-bullying policy (with the headmaster's assistance!), charity events, and ideas for improvements. Boddy himself has promoted the theme of leadership widely outside the school by his position in several organisations of independent schools' head teachers. The Lucca programme, which he founded, has now spread around the world. The *Good Schools Guide* places the school in the top six for leadership training. Behind these developments lies Leon MacLaren's aphorism that 'Those who speak lead; those who don't follow'.

On becoming headmaster, Boddy found that the School no longer provided many teachers for St James. He seeks them elsewhere, amongst spiritually inclined teachers of all backgrounds. The sixth form master at present, for example, was previously a Benedictine monk. The head of English is an Australian Sufi. In this sense, at least, the 'experiment' continues! At the same time, the school continues to succeed academically. New subjects, such as geography, drama and German have been introduced at GCSE, whilst there is more flexibility in choices around the usual core. In sport, boys can now practice judo, basketball, badminton and golf as well as the mainstream games.

Only about a quarter of the staff of St James' Schools are now members of the School. The broadening of the philosophical approach has helped to resolve any earlier problems about this. In-service training has been introduced, which can be seen as replacing the teachers' group, which no longer includes secondary teachers. This change has probably raised the level of professionalism amongst teachers by giving them access to the latest 'best practice'. At the same time it represents a departure from the original aim of

finding the point of the subject by referring back to original authorities, in so far as teachers are now readier to conform to the content
and methods that prevail elsewhere. There is perhaps an inherent
tension between seeking the most truthful expression of subjects
and achieving the best examination results for pupils. This question
remains to be settled.

Whatever the difficulties and errors, many of which were
common to schools throughout the country, the pupils – and staff –
of St James' and St Vedast Schools have been privileged in belonging to a unique experiment in education. Academic results have been
outstanding in relation to the intake. A substantial majority of pupils
have gone on to university, often to the best of these. Many of the
others have trained for creative careers, as artists, musicians, actors or
film-makers. Some have been especially drawn to philanthropic work
for charities, educational projects and so on. All have participated in
what might prove to be a turning point in the history of education,
at a time when in many respects it is degenerating rapidly in the
world at large.

In one respect in particular the schools have not yet fulfilled the
original intention. The fees gradually rose from a level that enabled a
family on a modest income to choose St James' to a point where they
are now comparable with similar independent schools, which is well
beyond the means of such a family. This was perhaps inevitable in
view of the need to recruit more teachers, especially when salaries
have to take account of soaring house prices. Whilst St James' is still
committed to welcoming all children who might benefit from its
special form of education, the brute fact remains that many parents
cannot afford to pay. Clearly bursaries could provide the answer. For
example, at present 18 per cent of pupils are on bursaries at the
Senior Girls' School.

Further afield there have been remarkable developments that
stem from the model of the London schools. Founded on the same
principles, but adapted to conditions of time and place, new schools
were opened in Dublin, Leeds, Stockton, Sydney, Melbourne, Auckland, New York, Durban, Johannesburg and Trinidad. Education as
prescribed by the Shankaracharya, Plato and Leon MacLaren, and
as administered with devotion by the head teachers and staff in
London, has become a worldwide enterprise.

CHAPTER TWENTY-ONE

Global Expansion

F OR OVER half a century the teaching developed by the
School has been spreading around the globe by means of new
Schools, opening as independent institutions but remaining in
a unity of spirit and intention. As Donald Lambie said at the leaders'
conference at Waterperry in 2003:

> It is remarkable to note that there is no constitutional link between
> the international Schools and London. It is solely the common
> search for truth which keeps the Schools unified.

At first the new Schools were mainly in English-speaking
countries. Gradually, however, others began in places where tongues
vary from Dutch to Hungarian. Leon MacLaren travelled widely and
regularly to offer wisdom and inspiration; occasionally as an arbiter
when difficulties arose. Donald Lambie continues to offer the same
leadership. What has helped further to preserve the unity of the
whole movement has been the provision by London of material,
largely based upon the Shankaracharya's conversations.

Advice was given by the Shankaracharya himself about the local
leadership of the Schools. There are two factors involved, he said.
The first is the aim of realisation of the Self, or movement towards
ultimate unity. This can be assumed as the purpose of the School and
its associates. The second is a question of conduct, especially of the
leaders themselves. Their words and their actions must be the same.
Any falling short, lack of discipline or misconduct would be spotted
immediately by their students. What they do is even more important
than what they say.

An amusing story was told of this. A mother had a son who ate
too many sweets. She took him to see a wise man. They were told to
come back a week later. When they returned, the wise man simply
told the boy to give up eating sweets. The mother thought that he

could have said this the week before, so she asked him about it. 'But I also was eating sweets,' was the reply. 'In order that my words should be effective, I had to give up eating sweets myself!'

Most overseas Schools began when a student from London went abroad, either back to his or her native country or as a career move, and decided with Leon MacLaren's approval to open a School. The very first one, in Wellington, New Zealand, began in this way, when Nolan Howitt returned there in 1956. It grew steadily until 1972, when under Howitt the majority of students elected to leave the School in order to come under the authority of Dr Roles and the London Study Society. Slowly the small group remaining, led by John Walter, rebuilt the School, despite 'it seeming to have lost everything', until it now has about 250 students. In 1982 a very fine neo-Georgian building owned by the Salvation Army was acquired. It looks over the harbour to the Tararua mountains. A native Pohutukawa tree on the front lawn symbolises the School's revival. After savage pruning by over-zealous students, it was reduced from a tall, proud tree to an ungainly stump, but has since grown to its former stature.

The present leader in Wellington, Bruce Dean, has introduced a cultural day, which includes Sanskrit, calligraphy, Tai Chi and much else. Wellington had the distinction of being the first School any-where to run a residential week. John Russell, later leader in Auck-land, organised this at a City Mission camp at Otaki. There were other occasions when Leon MacLaren tried out some new ideas in Wellington. A glimpse of his lighter side is given by a student:

> We sat in the sun at Otaki drinking cups of tea and eating fresh scones with strawberry jam. Mr MacLaren regaled us with hilarious stories, often with a punch line to raise laughter even more. All the time he was dispelling our gloomy attitudes and opening our minds. I had never been happier and the joy seemed to come from the discovery that, at long last, we had found a true teaching.

John Russell served as leader in Auckland from 1968 for no less than forty years. He gave up the prospect of a diplomatic career to follow his father-in-law, Dick Ryman, who had opened the School in 1960. The present leader is Barrie Preston. For many years Leon MacLaren wrote material for the overseas Schools that was initially tested on the senior group in Auckland. This, of course, led to close

1 'Convivium', School of Economic Science, No. 5, p.39..

communication with London. The School has a property of several acres at Glendowie. In 1997 the Ficino School for children was opened in Auckland.

Wellington has a branch across the mountains in Masterton, another in Palmerston North, a university city to the north, and recently a branch opened in Christchurch, the largest city of South Island.

In 1971 Peter Green, then Principal in London, after spending two weeks in South Africa, made a remarkably outspoken comment on the conditions under which the School operated there. The apartheid regime was, of course, still in place:

> The experience is very instructive for one realises what enormous odds the students and their teacher have to work against, and also how vitally necessary the School is to the future of such places. For mentally and spiritually they are deserts, and there are virtually no values or influences from culture and tradition to guide and support the people. Indeed the circumstances in which they find them selves are in every way adverse to development whichever side of the colour-bar they may fall.[2]

The School began in South Africa when Henri Schoup, a native of Belgium, and his English wife Joan went to Johannesburg from London in 1957. The following year he started a Philosophy group in the American Library, which had diplomatic immunity. In 1960 came the Sharpeville massacre. As a professional journalist, Schoup was amongst the first to arrive there, and sent reports to United Press. Soon he was served with a deportation order, which gave him 24 hours to leave the country. His wife stayed behind briefly in order to help arrange for the handover of the School. The Schoups moved to Amsterdam, where they helped to found the School there, but soon returned to London.

Meanwhile the Johannesburg School grew under the new head, Elaine Martinsen, followed by Anton Voorhoeve, who oversaw the introduction of meditation and a wide range of new practices, including the study of Sanskrit, Plato, the Bible, mathematics and music. A new branch opened in Pretoria in 1978 under Bevan Bergstrom, also leader in Johannesburg from 1993. Lenasia, with a strong Indian community, housed another fast-growing branch. Unfortunately Bergstrom died suddenly from a heart attack. His

2 Report to Annual General Meeting of the School, 22 July 1971

place was taken by Edward Thomlinson, previously leader in Cape Town. From his initiative a children's school, called St James, opened under the energetic headship of Pieter Steyn. Mark Grace has recently succeeded him. So too a programme for 'uplifting and fellowship in the community' began to help local under-privileged children. A fine School house was given over to these two projects. Philosophy students then worked on extensive renovation of the adjacent Salisbury House for their own use. A branch at Benoni to the east of Johannesburg also opened. Thomlinson retired as leader in 2007, to be replaced by Mukesh Bhavan.

In Cape Town Edward Thomlinson had begun with a lecture in 1972 in rooms at 'The Friends of Italy', decorated with prints of Leonardo da Vinci. After difficulties with various houses, suitable premises were found at Claremont, although a great deal of cleaning and renovating was needed there. Branches were set up in nearby areas. A Montessori primary school, called Auburn House, founded originally by a lady from the Cape Town School, was offered philosophical material and help with buildings. From the time of Thomlinson's departure to Johannesburg, Dr Shannon Kendal has led the Cape Town School.

In Natal the School meets at Durban and Pietermaritzburg under the name Kwa Zulu Natal. It began under the leadership of Lawrence Stretton, an architect who had attended the School in London for some years, and was an inspirational leader until his early death. The present leader is Graham Moore.

Leon MacLaren was a regular visitor to the South African Schools, holding residential weeks, and even having brief moments of relaxation on the coast at Durban. A story he told of a visit to Johannesburg during the apartheid era illustrates the difficulties even School members had in getting a true perspective on life there. A lady was driving him down one of the main streets of the city. She said, apropos the race situation, 'Of course, this is a white city.' MacLaren looked out of the car. Every face he could see was black!

The 1960s were a period when the School teaching was welcomed in many venues throughout the world. Holland, New York, Ireland, Australia, Malta and Belgium all saw Schools open in that decade. That in Holland began in 1962 under the leadership of Mr and Mrs van Oyen, who had joined an Ouspensky group in London in 1938. In 1961 Dr Roles suggested to them that they should meet Leon

MacLaren, with the consequence that a School was soon formed. MacLaren had a special relationship with the van Oyens, and was always pleased to visit them in Amsterdam, where, perhaps uniquely, he seemed to enjoy a kind of family atmosphere. Indeed in 1972 their daughter, Dorine, became his personal assistant, serving him loyally till his death in 1994.

The Amsterdam School thrived for thirty years, at one time having more students than London, and opening branches across Holland at The Hague, Deventer, Groningen, Breda, Utrecht and later at Leeuwarden. The van Oyens acquired legendary status as tutors. The model of London was followed in most respects, strengthened by the frequent visits of MacLaren, and also of Bernard White, who for thirty years flew over regularly to initiate students into meditation. A publishing section, Ars Floreat, produced books that included Dutch translations of Plato. A large country estate was bought at Oxerhof, near Deventer. In 1983 the Plato school for children was established with its own site. The leadership of the School of Philosophy passed from the aging Mrs van Oyen to her son, Paul, in 1991.

In the mid 1990s trouble appeared. Opposition to Paul van Oyen grew within the School, and hostile publicity arose about the Plato school, fuelled partly by earlier difficulties over St James and St Vedast in London. Donald Lambie inherited the problem of Amsterdam when Leon MacLaren died. Paul van Oyen resigned in 1997, but the opponents were not satisfied. They claimed legal ownership of the School properties and assets, so the dispute lingered on with those still loyal to London. Mrs van Oyen agreed to return as interim leader, until in 1998 Rob Kruijk was appointed by Lambie. Eventually a legal settlement was made, leaving all the property in the hands of the opponents, except Oxerhof. Under the pressure of these circumstances the Plato school lost pupils, and had to close in 2002. Its teachers had contributed much to the annual teachers' conference in the UK, and were sadly missed.

Rob Kruijk and his senior colleagues set about rebuilding the School. They took as their text some words of the Shankaracharya:

> Having understood the situation, one must form a resolve, use the discipline systematically, keep on looking back at one's own shortcomings and thus keep one's gates open to move towards liberation and give freely to others, so that they may also move towards Self-realisation.

Encouragement came with the opening of a new branch at Eindhoven. In Deventer the School acquired premises once used by the Dutch teacher, Geert Grote, founder of the *devotio moderna*, a movement that gave rise to the Brethren of the Common Life, to which Thomas a Kempis belonged. Significantly the Dutch School began to put much emphasis upon meditation and service. At Oxerhof a service of dedication for the members of the Dutch resistance who died there at the hands of the Nazi SS is held every year. From such roots the revived School continues to grow. In 2009 it hosted at Oxerhof the International Justice and Equity week, led by Ian Mason as head of Economics in London.

An American who attended the School in London, Tom Gerst, began Philosophy classes in New York, under the title Adult Study Workshop, when he returned there in 1964. Assistance was given by a Study Society group, led by Joy Dillingham, one-time personal secretary to Ouspensky. Various locations in New York were used as the School grew, including one in the kitchen of a *Cordon Bleu* chef, until in 1975 the School acquired its own property, a mansion in Manhattan's Upper East Side, just off Central Park. By then there were 600 students. Leon Maclaren took residential courses from 1965 onwards, usually at a brownstone house on West 80th Street, until 1978, when a very fine estate in the Hudson highlands in upstate New York was purchased. This property had been owned by a well-known entrepreneur, John Borden, who had a vision of a place of retreat from the hectic world of American business. In an interview he described this ideal that the School of Practical Philosophy has helped to realise:

> Borden conceived the idea of establishing his enterprise near the great commercial cities of New York, Philadelphia, Boston, Washington, our own capital, and in such close proximity to our large river and railroads to be built in the future, so that the farm which he would select should at the end of one hundred years or less be of such easy access that it would become available as a home, a park, a resting place, a place of retreat from business and all care for the Sir Knights of the United States and of such others as might in the far future visit our country from foreign parts. To do this a place must be selected, both healthful and agreeable, embracing all the beauties of nature, scenery and quiet that would be possible to secure...
> 'This being my purpose, I began to search through the hill country
> ... for the site of this dreamed of and hoped for place; and not until

the year 1881 did the location present itself; namely our most beautiful and unsurpassed Wallkill Valley in old Ulster.'

Tom Gerst had handed over leadership of the School to Joy Dillingham in 1966. For almost three decades she oversaw the School's expansion, both in numbers and in the range of practices introduced. Her drama training and ready wit made her a welcome companion for MacLaren on his annual visits and at leaders' conferences in the UK. In 1993 she stepped down in favour of Neal Broxmeyer, who unfortunately died three years later. He was succeeded by Barry Steingard, under whom the School has flourished in conditions very different from those it faced as the Adult Study Workshop. Much attention has been given to making the teaching more accessible and attractive to the public at large, and especially to young people, for whom there appears to be less free time for philosophical pursuits. This has been successful, with students in 2010 numbering 830.

Three new projects are of special note. A children's school on East 79th Street, under the headship of William Fox III, now accepts pupils from nursery age to fifth grade. Fox taught for many years in St James in London, where he was a highly popular form master, and has introduced both content and methods from there. Secondly, a highly original effort to widen the net for Philosophy students commenced in 2008 with a distance-learning programme using internet technology. Philosophy 'classrooms' are created, where individuals 'meet' for on-line discussion with a tutor once a week for one hour. This has considerable potential for Schools around the world, especially in countries, like the USA, where students might be very long distances from the nearest branch. Thirdly, in 2009 an International Young Professionals week took place at Wallkill, with students under forty years of age attending from the USA, the UK, Holland, South Africa and Australia. Businessmen, teachers and lawyers formed distinct groups. Economics, public speaking, writing and exploring one's talents were on the agenda. Such conferences may become biennial events.

Another School in the USA opened in 1970 in Boston, Massachusetts, when Cedric Grigg and his wife Evelyn were asked by his employer to move there from London. After a slow start, it prospered under the title 'The Philosophy Foundation', but in 1989 the Griggs had to move again and handed Boston over to Dr John

Lehmann. This time they set up the 'The School of Applied Philosophy' in Rochester, New York State, which is situated on Lake Ontario, and noted historically for being the northern terminus of the famous 'underground railway' for fugitive Negro slaves. Compared with Boston, students in Rochester tend to be 'older, involved in other organisations, and less willing to commit to disciplines', but –more importantly – they are friendlier! Most new students come by personal rcommendation. For residentials the School was fortunate for several years to be able to use William Fox's property at Niagara-on-the-Lake in Canada. The Griggs attest to the 'enlightening and life-transforming teachings of Shantananda Saraswati' and to the constant support of the School in London. They now await the next summons to move and to establish a new School: 'We cannot help wondering how God will decide to dispose of us next!'

In the early 1960s a group of people began meeting in Dublin to discuss Philosophy. When a student from the School in London joined them, a connection was made that led to the formation of the School of Philosophy and Economic Science. A tutor from London went over regularly, until in 1967 the doors were opened to the public. Under its leader, a Dutchman, Kurt del Monte, the School grew rapidly, but in 1972 half the students opted for meditation alone, whilst the others preferred to continue with the School programme. Konrad Dechant took over the leadership of these, and the numbers attending were re-established at about four hundred. Peter Glover, a senior tutor from London, gave considerable help during this period.

A magnificent Georgian house with 65 acres near the river Boyne, north of Dublin, which John Betjman described as 'the most dignified, restrained and original in Ireland', was bought by the School in the 1980s. Not only residentials but a variety of events are held there. Most notable perhaps are the Plato days, which attract over three hundred people. Students have written ten plays and four films dramatising Platonic dialogues. Weekends presenting Plato have also been held in Dublin Castle and elsewhere. These have now been offered to Schools abroad, with a most successful fortnight in Delphi recently, when the main text studied was *Timaeus*. A generous benefactor has enabled a senior Dublin student to devote ten years to translating the whole of Plato's works. All this recalls the strong tradition of early Irish scholarship, which preserved Greek learning for Europe in the Dark Ages.

Indeed, John Scottus Erigena, the great Irish Platonic scholar of the ninth century, has given his name to a children's school founded in Dublin in 1986. Under the headships of Michael and Mary Telford this provides a full education, grounded in Philosophy, for both primary and secondary pupils. In 2010 it had 420 pupils. Irish teachers provided stimulating company at the teachers conferences at Waterperry.

In 1992 Shane Mulhall was appointed leader of the Dublin School. This was at a time of opportunity for expansion. Courses were offered throughout the Republic of Ireland, and at present there are nineteen locations with about fifteen hundred students. A branch also opened in Belfast. Altogether 35,000 students have enrolled since 1967. Mulhall has frequently been asked to lecture beyond Ireland. From 1999 an annual cultural day has attracted wide interest within and outside the School. A choice of lectures on a wide range of topics in world culture is offered. Talks on the practical application of Philosophy are given in many parts of Ireland. About 30,000 CDs of these have been sold. Public courses are also held currently on Plato, Christian mysticism, parenting, business, Sanskrit and health.

Australia has been fertile ground for the teaching of the School. Sydney was the first city to try it. Michael Mavro, who had spent time in the London School, led a rapid growth of membership from 1967. Much emphasis was given to attention in physical work, and a remarkable range of activities developed, including illuminating manuscripts, making lace, dressmaking, spinning and weaving and wood-carving. Music and drama widened the scope further.

For residentials the School acquired a property at Mount Wilson in the Blue Mountains, two hours from Sydney. Much labour was needed to clear the site and to build. A large roof was bought from an amusement park, dismantled and re-erected at Mount Wilson, with a house on a concrete base beneath it. The School also bought a wool warehouse in the centre of Sydney, which was stripped by hand and fitted out with group rooms and halls. Architects and volunteer labour within the School performed all these feats, an achievement acknowledged by Leon MacLaren, who opened the Sydney building in 1980, and subsequently made telling comparisons with the somewhat slower progress of work on School buildings in the UK.!

Study groups in Plato, Sanskrit and the Bible developed meanwhile, with a lively youth group, several of whom later became

School leaders elsewhere. In 1985 John Colet School for children was founded under Gilbert Maine, a lawyer who has turned his mind to whatever studies have been needed. William Fox junior donated his house as the first school premises. John Colet now thrives as both an infant and primary school.

In the mid 1980s there was a crisis over the School leadership in Sydney. Mavro had provided disciplined and uncompromising training, but others looked for more responsibility, and some regarded the regime as harsh. MacLaren needed to intervene, so after a period of supporting Mavro he decided that change was appropriate. Malcolm Tolhurst took over. Greater emphasis was given to self-examination, contemplation and reflection, and responsibility for departments was more widely distributed. At this time, Mahratta, a beautiful art deco mansion with four acres of landscaped gardens in the north suburbs was purchased with the proceeds of the sale of the other city properties.

After fifteen years Tolhurst handed over to Anthony Renshaw in 2001. Since then meditation, especially, has been given a new emphasis. Rooms were acquired to enable introductory groups to meet in central Sydney. Regional branches throughout New South Wales and the Australian Capital Territory grew up: at Wagga, Newcastle, Canberra, Penrith and most recently at Leura in the Blue Mountains. Open garden and cultural events, symposiums and public performances of Shakespeare plays at Mahratta have attracted the public, sometimes with their participation. The Sydney School has sought to combine a universality of outlook with the capacity to meet changing circumstances.

Leon MacLaren remarked that Melbourne would be 'good soil to plant a seed'. In 1977 John Jepsen, then a young man in the Sydney School, opened the School in Melbourne, where he has remained as leader for over thirty years. Encouraged by visits from MacLaren in the 1980s, the School flourished, taking over a new house, called 'Illoura', at St Kilda. A combined residential for all the Australasian Schools was hosted by Melbourne in 1991, and became a regular biennial event. Then the Erasmus children's school began in 1996 and grew rapidly to over 100 children. They have produced fine dramatic performances, such as the *Ramayana* and *The Magic Flute*.

A branch of the School was opened at the port of Geelong in Victoria in 1996 under the leadership of John Tippett. It began in the Old Court House in the heart of the city, but soon moved to

Dalgety House, near Johnstone Park. As a past headquarters of wool brokers, it needed a great deal of cleaning and restoration, carried out, of course, by students in good Australian fashion. A large merino sheep property near Ballarat has become a residential centre. The spirit of the Geelong School is best summed up in an observation by a student when asked to clean wood. His father had been a carpenter. 'The love being transmitted through the damp cloth was the same as that which my father had poured into the wood as he worked with it. That love was the vital ingredient that made everything he created full of beauty and grace.'

At Perth in Western Australia the School began in 1991. The leader, Phillip Kruger, had come across the School in London, after he met a man 'who never criticised anyone or anything.' Subsequently he returned to his native Australia, and attended the Melbourne School for ten years. It was suggested that he might start a School in Perth, so he went there with his wife and five children. On the first night, when the students were asked to feel the play of air on the face and hands, the air conditioning went off! However, the School has prospered with now about two hundred and fifty members. Introductory courses are held in rented premises in the central business district, whilst senior students have an old house in the inner suburbs. Restoration work has been done by the School. Meditation, Sanskrit and Plato studies are prominent. Cultural days, open to the public, follow the model established in Melbourne, including Zen, Vedic mathematics, parenting, and business ethics. The leader aims especially to hold to Leon MacLaren's original vision of finding and teaching truth and justice.

The Brisbane School, in the tropical north, opened three years after Perth. Prior to this, a small group meeting as a branch of Sydney met at the home of a student originally from the London School. Rex Howard, a senior member in Sydney, was asked to establish public courses in Brisbane, so for a year he flew there every Thursday, a distance of 900 kilometres. He then moved north with his family. Various premises have been used, often those of churches or schools. Student membership has fluctuated between 80 and 180; at present it is about 140. Sanskrit has aroused strong interest, enabling Brisbane to provide tutors for Sanskrit weeks in Sydney. Shakespeare, too, is strongly supported, with five comedies being produced in recent years, three at a theatre on the University of Queensland campus. An annual cultural day enables students to make presentations to the public of subjects from the standpoint of Philosophy.

In sharp contrast to the vast continent of Australia, the little island of Malta in the central Mediterranean is also home to a Philosophy School. It, too, began in the late 1960s, but has experienced a much more turbulent history than most of its fellow schools. June Matthews, an English lady whose husband took up a post in Malta, began the School, and saw it through a lengthy period of difficulties. After it had grown considerably in numbers, the Catholic Church and other people on the island became suspicious of its activities. The School was accused of seeking to replace Christianity with Hinduism throughout Malta. This largely stemmed from the attitude of the nonagenarian Archbishop of Malta, who clearly regarded the School as a threat to the Church and perhaps, in particular, to his authority. Persecution of School members began, including threats to dismiss them from employment. Many students left the School. A handful remained, determined to preserve the presence of the School's teaching in their country. As in the story of the king who held to the truth (see pages 163-4), their courage won through. A more reasonable view prevailed amongst the island's authorities, and the school began to grow once more.

Leon MacLaren visited Malta in 1981, and appointed Joseph Sapienza as the new leader. June Matthews returned to the well-deserved peace of Bath, where she promptly became leader of another branch of the School! The Malta School now owns an eighteenth-century house, extensively renovated by students, which looks out over the beautiful harbour of Marsamxett, a popular sailing venue. About a hundred students attend groups that use both English and Maltese. Sanskrit has taken root, exemplified by a senior student's translation of the *Gita* into Maltese. The island remains a meeting of cultures and trade routes, where the teaching may assume an importance that belies the size of its land and population.

Henri Schoup returned home to Brussels in 1967, working still as a journalist with United Press, until he and Joan both became freelance writers. Meanwhile they received Philosophy material from London, and naturally opened a School once more in 1970, which at first used only the English language. Later French and then Dutch were introduced, so that the Belgium School became tri-lingual, with much translation activity. Several students attended who now are senior members in London, including Christine Lambie. In 1974 a generous student financed the purchase of a town house. Seven years later courses in Dutch began also in Antwerp, where a house was bought in 1985. For a time branches opened at Bruges and Aalst, and one still continues at Dilbeek, near Brussels. Total numbers grew to about 500, but in 1986 a national magazine produced a critical article that led to a significant exodus of students. There are now about 150. Henri Schoup handed over the leadership to Alain de Caluwe in 1995, and found a quiet retirement with Joan on the island of Arran in western Scotland.

The School in Cyprus, like Brussels, celebrates its fortieth anniversary in the same year as the whole School worldwide celebrates the centenary of Leon MacLaren's birth. It was founded by a Cypriot student who had attended the London School. A house is now owned in Nicosia. Cyprus has long been beset by disunity, particularly between those of Greek and of Turkish origin. Appropriately enough MacLaren sent a message to the Cyprus School in 1992 that resonated with the students there:

> The truth is always one and not divided. When the ego arises, it always divides and sets limits and so people find themselves divided and in opposition to each other, thus leading to confrontations and warlike activities. But in unity there are no enemies; there is the one truth and no second. So, in a divided world, there is a special need for the realisation of unity at all levels. This is the particular work of the School. Blessings and good wishes with you.

Cyprus was well prepared for the teaching of Advaita, through its traditional Greek Philosophy, on one hand from Plato and on the other from the texts of the Orthodox Church, notably the *Philokalia*. Both of these sources supplement the material used by senior groups. Courses are conducted mainly in Greek, but a few groups in Nicosia and Limassol provide for English-speakers. Turkish is available if needed. Sanskrit, Platonic practical Philosophy, Christian scriptures and the Conversations support study groups, with the Shankaracharya's *Good Company* for children. A ladies handicraft group is also popular. The School offers courses at Larnaca, the birthplace of the Stoic philosopher, Zeno. In addition to the School leaders from London, Bernard Saunders has also made many instructive visits to Cyprus. The School made a major step forward recently, when a donation of land and the services of a lady architect enabled a house for residentials to be built near the Troodos forest. Many other students gave money, time and skill to completing the work there. Vanias Markides is the School leader in Cyprus.

Geoffrey Ramsay left Toronto as a young man, and found himself in a Philosophy class in London in 1960. Sixteen years later he returned home and started a school there. Frequent changes of venue in Toronto followed, each one requiring repairs and renovation. With few resources the School grew slowly but surely. Ramsay retired through ill health in 1991. Leon MacLaren asked William Fox junior and his wife Carol to move to Toronto from comfortable retirement in New York. Abandoning their work on restoring the New York property at Wallkill and with the newly formed children's school, they left to brave the cold winters of Canada. Fox soon endowed the School with a building on the first heritage street in Toronto and another for a branch in St Catherine's. His property at Niagara-on-the-Lake was made available for residentials, until it was sold when William and Carol moved to Israel. Paraic Lally, the new leader, continues the work of his exemplary predecessors.

The School in Trinidad was likewise begun by a native of the island, who returned home after a spell in the London School. Wendel Henckel opened the Trinidad School in 1976 in a music room in San Fernando. Before his lecture, he pointed out the poor state of the room, and proposed that it might be cleaned. With the advice to let the attention rest at the working surfaces, the prospective students put the room to rights before even hearing the opening lecture. Shortly afterwards Henckel was asked to give a talk at a martial arts centre. Under the title of 'Self Defence', he explained how the Self, having no form, needed no defence!

Various venues were used for some years while the School grew rapidly, until eventually a building was constructed by students themselves at Morvant. For a while residentials were held at an estate in the Santa Cruz valley. Finally, the School returned to a new location in San Fernando. The leadership changed in 1992, when Henckel, who later rejoined the School in London, handed over to Brian Cameron. Since then, residentials in the USA and Canada have given fresh impetus, as did visits by Leon MacLaren in 1979 and 1984. A children's school has also been founded. The first class completed their primary training in 2009. Emphasis in the Philosophy School continues to be on the teaching of Advaita, supported by meditation and service.

It is unlikely that a Philosophy School would have been allowed to operate in the Spain of General Franco. Church and State alike made it almost impossible at that time for ideas of unity and human freedom to be expressed, let alone taught. By 1979, however, the monarchy was restored and democratic institutions revived. Jocelyne Laffitte, impressed by the calm behaviour of a friend from the School during a fire, joined the School in London, and soon returned to Madrid to start classes there. Students keen to meet new and creative ideas came in large numbers. A choir and a theatre group were set up.

Unfortunately a crisis occurred in the Schools affairs in 1993. Senior students felt that a gap was opening between Madrid and London. Donald Lambie visited the School and Jocelyne Laffitte agreed to step down as leader. Pedro Martin was appointed to replace her. A week at Waterperry under Lambie enabled the senior group to discover a new strength and enthusiasm. Brian Joseph from London has since visited Madrid many times to assist. Sanskrit was given more attention, and art and *Abhinaya* dance have begun. In 1998 a house in a beautiful area north of Madrid was purchased for residentials. Much work of restoration has been done by students. In particular, a brick pavement, traditional in Spanish gardens, was laid by hand. The Discantus choir have performed in the Anglican Church in Madrid, and an *Abhinaya* week attracted ladies from around the world. More recently the Spanish School has published a Spanish edition of Volume 1 of *The Letters of Marsilio Ficino*, the launch of which was a major cultural event, with copies being sent to Queen Sofia, the Prime Minister and others. By such work Spanish speakers – no less than 700 million – have access to the Philosophy of the Florentine Renaissance. Spain once more is being reconnected with its spiritual tradition.

Translation of Philosophy material into Spanish in Madrid has been an important factor in the success of the School in Venezuela. This began in 1993, when German Alba returned there after many years studying engineering and working in the UK and elsewhere. His School tutor in Manchester had said that a School should begin 'as a natural event in response to the need of the people'. In Venezuela philosophical questions were coming to the fore, so classes began at Alba's home. In 2005 a house was purchased, creating a new need for service and care in managing finances. Some students provided country residences for weekends, but then a

Cistercian monastery offered retreat facilities, with panoramic views of the Venezuelan Andes for good measure. Locally the School at Merida is known as a practical institution, relevant to everyday life, where both the stillness of meditation and the laughter of good company are found together.

Spanish reappeared as the language of Philosophy when a School opened in Buenos Aires in 1996, led by Guillermo Berardone, who had studied at the School in Durban and London. The Durban leader had said to him that for a new School 'all that is needed is a real love for the truth'. Berardone's participation in Economics, music, the choir and Sanskrit in London also helped to qualify him as a future School leader. So, too, did his marriage to Neda, a star pupil at St James and a Cambridge science graduate. After some years using rented rooms, the Argentine School moved to the Berardones' new house in central Buenos Aires in 2004. The main obstacle has been the habit of working late in the busy city. Nevertheless, many study groups now accompany the Philosophy classes there

A unique project was initiated after the Sanskrit group realised that there was no Sanskrit-Spanish dictionary. The Monier-Williams dictionary has been made available online, which allows interested collaborators to translate it into Spanish, or into other languages. Students from around the world are co-operating in this. Another project is to develop a centre to be used for residentials just outside Buenos Aires. A hectare of land has been cleared, and trees and vegetables planted. The idea is to create an educational centre on 'green' matters, such as sustainability and recycling, whilst nurturing respect for nature amongst children from underprivileged backgrounds. The Berardones themselves have even designed and built a small cottage using recycled and non-toxic materials. A larger building is projected. The School is still fairly small, but the quality of the people is remarkable, and they are proud to belong to the global family of Schools.

In the fifteenth century King Matthias of Hungary, under the influence of Marsilio Ficino, whose follower Bandini stayed at Matthias' court in Budapest, presided over a cultural and political revival of his country. Five hundred years later the words of Ficino appeared in an advertisement there: 'Philosophy is the ascent of the mind.' It was the beginning, in 2003, of a new School under the leadership of Miklos Varadi-Beothy and his Australian wife, both long-time students of the School in Sydney. Translation of material into Hungarian had begun some while before. After decades of Communist rule, the country welcomed new ideas. The School in Budapest has grown now to about 70 members, with studies in Sanskrit, the *Gita*, parenting and Economics also under way. Donald Lambie visited in 2005, and accompanied a group to a Gregorian Mass and to lunch with the Abbott at an 800 years old Benedictine monastery at Pannonhalma. Brian McGeogh from Dublin and Ian Mason have been visiting lecturers, the latter at the Hungarian Academy of Science. Much enthusiasm has been generated for bringing practical Philosophy to Hungary, exemplified by the translation into Hungarian of *Good Company*.

In Israel a small Philosophy School has also been established, which keeps in touch with the School in London. After some years retaining a connection, the School in Athens under Nicholas Kazanas no longer has any association with the UK. Likewise, the School in Boston, originally set up by Cedric Grigg from London and his wife, ceased to be a part of the worldwide association of Schools in 2005.

What has particularly sustained these diverse Schools for over half a century has been a regular series of conferences, usually held at Waterperry, for the School leaders. For a period of three or four weeks, they have experienced intensive studies in major disciplines, like Sanskrit, Economics or music, with the emphasis always on the Advaita Philosophy of the Shankaracharya's Conversations. Service teams have enabled them to meet the demands of an uncompromising programme, first devised by Leon MacLaren. Naturally there has also been the opportunity to share information on tutoring, organisation and the problems that have arisen in their respective Schools. The leaders have enjoyed the rare opportunity to become students once more. 'The common search for truth' has certainly been a binding force for unity.

CHAPTER TWENTY-TWO

From Untruth
to Truth

THE NEXT conversations between Leon MacLaren and the Shankaracharya took place in 1980 and 1982. They opened with a question about many students who were experiencing a deeper understanding and peace when in the immediate environment of the School, but who lost these when outside it. What stood in the way were the convictions that 'I am other than the Self' and 'I am the doer'.

All forms of pleasure, pain, suffering and so on are experienced as though real when there is association with something other than the Self, was the reply. Memory of the Self keeps them at bay. The Shankaracharya recited a Sanskrit prayer that helps this memory. In English it reads:

> Lead me from untruth to truth.
> Lead me from darkness to light.
> Lead me from death to immortality.

The three parts correspond to the three aspects of the *Brahman*, namely truth, knowledge and bliss. Untruth, the darkness of ignorance and death are attributes of the world, and appear to limit the individual. In reality they do not exist, for the Self knows nothing of them. The prayer asks for realisation of what is permanently true, of knowledge that dispels fear, and of recognition that one is eternal, which produces bliss.

From this salutary opening the Shankaracharya went on to re-introduce the subject of three types of men and women: the active, the devotional and the intellectual. These are determined by *sanskara*, the accumulation of the effects of past actions. In Indian tradition, when a child is six months old the parents place before it objects like tools, utensils and books of various kinds, and observe which ones the child naturally picks up. This gives a clue about its *sanskara* and tendency in life. With the aid of such information, the child's educational progress and vocation can be guided.

A person who is naturally devotional has already advanced on the way of action, but is not yet ready for the third way of knowledge. Yet, it was emphasised, these three ways are not to be practised each in turn in isolation. In the School all three are required. A day may be spent on three kinds of practice, for though one aspect is predominant in a person the other two play a subordinate part. The School should allow, however, for the predisposition of one to prefer dedicated action, another to follow devotional works, and a third to prefer ideas, which would only be turned to devotional use when the reasons for that are fully understood.

And yet, asked MacLaren, surely all three ways must use reason to direct them? Reason is common to mankind, said the Shankaracharya. If a man is called a beast, he naturally responds that he is a man. Reason informs him of this without aforethought. Ultimately the aim of the teaching of Advaita is that one should know in this immediate way that all is *Brahman*, including oneself.

Even some great teachers have kept to a way of action or devotion. Ramananda, for example, remained a dualist, who taught that on the way of devotion the beloved and the lover are separate. The latter devotes him/herself to seeking the presence of the Lord. He interpreted the scriptures in this way. On the other hand, Sankara was a thoroughgoing teacher of the unity of the *Atman*, or Self, and the *Brahman*. For him knowledge was the final step that brought liberation, and it is this tradition of Advaita Vedanta that the Shankaracharya himself endorsed. In support of this, he cited the final chapter of the *Gita*, where Krishna enjoins Arjuna to give the knowledge that brings unity only to those who are prepared to listen, accept discipline and have faith. Such knowledge is acquired only through experience, and it alone is permanent.

In order to stress once again that the three ways are not to be seen as independent paths to self-realisation, the Shankaracharya reminded MacLaren of the key practice of giving attention to whatever is to hand, be it physical, devotional or intellectual work. At the point of attention all powers operate. There is no need to try to remember all three ways as one digs or prays or reasons; attention does the work.

MacLaren's study of the *Laws of Manu* led him to ask about the institution of marriage. In British society young people, he said, no longer had the idea that it was a profound relationship, and believed that they could terminate a marriage when they chose.

The Shankaracharya began with the categorical statement that marriage is a partnership for life, and that there is no natural provision for divorce. Natural law allows only for one-spouse relationships. When questioned about historical and literary examples to the contrary, such as that of the three wives of Rama's father and the five husbands of Draupadi in the *Mahabharata*, he explained that in special circumstances exceptions to the law might be made. Rama's father needed an heir, and his first two wives did not give him one. Rama himself was a powerful example of a husband loyally devoted to his one wife, Sita. Indeed, the central theme of the *Ramayana* is the unstinting efforts to recover Sita from the hands of her demonic captor, Ravana. In the case of Draupadi, she had mistakenly asked five times for a husband, in the course of a religious ceremony. Nor should one be misled by stories about the gods, the Shankaracharya went on, for marriage only applies to human life. Higher and lower creatures come under other laws.

Leon MacLaren was keen to know what advice could be offered to families and young people themselves about the choice of a partner. Once more the answer was unequivocal. Romantic ideas about selecting a spouse, regardless of any consideration beyond personal attraction, were dismissed. The families concerned should have a strong bearing on the issue. Parents or guardians should consider five aspects of the prospective bride or husband: the cultural background of the family; the education and ability of the individual; his or her nature or character; age – ideally the man should be somewhat older – and the economic resources of the proposed household. On the last point, the Shankaracharya was quick to add that, particularly in the West, too much attention was given to ensuring that resources were acquired before marriage, so that the age of marriage was delayed unnecessarily. Indeed, he said that spouses should be selected by the age of sixteen. This had been the tradition in India until recently. It ensured that, when fully mature, the sexual and emotional impulses could be directed towards one person only. Moreover, it prevented the destructive activity of competing for partners, and indulging in vanity and deceit. If this degenerates into looking for objects of passion, it demeans the dignity of men and women.

This traditional and stringent view of marriage was concluded with a powerful justification. Marriage, he said, was not for the purpose of the gratification of the partners. One purpose was, of course, the continuance of human life, but it had also a finer role to play. Everyone faces difficulties, personal and social tragedies, problems of all kinds. In marriage the partners face these together, and should never consider leaving the other to suffer alone. The Shankaracharya gave the example of a doctor with a senior position in a hospital, who personally cared for his paralysed wife for twenty years, and always remained happy in this service. This is why it is a partnership for life and not a fair-weather relationship

Later MacLaren asked about the use of marriage ceremonies. The local law and custom should be observed, said the Shankaracharya. Above all the creation of an atmosphere in which love and unity are impressed on the couple concerned is vital. They need to be aware of the philosophical basis of marriage, namely that the man represents the *purusha*, or spiritual aspect of humanity, and the woman the *prakriti*, or nature. Their union leads to fulfilment and harmonious life.

The conversation moved to the topic of controlling the mind. Arjuna's frustration in the *Gita* at the turbulence and obdurate nature of the mind was cited; at which the Shankaracharya referred to Krishna's answer that renunciation and practice may nevertheless bring it to rest. There are three main ways to achieve this: firstly by renouncing favoured subjects to which the mind continually returns; secondly by letting go of desires; and thirdly by bringing the mind back to the *Atman*, the Self. This last is the master step, for the other two should lead to it. If, on the other hand, the mind is allowed to dwell on remembered experiences and anticipations, it may become obsessed, like a rich miser whose mind perpetually gets caught on images of his wealth, even whilst he works, plays or sleeps.

What then does Krishna mean, asked MacLaren, by telling Arjuna to have the mind intent on Me, even while he fights? He meant, was the reply, that the private ownership of the mind should be given up, or surrendered, to the one Self. This is not to engage the mind in two places at once, but to allow the will of the Absolute, rather than the *sanskara*, to determine the action. Without the ego there is no question of the mind being divided. It simply becomes the tool of the Absolute.

An illustration was taken from the *Ramayana*. When Rama abandoned his rightful throne and entered the forest, he told his brother Bharata to rule the kingdom. Bharata was reluctant, but he took the wooden sandals of Rama, and placed them in the position of the sovereign. With this token of the true kingship ever before him, he ruled as regent. Any private claim to the throne was surrendered.

A more commonplace example was added. The owner of a business may do little or nothing; yet he takes full responsibility for it. This leaves the manager free to deal with all the day-to-day matters, using his talents to the full. He devotes his efforts to the service of the proprietor, free of the pressure of carrying the final burden. Likewise, we are all managers, and should leave the Lord to take care of the future. This is the sense in which one is not the doer.

Discussing control of mind naturally led on to a question about resolution or intention – *sankalpa* in Sanskrit. Is that the source of the agitation that diverts the mind? The Shankaracharya replied that it is bad resolutions that create agitation, those arising from personal desires or aversions, like anger, greed or attachments. Good resolutions are conducive to self-realisation. Even these, however, have finally to be surrendered in favour of *nir-sankalpa*, the absence of any resolutions. This last condition is one of following only the will of the Absolute. One has to give up everything. It is like the attitude of a child, whose needs are all cared for by a mother, because the child is incapable of forming intentions. Nature and the *Atman* take care of those with *nir-sankalpa*. This is rare. Most people make many resolutions each day. They should be minimised, so that glimpses of good resolutions may emerge.

A strong good resolution, which is one that has moved beyond the small circle of oneself into a larger circle where others are helped, may last a lifetime. It can be overridden by a new resolution for a good reason, but otherwise it continues until fulfilled. Sometimes imagination may seem to present a *sankalpa* of real substance, in the form of some vision or apparently divine dream, but these are transient. The test of authenticity is submission to reason. A genuine good resolution cannot be lost. If difficulties stand in the way, they will be overcome, even if another lifetime is needed for the work to be completed.

Leon MacLaren asked about his resolution to found the School. That was a good resolution, he was told. Yet it is right to enquire how it may be released. Allow the School to flower of itself. It is not a matter of withdrawing from action; rather of dropping all attachments and desire for results. Actions done for no reward help the whole universe. Create men and women who are strong, and capable of proclaiming with dignity the spiritual message to as many people as possible. They need to be practical people, who combine spiritual knowledge with efficiency, speed and simplicity in action. Such people may give rise to a society that truly values idealism. You have the right also to turn to me, the Shankaracharya added, for it is my duty to work wholly for the cause of spirit.

On hearing of the progress of School students towards a more disciplined and blissful life, the Shankaracharya spoke of the divine world that may be revealed to those who follow natural law, and face up to the obstacles that are presented. The divine world is not external; it exists in oneself. Its qualities belong to the Self, and are revealed by knowledge. In the *Gita* they are enumerated as divine virtues, beginning with fearlessness. As subtle forces they are ever-present, but may be hidden by impediments. Ego expels divinity. So, too, does disparity between thought, word and action.

Although they are beyond the physical world, these subtle forces may be associated with particular locations or organs in the body. For example, creative art results from the regulated use of vision, when a godly power may come to the help of the artist. Musicians often have a sense of such powers playing a part in the creation of harmony and other qualities of sound. Similarly, if the rules of grammar and reason are followed, even the goddess of wisdom may assist the speaker or writer.

Demonic forces prevail in those whose lives are dedicated solely to their own personal ends. These people are distinguished by cruelty, by filthy habitations, by lust and so on. Ravana in the *Ramayana* was such a man. His power came from devotion to Shiva, but he was dominated by sexual desire, and so ignored the rules of civilised conduct. But there is no special race of demonic creatures; they are men of evil character and way of life.

In concluding his remarks on divine and demonic forces, the Shankaracharya gave this reminder: the ultimate sovereign is the Absolute; all derive their power from Him. Knowledge and meditation constitute the royal road to realisation, and any lesser powers are to be served only as a means of access to the ultimate truth

Finally, these conversations dealt with some questions about punishment, transmigration and death. Some students in the School have made a mess of their lives. What are the consequences? What can be done about this? MacLaren referred to some verses in the *Laws of Manu* that implied that fearsome punishments might be incurred after death. There are three possibilities in human life, said the Shankaracharya. Those who are wise practise detachment from their actions, and when they die are united with the *Atman*. Those who practise righteous actions without detachment are rewarded in heaven, but they return after a time to another life on earth. Those who indulge in sensuality, and are attached to evil actions are punished in hell, and also return to earth. Consciousness is the observer of all deeds, so all are recorded. The gods Dharmaraja and Yama are said to be the assessors of good and evil respectively, and through them reward and punishment are meted out.

Yet what the *Laws of Manu* prescribe is more of a warning or deterrent than a literal description. Through reason human beings, unlike animals and lesser forms of life, may come to recognise the choice between good and evil, and the possibility of detachment from both. Even those who have acted wrongly can become free from their sins and the consequences by heartfelt confession and surrender, in which a resolution not to repeat the offence must be paramount. A mass of cotton wool may take years to be collected, but a single match will ignite it, and in seconds it will be reduced to dust. Such is a true resolution.

As for death, the Shankaracharya observed that, like birth, it is never actually experienced. Others tell us of birth and death, but it is not of the Self, only of the body. The *Atman*, consciousness, persists throughout life and beyond, whilst the body passes through the stages of birth, growth, adulthood, decay and death. What is in mind at the moment of death, however, is crucial. Upon that depends the next life. If the mind is exclusively intent upon the Self, or *Atman*, then unity with that is the outcome. If it dwells on things of sense, then it will be born again to a life of sensuality. That moment is a result of what has been practised in the past lifetime. Practice turns to nature. Those who practise wisdom become wise; those who practise virtue or vice become virtuous or vicious.

When discussing good and bad resolutions, the Shankaracharya made the remarkable statement that Leon MacLaren's good resolution to create the School would be supported by a man of *nir-sankalpa*, one who works only for the will of the Absolute. He himself had taken on a good resolution that, through the agency of

Leon MacLaren, the school would reach its full development, and its students would achieve wisdom and serve their nation both practically and spiritually. MacLaren expressed the gratitude of all for this deeply heartening message.

CHAPTER TWENTY-THREE

The Years of Crisis

L IFE IN Britain in the nineteen eighties was turbulent. The turbulence reached at least to the doors of the School of Economic Science. Whilst Mrs Thatcher's Conservative government introduced an extreme form of monetarist Economics, presided over unemployment of three million, fought a successful war in the Falklands, privatised large sections of British industry and had a violent confrontation with the coal miners led by Arthur Scargill, the School was facing virulent criticism in the media. In both cases there were significant reforms. By the time that Mrs Thatcher was ousted in 1990 the doctrines of 'free markets' and of 'small government' had become shibboleths, and permanent shifts towards privately owned public services, like railways and power, were entrenched. Trade unions had been heavily regulated, and the banking system given free rein to create money for any profitable purpose, including buying houses. For the School the new direction was less obvious. It had listened to the criticisms and began, slowly perhaps, to respond to those that were valid.

The School's property holdings underwent substantial changes in 1986. An ex-student generously gave to the School a large country house with 30 acres of grounds at Nanpantan in Leicestershire, together with a fund for conversion and future maintenance. Looking out onto a beautiful heath-land escarpment, this property was a godsend for the provincial Schools especially, though it has been well used by London also. In the same year Stanhill Court was finally vacated, and St Augustine's studios were sold. The facilities at St Oswald's studios were improved.

During the 1980s there were over 1500 students in the London School and about 2000 in the branches. The latter had steadily grown throughout the UK. Many towns had branches under the aegis of the North East, North West, Essex and Guildford Schools, whilst Birmingham, Brighton, Canterbury, Edinburgh, Oxford, Croydon, Southampton and St Albans all offered classes. Activities like music, art, drama, Sanskrit and the Ficino Letters flourished in many of them. Some had bought houses. In general their teaching and development followed closely the pattern set by London, but there were regional characteristics and a variety of leadership that avoided stereotyping. Although constitutionally they remain under the control of the London School, so that appointments require confirmation by the London Executive, their leaders retain a fair degree of freedom of action. An annual conference of provincial leaders takes place at Waterperry. This helps to ensure that the School teaching is fundamentally common to all UK. Schools, and also to meet the increasing need for implementation of new regulations on such matters as health and safety.

All these developments of the School, which included making adequate financial surpluses in most years under the new Treasurer since 1980, James Armstrong, occurred despite a storm that blew up in 1983. Sporadic criticism of the School had appeared here and there in the press in the UK and abroad, but in that year the national newspapers spread alarming stories. A young lady student was having an affair with a man who was not a School member. She was advised by her tutor to break off the relationship. When her partner heard of this he was outraged, and informed the London *Evening Standard*. An investigation began.

Journalists appeared at the headquarters of the Liberal Party, after they had discovered that Roger Pincham, Chairman of the Party from 1979 to 1982 and candidate for the constituency of Leominster, was a leading member of the School. He invited them to a meeting attended by himself and the Secretary-general of the Party. They had a long and open discussion of how Pincham reconciled his membership of the School with his role in the Liberal Party. Following the meeting nothing happened for some while, except for the presence of *Standard* journalists at political meetings in Leominster. Then, on the day before polling for the general election of 1983, the *Standard* published a banner headline and groups of articles about Pincham and the supposedly sinister role that he and the School were playing in infiltrating the Liberal Party. Other School members standing as Liberals in either 1979 or 1983 were mentioned, in seats at Maidstone, East Grinstead, Ealing North, Paddington, Uxbridge and Streatham. On the following day, Pincham's deficit in the poll rose to over nine thousand more than when he had come within six hundred of winning in 1974. The Herefordshire papers had covered the same story as the *Standard*. In the other seats in 1983 no one from the School came anywhere near winning.

Was this a deliberate plot by the right-wing press to discredit the Liberal Party on the eve of the poll? There is no direct evidence of this, only the remarkable fact that the story was published on that day, when it could easily have appeared some while before. Certainly in Leominster it seemed to have a major influence on voting. Pincham himself, however, has said that he would probably have lost in any case, as the tide was running strongly for the Conservatives at the time. Nevertheless his political career was adversely affected by the publicity. Although he later received a CBE, he may have been denied the seat in the Lords that Chairmanship of the Party some-times earns. A complaint to the Press Council by an ex-School friend was not upheld. In the City Pincham's reputation remained intact, but he was obliged to answer awkward questions for some while to come. In 1985 he left the School when MacLaren asked him to take charge of the youth groups, which would have occupied many week-ends, and seriously inhibited both his family and political life. Yet for many years he remained as chairman of the governors of St James' schools, until replaced by Jeremy Sinclair. With MacLaren he stayed on the best of terms, and never ceased to admire his character and achievements.

Any appearance that the School was trying to infiltrate the Liberal Party can be easily explained. The School's Constitution expressly forbad political activity by the School or by members on its behalf. But nothing did or could prohibit members from engaging in poli-tics on their own account. It would be surprising for an organisation over three thousand strong, of largely middle-class people, not to contain some political activists. Moreover, the School had taught a radical form of Economics for over forty years, together with other subjects, like Law, History and indeed Philosophy, that impinge on political thought. What Pincham calls 'high Liberalism' of the variety followed by the old Liberal Party of J.S. Mill, Gladstone and Asquith had a powerful appeal to people with such a background. Leon MacLaren himself was certainly a Liberal of that type. Hence those who were politically inclined were quite likely to be Liberals. A few School friends of Pincham had helped him in Leominster, but their meagre political capacities belied any idea of a plot! In fact, particularly since the growth of Social Democracy and the emergence of a new, more populist kind of Liberal Democrat Party, many School members have probably grown more conservative in their views. Moreover, there has always been within the School some support for all the main political parties. Andrew MacLaren, of course, was a long-standing member of the Labour Party. David Boddy, the present headmaster of St James' Senior Boys School, had an earlier career in Conservative Party central office, with every prospect of greater political success, until he chose to leave politics. Any suggestion of infiltration of Parties is no more than the musings of conspiracy theorists.

Unfortunately for the School, politics was by no means the sole area where criticism surfaced. Other national newspapers had published stories. By 1984 two journalists connected with the *Standard* produced a book called *Secret Cult*, claiming to be a full exposé of the inner workings and influence of the School. This did not achieve a wide circulation, but it naturally attracted readers amongst people joining the School or seeing its advertisements, as well as those who had left. In general it interpreted the evidence in favour of its main thesis that the School was a cult. For example, the School rule regarding measured sleep is simply 'to get up when you wake up'. This was interpreted throughout the book as 'sleep deprivation'. On the other hand, there were some telling criticisms and genuine examples of distress following upon School membership.

In some cases churches spoke out against the School. This usually occurred when dissatisfied ex-students sought advice or consolation from clergymen. The Bishop of Woolwich, Michael Marshall, from his earlier experience as a vicar in central London, used strong language to condemn the School, but his reference of it to the Archbishop of Canterbury got no response. The Quakers stopped the School from using their Euston Road meeting house. The Dean of St Albans notified the Church of England General Synod of the press reports. When the Synod referred it to the Board of Mission and Unity, Peter Green corresponded with them. Not all church involvement was critical. Some churchmen, like Father Hewitt, vicar of St Augustine's, Kensington, supported the School. Many students have remained churchgoers.

A sub-committee had been set up consisting of Green, Armstrong, Debenham, Boddy (as press officer) and Leslie Blake, a barrister and leader of the Law group. David Boddy, in particular, did sterling work dealing with all press matters. They discussed with Leon MacLaren whether legal action should be taken against the *Standard*, but counsel advised them that, since the whole matter was already in the public domain, there was little chance of gaining an injunction against further publications. A further difficulty was that if there was a case to bring for libel, the libelling had been against individuals.

Undoubtedly there were examples of people who had become seriously disturbed during their time in the School, even to the point of having nervous breakdowns. To what extent these were a result of their School experiences, however, must remain an open question. Often outside circumstances, such as family relationships or careers, were difficult. Some people had mental or health problems that were in no way connected with School membership. When they sought help from School tutors, the advice given may sometimes have exacerbated the situation, but there have been a great deal more cases where tutors' help has been much appreciated. Probably the most common complaint concerned marital or sexual relationships. The School was blamed for the break-up of marriages. A statistical point made by Peter Green in a letter to the *Standard* is relevant here. He said that about fifty thousand students had attended School courses since their inception. In the social conditions of Britain of that period, how many of them would have experienced marital problems with or without being members of the School?

Nevertheless there were individual cases that did highlight a tendency needing correction. Senior students in particular were expected to carry out School duties, even at the inconvenience of themselves and their families. Up to a point this was a necessary requirement of an organisation that depended almost entirely on voluntary work. The range of activities in the School, including residentials, special studies like Sanskrit, Art in Action and the mere manning of regular classes required many days and hours of students' time. Yet these demands had tipped over into expecting School needs to take precedence over more or less everything else, even attending births, funerals, anniversaries and other major family or social events. This was particularly serious where children were concerned. Some families made very elaborate arrangements to share childminding with other students, but the frequent absence of parents could not be entirely made good. When only one partner was in the School, the problem was different. Resentment at being left alone was perhaps inevitable in some cases. The lighter side of this was shown in a newspaper cartoon pinned up on a School notice board. It showed a husband returning home after a day's work to find a note on the kitchen table saying, 'Gone to Philosophy class. Your dinner is unreal.'

For a brief period Leon MacLaren tried to follow the words of the Shankaracharya concerning marriage, where he spoke of the Indian practice of parents' selecting marriage partners for their children. The Shankaracharya gave a rational explanation of this, pointing out, for example, that parents have the experience to judge the background, character and financial prospects of a future partner. MacLaren obviously saw the merits of such a system, when compared with the common Western practice of relying almost entirely on the often immature emotional choice of the young people themselves. 'Being in love' was probably not a concept that appealed to him. He may have overstepped the mark, however, in taking upon himself the task of giving 'parental' advice. Very few marriages were influenced in this way, whilst one or two that were proposed foundered on the opposition of the people concerned. It was a short but unhelpful attempt to correct one of the many failings of contemporary British society.

All this was an aspect of the general practice of obeying what the School leader and the tutors under his authority asked of students. Discipline has always been a central tenet. Without it there can be little progress in the search for enlightenment. But the aim has always been self-discipline. To what self is the discipline due? Not, says the School, to the wayward self that is subject to desire and the claims of the world, but to the one Self, the *Atman*. The School offers guidance to students, until the authority of the *Atman* itself is clearly recognised. There is obviously a danger here that the individuals concerned, the leader and tutors, might appear to be infallible. Probably an aura of infallibility did surround Leon MacLaren. It may have extended to some tutors also. This was a mistake. Yet it has not changed the fact that for most of the time obedience to the School has been right and beneficial for most students.

Dorine van Oyen made a significant comment about School discipline, when she wrote:

Perhaps there should have been a more careful screening of people before they were subjected to the stricter disciplines.[1]

She also suggested that the advertisements for the introductory course could have indicated more clearly that habitual patterns of life would come under scrutiny.

What the *Secret Cult* emphasised most was 'destroying the personality'. In a sense this is correct, but once more the language used concealed the real point. The Shankaracharya's teaching is to replace action centred upon the *ahankara* or ego with action centred on the Self or *Atman*. The mind is then freed from the impediments that arise from the ego, particularly those based on personal desire. The personality is not so much destroyed as seen for what it is – a *persona* or mask – that can be seen through. Its proper function as a means of performing the various roles that we all need to play in life can then be established. Probably for some students the removal of impediments that have developed into hardened habits over many years seems too much to ask. The School may have been wrong to insist that they should be removed. But, of course, no actual force was used. The whole teaching of the School is by word of mouth. Anyone can walk away from a School meeting or event at any time. Some do!

Questions remain, however, about those who leave. For some while Leon MacLaren expected School members to ignore those who had left. This austere rule gradually fell into oblivion, largely through non-observation of it. He hoped that it would be a means of getting leavers to return, when they found what they were missing, including the company of old friends and fellow students. Some have returned, but on balance the ostracism of leavers, when it was followed, caused more trouble than it was worth. Few students were prepared completely to avoid long-standing friends. Those who were ignored were often resentful, rather than contrite. In the case of marriages, if one partner left, the logical conclusion was separation! Fortunately marriage proved stronger than the rule.

These aspects strengthened the critics' view that the School was a secret cult. They had already identified a cult as a body that gave unquestioning obedience to a leader, that made excessive demands on its members, that destroyed the personality and that used techniques like sleep deprivation. A key feature, they added, was secrecy.

1 Dorine Tolley, *The Power Within*, p.205.

Once again this was true in one sense and not in another. There was no attempt to make the whole project secret. Indeed thousands of advertisements went up every term on the London Underground and elsewhere. The School buildings are in conspicuous places in London and the provinces. No one was told to keep attendance at the School a secret. At the same time there was, and is, a rule that students should not speak outside the School of what is said within group meetings. This harks back to Ouspensky's view of the teaching, but also follows the simple principle embodied, for example, in the Chatham House rule for political meetings that protects speakers from public exposure of what is said in private. It would be quite wrong, and also inhibiting, if what students choose to say in their Philosophy groups were freely transmitted to all and sundry. Part of the problem of 'secrecy' has perhaps been the fact that many students have interpreted this rule too strictly to mean that one should not say anything about the School at all. This is certainly a misinterpretation, since students are also strongly encouraged to bring friends along to join the classes. Indeed this has been a major source of new enrolments over the years.

What turned out to be the most vulnerable target for criticism by the media was the children's schools. Roger Pincham's Chairmanship of the Governors provided an easy trail for the investigators, from the School to its interests in education. Here they settled on a few main aspects. Firstly, they asked, had parents been told of the connection with the School? The answer was somewhat ambivalent. It had usually been mentioned at interviews, but often by referring to the School's ownership of the premises used, such as Chepstow Villas or Queen's Gate. If parents asked about a connection, they were told. If not, the full extent in terms of staffing and curriculum was not made explicit. Of course, this was not an easy matter, since the philosophical nature of the whole project could not be readily made available to parents who had no experience whatsoever of it. Each subject was given a philosophical basis and introduction, such as the nine elements in the case of the sciences. Sanskrit invocations were used in assemblies. Pausing preceded and followed lessons. This was not a serious problem at the beginning, because all the parents were member of the School. As time passed, some left and new parents were increasingly not members. More could have been done to explain to newcomers what kind of education was being offered. In some cases parents of children who had not settled down well, for a variety of reasons, including their own personal difficulties, blamed this upon what was largely a failure in public relations.

The standard of teaching was also criticised. Most teachers were well qualified and experienced, but there were some who came from other occupations. This led to a certain lack of professional techniques, usually made good quickly enough. A few teachers were over-zealous, from very good motives, which led to excessive expectations and sometimes to unfair punishment. The idea that every child is an embodiment of the Absolute or *Atman*, excellent in itself, occasionally was taken to mean that the child could perform wonders in such matters as mathematics, Sanskrit or cross-country running. This was an unfortunate *non sequitur*.

More serious perhaps was an attitude by the head teachers and staff, stemming from the view of Leon MacLaren, that parents were not to be consulted a great deal on the education of their children. This view was not much at variance with that of many traditional independent schools of earlier times, but by the 1970s the idea of parent participation was making headway. Reinforced by a belief that many parents would not appreciate the special philosophical nature of the education, any failure to consult was likely to cause trouble from a vociferous minority. The public criticism of 1983 fed this. Most parents were well content with the schools' performance. Those who were not could now claim that their participation had been denied. In fact, there had been regular invitations to parents to all kinds of events, like concerts, plays and open days, together with termly reports that were exceptionally thorough, but these did not satisfy those demanding, for example, that the Schools introduce parent governors.

There were parents also who objected to meditation, which was introduced rather early – at the age of ten – those who adopted their teenage daughters' horror of long skirts; and other minor bones of contention. Most damaging, however, was the criticism of the discipline at the schools. At first corporal punishment by teachers was allowed, but this was restricted very soon to the head teachers only. The use of the cane at the two senior boys' schools caused most trouble. Once more they were only following a practice commonplace a generation before, but public opinion had changed significantly, and the cane was now prohibited in all State schools and some independent ones. Nicholas Debenham and Julian Capper both thought that on principle caning was useful to deal with serious offences, like lying, cheating and bullying. Particularly in St Vedast, it was in response to a small core of persistent offenders, some of whom should not have been there in the first place. All the schools were reluctant to turn pupils away, not just for financial reasons but because they genuinely wanted to offer a special education to all-comers. When both headmasters publicly defended the use of the cane, they became somewhat identified with this. Such an image was a travesty of what they really stood for. Yet again the problem was partly one of public relations.

Within a year or two, as a result of the adverse publicity, the two St Vedast Schools were forced to close through lack of pupils. They had borne the brunt of the criticism, probably because they had a higher proportion of non-School families. Some parents chose to transfer their children to St James' Schools. Several teachers also transferred; others had to find new teaching posts outside. St James was to suffer more later, when the problem re-emerged after a decade.

Whatever the journalists and others may have said or written about the children's schools, two facts are incontrovertible. The intentions of the governors, head teachers and staff were, and remain, to aim at the best possible education in the fullest sense of the word for the children in their charge. And, secondly, the vast majority of the young people coming out of the schools have been admirable in character, well informed, in good health and fully able to meet the demands of the modern world, including their next step into further education or a career.

The *Secret Cult* was not all gloom and doom. There were interviews recorded with ex-students of the School who admitted gaining much from their attendance. Some comments from the authors proved useful; for example, that in hiding from publicity the School made 'secrecy' its worst enemy. Other points were amusing, such as the description of young men at Art in Action all wearing dark suits, collars and ties and lurking behind bushes with two-way radios. These were the rather amateur team of students dealing with security. (Thieves have been a genuine problem at the event.)

The trouble of the early 1980s spread to some UK branches and to Schools abroad. Especially hit by criticism were Holland, Ireland, New Zealand and Toronto. Students left and enrolments fell away. In London numbers were similarly reduced for a while. *The Independent* and others refused to take School advertisements. Newspaper articles and the *Secret Cult* remained available, especially for new students curious to know more about the School. They received what can only be described as a heavily biased account. Even where the information was correct, it gave a false impression by omitting to refer to the valuable achievements of all the Schools in so many areas, and the testimony of thousand of students who would thoroughly recommend what they have understood and experienced.

Leon MacLaren had refused to be interviewed by the press. He took the view that the School should not respond to criticism, and quoted a letter of Ficino that referred to critics of his Florentine Academy as 'fleas'! After holding a meeting of the Monday evening groups to tell them of his attitude, MacLaren left Peter Green with the unenviable task of doing the same on the remaining four evenings! As always the Principal fulfilled his duty impeccably. Indeed, he showed remarkable steadiness and balanced judgment throughout the public relations crisis.

In fact, much was learnt during this difficult period. Despite his apparent insouciance, MacLaren took the criticism seriously enough to ask the Shankaracharya about it on his next visit to India. The answer – as always – was unexpected and illuminating. Treat it as a shot across the bows, and practise detachment. These were valuable instructions. The School began to look at the practices that had caused alarm in some quarters, such as ostracising those who left and not informing outsiders of what the School stood for. Tutors in general became more open and friendly, and less like the sentinels of righteousness that some had become. By and large the School became a happier place to be. It was a trifle ironic that this was at a time when the world was still being misinformed that it was a dangerous cult.

Roger Pincham summed it all up in his a letter to the *Evening Standard*, published as an appendix in the *Secret Cult*:

> Your people have not stumbled across a collection of battered and brainwashed lunatics but a body of generally respectable and respected people who have learned the value of sensible discipline, and choose to find time to study and work and think and converse together in common cause.[2]

The nineteen eighties were a time of stirring events for the School, as they had been for the Britain of Margaret Thatcher.

---

2 Roger Pincham, *Secret Cult*, Lion Publishing, 1984, p.287.

Meanwhile the School had continued quietly to hold classes, including a new Ethics course run by James Armstrong. Peter Watson became the General Secretary of the Fellowship in 1988. In the same year a loan of £5,000 was sent to India to help Jaiswal found a new children's school.

CHAPTER TWENTY-FOUR

Liberal Studies

A MOST valuable impetus was given to the work of the School by the formation in the early 1970s of youth groups and study groups for young people of about eighteen to the mid-twenties. These were led by Michael Nash and James Armstrong respectively. Their function was once rather crudely summed up, probably by an ex-member, as 'Mr Nash kicks their backsides, Dr Armstrong feeds their minds, and the School takes them to the realisation of their true nature.'

Michael Nash, as an ex-sergeant in the British army, was well fitted for his task. He did not hesitate to berate the students who attended the Saturday classes for any unpunctuality, sloppiness, laziness, greed or bad manners; nor, of course, for more serious offences like drug-taking. He even forbad any partiality towards favoured partners during School functions, explaining this on the grounds that it was unfair on those excluded. Yet his somewhat robust treatment was rarely devoid of reason and good humour. Much effort went into getting these young people, who came from a society in which standards of behaviour were in transition, to see the reason for the rules that he imposed. Why should you expect to enjoy a clean, comfortable house, if you do not first work to create it? Why should you receive a grant for your education that is paid from the work of others, if you do not give something in return? How can your life be well ordered, if each day is not properly measured out? Nash usually found that positive responses were forthcoming.

He also gave some substantial grounding in principles that were largely omitted from the education of his charges. They read Plato, Shakespeare and Blackstone. They drew straight lines and circles at calligraphy boards. They studied Vedic mathematics and practised sounding pure vowels. In the main, all this was received with a ready appetite. Nash himself developed a keen interest in British cultural history, which gave rise to some useful questions for the youth groups. What was one doing about the lives of future generations? The common law was the work of a thousand years, Parliament of seven centuries. What will my short life have served? Economics was given some precedence, especially the ideas of a natural hierarchy in humanity and of economic duties owed to others and to society. And what are the causes of poverty and of oppression? Good questions for an age group that experienced the 'Winter of discontent' and the coal miners' strike.

Outstanding examples of the work of the youth groups were two major events. At St Augustine's church in Kensington they performed Vivaldi's 'Gloria', and at Sadlers Wells theatre a 'Celebration of Youth', including piano and choral pieces, songs by Flanders and Swan, a shortened version of *Macbeth* and a piper playing 'Scotland the Brave' in honour of Leon MacLaren.

'Whatsoever a man soweth, that shall he reap' was a favourite text of Michael Nash. At the same time he was keen that his students should succeed in life. He typically described the aim of the youth groups as 'the intention of this organisation is not to fit you with crutches but with skates.' Here you will learn that which is vital to your future life. If nature has suited you to be a bus driver, then be the best bus driver. If you are to be a judge, then be the wisest of all judges. One wonders how Donald Lambie, a member of the youth groups, saw such advice!

From the somewhat martial tutelage of Michael Nash, the young people progressed to the more academic care of James Armstrong, an Honorary Fellow of Harris Manchester College, Oxford. The single instruction he had received from Leon MacLaren was 'to get them to think'. This he proceeded to do with considerable energy and ingenuity. Courses on ethics, reason, dialectic and geometry, all of which were related to his activities in the School itself, were developed for their benefit. Often he would enthuse a student whose own course at university was found to be disappointing. Only too often the principles of a subject were strangely omitted, and Armstrong was quick to notice this, and to offer a source or formulation that filled the gap. His long-term aim was to help in the creation of a new university, based upon the fundamental principles that the teaching of Advaita was bringing to light, but this was not to be attained, at least within his lifetime.

A parallel development of groups for young people began in South Africa in 1978, when Leon MacLaren was in Johannesburg during his annual tour of overseas Schools. Inspired by his teaching, some young teenage ladies asked him the following year to help them practice spiritual work in their daily lives. He devised a ceremony of commitment, which he later referred to the Shankaracharya, and a special group was formed. The intention was to offer them a foundation for life. Soon afterwards some young ladies in the London School asked to follow suit. Ian Mason, who accompanied MacLaren on his world tour for several years, was put in charge of them, and a close connection with the Friday group (see pages 307-8) was established when this new foundation group began acting as a service team for them. MacLaren wrote the material for the young ladies, and continued to take a close interest in their progress. One member, Catherine Thomlinson, has recently become headmistress of St James' Junior Schools. Ian Mason remained in charge for about twenty years. He was succeeded by Oliver Saunders and then by Martin Kettle.

A similar foundation group was led by Donald Lambie and Suzanne Woods from its inception, until it, too, was handed over to Martin Kettle. Both foundation groups then began to recruit especially pupils who had attended St James' Schools. After Michael Nash retired from taking the youth groups, the foundation groups were then opened to anyone in the School between the ages of about seventeen and twenty-four. They have met weekly to hear the introductory Philosophy courses and also special material, written recently by Christine Lambie. The ground covered has included 'Relationships', 'Finding Direction', 'Secrets of Success' and 'Meditation'. Kettle has adapted the style of meetings to suit his charges; for example, by having freer discussions in which pairs of students talk together and then report back to their group. An annual Foundation Week is held at Waterperry, and an International Youth Week every two years has been located as far afield as Niagara and Sydney.

The dialogues of Plato have been an essential ingredient in the School Philosophy material from the beginning. Witness the early enthusiasm of Kenneth Jupp! A Platonic input remains in courses throughout the School. For example, the view of beauty as a fundamental Idea or Form beyond empirical observation, as depicted in the *Symposium*, is a prominent feature of the Part One course. Also, Plato's conception of government, particularly of the degenerate movement through stages from aristocracy to tyranny, has been presented many times in Economics and Law courses. His whole philosophical outlook, exemplified in the 'analogy of the cave' in the *Republic*, that a transcendent or noumenal world lays behind or within the world of phenomenon accords naturally with the teaching of Advaita.

Groups have studied Plato texts for some years under the leadership of Will Rasmussen and then John Meltzer. English translations have been used, but help is occasionally obtained from Greek scholars both within and outside the School, notably from Professor John Dillon of Trinity College, Dublin. Generally the method has been to read a dialogue together, and then to discuss its meaning and implications in depth. Each year a Plato day has been held at a Cambridge College, with guest speakers from universities and the School. These have given a major stimulus to the work, one fruit of which has been a comprehensive ten year project to translate the whole of Plato's works into English, undertaken by a senior member of the School in Ireland. For such an ambitious task he has, of course, sought assistance from other group members when required. Platonic studies in the Dublin School provide a very strong backing for his efforts.

Yet another aspect has been the intricate study of Platonic solid geometry carried out, especially by Dr James Armstrong, as early as the 1970s. By examining the angles made by radii at the centre of each of the five regular polyhedrons, Armstrong gave a thorough account of their structure. From this he developed a system of three-dimensional geometry that he believed should replace the Euclidean system in mathematical education. This contributed to the establishment of mathematics in St James and St Vedast Schools, of which Armstrong was a governor. Clearly such geometry has important implications also in such fields as architecture and engineering, his own profession.

In 1994 some students became interested in the question, 'Is Advaita in harmony with the Judeo-Christian tradition?' This was clearly an important issue, both for the School itself and for its relationship with society in general. Study groups were formed under the leadership of Rosemary Cox. There are now ten small groups, which meet together at least once a year to share the insights gained. Each group reads texts aloud, with the emphasis on listening 'beyond the familiar', investigating key words, and speaking of any practical experience of the meaning. A wide range of sources have been used, including the Tyndale and King James' Bibles, the Gospel of Thomas, Philo of Alexandria, Origen, Maimonides and Paramahansa Yogananda's commentaries on the Gospels. New Testament Greek has been studied also.

In the Old Testament the Pentateuch and the Prophets have been seen especially as a source of moral principles, whilst in the Psalms such clear statements of Advaita as 'Be still, and know that I am God'[1] have recalled the original question of the study. There was research into the historical and geographical conditions of Israel prior to the birth of Christ. The idea of His dual nature as Man and God has led to an appreciation of the meaning of Him as Son of Man (Humanity) and Son of God (Absolute). St John's Gospel has been a fruitful source of references to Advaita, such as:

> That they all may be one; as thou, Father, art in me, and I in thee, that they also may be one in us.

From this study a confidence has been established that the Judeo-Christian tradition provides the moral teaching for a righteous life, at the same time as being founded upon the principles of Advaita. This conclusion is summed up in a quotation from the Gospel of Thomas:

> Cleave the wood, I am there;
> Lift up the stone and you will find me there.

Another field explored by James Armstrong was that of Ethics, in which he created a public course. He analysed the subject under four headings: duties implicit in self-consciousness, the ability to care for the creation, the relationship between freewill and duty, and decision making guided by the context and consequences of action. The key to all of these is the use of reason. Hence Armstrong examined what this is and how it is to be found. One of his favourite quotations came from Isaac Newton's rules of reasoning:

> We are to admit no more causes of natural things, than such as are both true and sufficient to explain their appearances. To this purpose the philosophers say that Nature does nothing in vain, and more is in vain, when less will serve; for Nature is pleased with simplicity, and affects not the pomp of superfluous causes.

1 Psalm 46.
2 *John*, 17:21.

The course also looked at value systems, both personal and cultural, how they are formed and how they influence decisions. This was related to the hierarchy of humanity already taught in the Economics course. In particular, ethical views often depend upon theories, opinions and beliefs at the level of a nation, but beyond these are the more powerful forces of integrity and justice. Above all stands wisdom. Armstrong was himself motivated by a desire to see truly educated men and women at the helm of a nation. In many ways in the School, not least in his work with young people, he furthered this aim.

Some time after an Ethics course was introduced, an interesting extension of this occurred, when two businessmen in the School, Paul Palmarozza and Christopher Rees, established a course in Business Ethics. They also wrote a book, *From Principles to Profit*, on the subject. In essence the content had been summed up in a professional oath taken by Palmarozza many years before, when he qualified in the USA as an engineer:

> I believe that my profession requires in its very nature particular sensitivity to moral obligations and to the broadest human welfare and progress, that our world, with its material things and things of the mind and of the spirit, may be a better place to live in.

Such a recognition of moral obligation, the course taught, should be present in all professions. Without it business degenerates into a race for profits, with each person seeking his or her own ends exclusively. There have been many examples recently of unethical behaviour, often by very large firms, causing profound hardship for clients, employees and the public. In one fraud case the defendant said that he knew what he was doing was wrong, but he had not thought that it was illegal!

Should a firm not consider the impact of its policies on all who are affected by them; whether, for example, to provide services to less profitable remote locations, or to care for disabled people who come within its ambit? The engineering industry is a particularly relevant case, for today so many services in, say, telecommunications are so integrated that one fault may bring breakdown to huge numbers of people. The threat of terrorism intensifies this issue. How much would it change company policy, if the welfare of the whole nation were in the minds of directors?

Business Ethics draws on both the Philosophy and Economics

material of the School. Viewpoints, for example, can expand from 'me' to the family, community, nation, mankind and the universe. Palmarozza quoted a graphic statement by Albert Einstein:

> A human being experiences himself, his thoughts and feelings as something separated from the rest – a kind of optical delusion of his consciousness. This delusion is a kind of prison for us, restricting us to our personal desires and to affection for a few persons nearest to us. Our task must be to free ourselves from this prison by widening our circle of compassion to embrace all living creatures and the whole of nature in its beauty.

When an action is for the benefit of others, its quality becomes refined. Even for someone with little authority in a firm, the example of such an action affects colleagues and clients, spreading like a ripple to touch everyone. Need firms see such a principle to be in conflict with making profits? Action on a larger scale, finer work and generosity add to the reputation of a firm. One well known for its integrity does more business, not less. This is not the reason for being honest and truthful, but it is a by-product. Success is necessary for firms; it is not, however, an end in itself.

Several businessmen from all kinds and sizes of firms have been drawn to this course of Business Ethics, and some now form an advance guard, prepared to share experience of how morality may be introduced where it is lacking. This may become a vital element in the School's contribution to the economy, in addition to the long-standing principles of Economics.

A somewhat different field of study arose when Brian Joseph agreed to lead a small group interested in modern academic Philosophy. Starting with Descartes, they have examined leading philosophers of the Enlightenment and beyond. The aim has been to look for some connection with the principles of Advaita – an elusive assignment! – whilst retaining as much objectivity as possible. Amongst significant discoveries, they have noted Spinoza's recognition of absolute unity, Kant's understanding of space and time as 'in us', and his concept of the transcendental unity of self-consciousness, and Wittgenstein's repudiation of a language of private experience. Schopenhauer, in particular, who was acquainted with the Upanishads, was found to express an awareness of the world as appearance and of the self as a substantial reality under the form of will, both of which more or less conform to the Philosophy of

Advaita. How these studies will progress remains very much an open question.

As far back as 1973 a law group was set up by Leon MacLaren, and has since been tutored by two barristers, Leslie Blake and Ian Mason. In his initial address to the group, MacLaren said this:

> This study is about how first principles have been used in English law and how it has worked out. Law is the Will of God and the whole of creation is the manifestation of that Will. Every creature owes its life and its being to that Will. To appreciate this is fundamental to law.

MacLaren had much reverence for the British Constitution, common law and monarchy, all of which he viewed through the eyes of Philosophy. For example, he saw that the law of three applies throughout the system as Queen, Lords and Commons; legislature, executive and judiciary; claimant, defendant, judge, and so on. He appreciated the subtlety with which the common law advanced human freedom over the centuries; and, of course, knew of the hierarchy in humanity that reflected the law of seven.

At the same time his critical appraisal was turned on the difference between civil and economic freedom. He saw that the latter had been thwarted by landed interests, using the power of government through Parliament to protect a stranglehold of land monopoly that impoverished the great majority of the population. Self-government, as the outcome of freedom, he insisted, was the best form of government.

Whilst concentrating on principles, the law group has also spent some time on discussing their application to current legal issues. These have ranged over trade union rights, the law of privacy in relation to the press, the Constitution of Namibia, the reform of the House of Lords, the nature of the European Union, and international law as regards the situations in Kosovo and Iraq. An important aspect has been the contrast between the English principle that the monarch is under no man, but under God and the law, and the rule often prevalent on the continent that what pleases the prince has the force of law. Authorities used have included the scriptures, Plato and the great English jurist, Sir William Blackstone. Books have been written, especially for young people, on the British Constitution, common law and sovereignty.

Natural law has been an essential focus of the law group's

thinking. From this the principle of the common law, that law is discovered not made, has been emphasised. Recently the group has looked at the way in which ancient peoples, including those who survive today, have retained their understanding of natural law. With Ian Mason's initiative, the group has visited African communities to study this. Amongst them they found the concept of 'earth jurisprudence', a 'philosophy of law which approaches law and law-making from the standpoint that the primary source of law is nature, particularly, though not exclusively, the planet Earth.' Such a fresh look at the concept of law accords well with the founding purpose of the School.

Soon after Kenneth Verity wrote a book of sonnets in 1973, following Shakespearean form but drawing on philosophical concepts for meaning, Leon MacLaren appointed him to take charge of a writers' group. Over the years the membership changed considerably, so that any effect it had on students' writing has been difficult to trace. Several books, however, have been produced, together with contributions to journalism, broadcasting and other literary professions. One member, for example, was the art critic of a national newspaper for many years. Another wrote the script of a weekly TV drama.

The method used to elicit creative writing was for the group to be presented with a quotation, statement or idea, to which they were asked to respond in writing in any form they chose. Discussion of the results was often brief but potent. This process yielded anything from a haiku, sonnet or blank verse to an essay, dialogue, short story or even an incipient novel. Such a practice undoubtedly fostered the idea of creating literature that could be, as Leon MacLaren declared, 'the handmaid of Philosophy'.

One of the few specific pieces of advice was that of MacLaren himself – to cut out every unnecessary word. Once when Verity was asked about the social limitations of Jane Austen's field of literature, he gave an analogy: if you shine a light in a small enclosed space, its effect is immensely powerful. Similarly, the seventeen word haiku was a form that both he and the group especially enjoyed. Contrariwise, he himself has written a vast survey of poetry through the ages!

None of these studies were initiated by Leon MacLaren, although usually his advice had played a significant part. Nor has there been any intention of the School deliberately to become a kind of university of liberal arts. Their origins appeared to be the keen interest of a particular student or group of students that had arisen under the stimulus of the Philosophy of Advaita. An insight that penetrated the usually opaque material of modern scholarship and literature had been gained. From this seed a new study was created.

CHAPTER TWENTY-FIVE

The Voice of
the *Atman*

WHEN Leon MacLaren went to India in 1985 to see the Shankaracharya, his account of the criticism received by the School and of the policy of not actively responding to it was met with a reply that gave a new direction. The 'shots' that had been fired may have indicated some impediments within the School that needed examination. But this step could be taken further. The whole way of liberation could be understood as a process of removing impediments. Identifying impediments was a matter of self-examination. That could be seen as the way forward for both the School as a whole and for its individual students.

All impediments arise from *ahankara*, the ego, the Shankaracharya went on. By setting up limits the individual defines his own ego. So the limits need to be seen, and then transcended. They stand in the way of union with the Absolute. Yet they are very attractive. The *Isa Upanishad* even describes the ego as a golden sheath that stands between a man and *Brahman* (referred to here as *Pushan*):

> Between you, O *Pushan*, and me the light of truth does exist, but it remains covered by a golden sheath. I and thou are ultimately the same, but please help me to remove this golden cover, so that I may see the truth of unity.[1]

MacLaren pursued this further by asking about the energy that might be used to meet the needs of the world, if the limits were transcended. The reply used the analogy of channels for the passage of water. They must be clear; the gate must be open. A strong resolution is required to open it, for the gate is *ahankara*. Whilst the gate

1 *Isa Upanishad*, 16, 15.

remains, the individual is barred from realising his unity with *Brahman*; nor can he fully communicate with others. Yet the unlimited source of energy is ever present. Resolution, discipline and self-examination make it available.

Transcending the ego gives the individual access to inner energy, at the same time as enabling him or her to meet the needs of others. But, asked MacLaren, what of the warning of both Krishna and Christ not to give the teaching to those who have no wish to hear it, to those who would trample the pearls of wisdom under their feet? There is no need, replied the Shankaracharya, to open a propaganda front at the crossroads to preach the wisdom of the *Gita*! It is simply a question of opening the treasury of knowledge to those who seek it

Senior students in London were told after this conversation that the *ahankara* must go. Instructions were given to men's and women's groups, but with differing outcomes. The men frequently saw the main impediment as a belief that liberation and full consciousness were incompatible with earning a living. The women noticed that they always reserved something for themselves, even when seemingly devoted to serving others, including their husbands. When told of this later, the Shankaracharya insisted that observation needed to go deeper, so that the *Atman*, rather than the senses or mind, is the real witness. Then, he added forcefully, reason can clear the decks of the rubbish of impediments. He added a word about the observation concerning women. If something is going to be reserved for oneself, then at least let it be of a *sattvic* nature!

A practice that MacLaren had introduced earlier to some students was reflecting on words from the scriptures, particularly the Upanishads. He now wanted more advice on this from the Shankaracharya. It was confirmed as a valuable practice having two constituents. The first, following on the actual hearing of the words, is allowing the meaning of the passage to resonate in the mind. The second is the absorption of that meaning into the very being of the practitioner. These are known as *mananam* and *nididhyasanam*. Without the latter the words are forgotten, but as part of the being they bring constancy, clarity of mind and much else.

The Shankaracharya gave several examples of suitable passages for reflection from the Upanishads. These included:

Crave to know that from which all these beings take birth, that by which they live after being born, that towards which they move and into which they merge. That is *Brahman*.[2]

Reflection on this may lead to a recognition that all phenomena arise from *Brahman*, are sustained by it, and finally are dissolved in it. This may then be seen in such diverse areas as dawn, daytime and sunset; waking up, daily activity and sleep; and the play of the three *guna* in one's life. Throughout all of these the *Brahman* remains as the constant substratum.

The four *mahavakya*, or great sentences, of the Vedic scriptures were also recommended for reflection. These all assert the identity of the individual and the universal Self, in the form of 'Thou are That', 'This self is *Brahman*', 'I am *Brahman*' and 'Consciousness is *Brahman*'. In a verse, quoted by the Shankaracharya, that contains the second of these, the Self is also identified with 'the witness of all'. MacLaren asked about this last description. This witness watches over the elements, senses and mind, motivating all and yet itself unmoving, he was told. Like the fragrance in earth, the taste in water and the essence of each element, the witness prevails everywhere, in all things. The Shankaracharya then quoted a similar verse in support:

> God, who is only one, is hidden in all beings. He is all pervading and is the inner Self of all creatures. He presides over all actions and all beings reside in Him. He is the witness, the pure consciousness free from the three *guna* of nature.[3]

What MacLaren had already found was that students experience two results in reflection: the illumination of obstacles, and glimpses of the nature of the *Atman*. These both indicate that much more may follow, was the Shankaracharya's comment. There is no limit to the ultimate. Who says he knows knows nothing; who says he does not know is ignorant!

Reflection, he continued, may be on the *saguna* or the *nirguna Brahman*. The former is an incarnation of the Absolute, who may be the object of reflection, so that the disciple partakes of his nature and emulates his life. The latter is the Absolute beyond all creation, devoid of all qualities, pure and unimaginable. Reflection on it is like deep sleep in which all experience of objects has gone, yet with the

2 *Taittiriya Upanishad*, 3, i, 1.
3 *Svetasvatara Upanishad*, 6, 11.

presence of the Self. *Nirguna Brahman* is consciousness without form, the precondition of all manifestation.

A brief analogy followed. Two artists were commissioned to paint murals on opposite ends of a hall. A partition separated their work. One applied undercoat, then drew and painted. The other simply made good any faults in the wall, and then proceeded to do nothing but polish it. After a month the partition was taken down. The two walls showed the same picture, down to the last detail. One artist had completed a physical work; the other had allowed the wall to give a perfect reflection. The painter represents reflection on an incarnation. He seeks the divine qualities, like the nature, name, character, actions and place of the divinity. The other seeks only divinity itself by a kind of negation of all qualities, revealing the divine light itself.

A question from MacLaren about the *Brahma Sutra* led to a far-reaching answer on Advaita. The Shankaracharya's advice was that the *Brahma Sutra* should be studied only after a thorough acquaintance with the *Gita* and the principal Upanishads, as it deals with unresolved problems or apparent contradictions in these scriptures. He went on, however, to discuss the question about creation with which the *Brahma Sutra* begins. Advaita explains creation, not as the emergence of an illusory world from the *Brahman* – for how could illusion arise out of truth? – but as the superimposition of a transitory, ever-changing appearance on an eternal, unmoving reality. Several analogies were offered. A rope appears as a snake. Only the rope exists, even when it is mistakenly being seen as a snake. The creation is a drama, in which all the characters, good and bad, have equal status in so far as none are real. Waves on the surface of the ocean have no independent existence; they are just a form of the ocean.

A profound explanation followed that had a strong bearing on the challenging 'problem of pain' that so occupied the Buddha and other great teachers. Pain and pleasure, suffering and worldly happiness, may be both known and experienced. Yet the knowledge may be present without the experience, as when a doctor knows that a patient is in pain without he himself experiencing it. The Self knows pain and pleasure, but has no experience of them, for they are only in the body and mind. Were this not so, then a person under an anaesthetic would still experience the pain, for the Self is beyond anaesthesia. In fact, only the body and mind, where the pain lies, become unaware of it, and this is sufficient. In terms of language, knowledge is embodied in the word, and experience in the meaning of the word. The word 'lion' causes no trouble, but the meaning, the lion itself, does! The Self as consciousness is formless, and therefore cannot have experience that depends upon form.

The Shankaracharya quoted a verse from the *Gita* that illustrated this explanation:

> 'I do nothing at all,' thus would the truth-knower think, steadfast –
> though seeing, hearing, touching, smelling, eating, going, sleeping,
> breathing, speaking, letting go, seizing, opening and closing the eyes
> – remembering that the senses move among sense-objects.[4]

Only the ignorant man, he added, acts as though everything were real and true. As a result he has no chance of escaping from involvement with pleasure and pain, and the worries that go with them. One way of dealing with pain is to replace the thought or feeling with another that is pure. Better still is complete detachment. The *Atman* never suffers. In Advaita one simply watches everything as it is. Others may be helped, if one joins in the drama but plays the part without attachment to it. The drama is all *prakriti* or nature, and in itself causes no stress whatsoever.

Later the Shankaracharya related this concept of drama or illusion to the states of waking, dreaming and sleeping. In all three the *Atman* as witness is present, even in deep sleep, as we imply when we say, 'I slept blissfully, but I do not remember anything.' Error creeps in, however, when an image of the witness appears in the *buddhi*. Then we think that this imaginary witness experiences all the situations that occur in any of the states – that it is I who really am awake, in a dream, or in deep sleep. In reality I, the Self, has no change of state whatsoever. I am not the experiencer or enjoyer, any more than I am the doer. The image of the witness is a pretender; he is the ego. Hence the ego – *ahankara* – must go! The real witness is one. If there appear to be many witnesses, then this must be a mistake. There is no individual acting as witness, for the single witness is the *Atman*, which is the Self in all creatures, presides over all actions and exists in everything.

Yet another approach to the concepts of illusion and reality was taken when MacLaren asked about the *hita* nerve that is referred to

4 *Bhagavad Gita*, 5, 8-9.

in the *Brihadaranyaka Upanishad*. This, said the Shankaracharya, is the
location of all forms of dream or imagination. They may arise in
several ways – from sight, feeling or drugs, for example – but all are
stored as past impressions, including those from previous lifetimes,
in the *hita*. When they emerge as later experience in dreams and
imaginations, they can all be categorised as ignorance. Only the
subject that observes them, the *aham*, is real. This, however, is by no
means the end of the story. In truth the whole creation is an expression of dreams.

This sweeping conclusion was further explained. On waking from
a dream, one regards the waking state as reality, and looks back on
the dream as an unreal world of imaginary things and events. So, too,
ordinary life, the world of the waking state, is really another dream
that appears to last much longer, but has little duration when seen
from the standpoint of reason. For it is reason that reveals the
unreality of life, by showing that the only reality is the witness or
observer of it. Even transmigration, the movement from one life to
another, is no more than a dream. The *Atman* goes nowhere in time
or space, for it contains time and space. Where could it go?

MacLaren asked how one might see the world so differently. The
answer gave rise to a new and fruitful practice in the School, when it
was later introduced to senior groups. A realised man does not
recognise differentiating qualities as marks of cognition. In him
such impressions do not arouse the emotions or desires that govern
the lives of others. The only identity that he recognises is that of
consciousness or *aham*. A practice that may lead to this knowledge,
to the awakening of reason, is twofold. It consists of *vyatireka*
and *anvaya*, or what in the West could be loosely called analysis and
synthesis.

One begins with the fundamental question, 'What am I?'
Vyatireka then proceeds with the systematic elimination of one
element after another –'Am I the element earth?' and so on, until the
final 'element', consciousness itself, is reached. That is indeed the
Self or I. Having established this, one goes through the process of
synthesis, or *anvaya*, which brings back the elements to their true
place, as no more than forms of this one consciousness. In conclusion, the whole creation may be seen for what it really is, no more
than *maya*, the manifestation of *Brahman* in time and space, 'an
expression of dreams'. The Shankaracharya further remarked that
the whole process could also be seen as a movement through the five

sheaths given in Sankara's *Crest Jewel of Wisdom*, namely body, breath, mind, intelligence and blissfulness. Leon MacLaren was later to devise a practice in which a passage from the *Gita* was taken as the subject matter.

In these conversations the question of verification of the teaching was raised. There are four criteria for ensuring that knowledge is genuine, said the Shankaracharya. They are adherence to scripture (*sruti*) and to other sacred or inspired works (*smriti*), such as the *Gita* or the *Puranas*; the assent of a self-realised teacher; and recognition by the individual based on his or her own experience. Scripture is the Veda, the revealed knowledge that has no trace of individual authorship and is true for all time. The purport of the Upanishads and of the Gospels is Veda. *Smriti* usually have a known individual author, such as Valmiki of the *Ramayana*, whose writing retains signs of individuality whilst being universal in scope. The *mahapurusha*, or teacher; is especially available in the present, and may resolve apparent difficulties or inconsistencies. He makes the meaning of the sacred literature intelligible – in a way that the Shankaracharya himself clearly exemplified. Finally the acknowledgment by the aspirant of the truth of a judgment or decision must complete the verification. Without this there is doubt. Yet this last step does not validate the others. They state the truth of the matter; the doubt arises in the individual's mind, and reflects his honesty or his ignorance. Free will depends upon this personal assent, or *anubhuti*. Only after it takes place can the individual proceed with confidence. The Shankaracharya added later that the final judgment must include logical correctness and agreement with cause and effect. Reason is the key to this completion of verification. If it is based on devotion alone, for example, this may lead to problems later.

A question related to verification was asked by Leon MacLaren on behalf of a scientist in the School. How should a science teacher deal with the description of the universe as given by the circle of nine points, in view of modern scientific knowledge? The answer recalled what the Shankaracharya had said earlier on the same subject. Scientists treat empirical tangibility as a measure of certainty, ignoring the fact that certainty itself cannot be established empirically. He now said more. They use only the three tangible elements, and leave out all the rest. The other five can only be recognised by metaphysics, explained through language and Philosophy. Until scientists accept the presence of metaphysical elements they cannot proceed further.

Hence they can never find out how creation comes about, nor how emotion has a place in it. Nor does duality of mind and matter enable a comprehensive system to be established. The four elements of mind – *manas, buddhi, chitta* and *ahankara* – are used all the time; yet they cannot be verified by empirical instruments. Hence one turns to the authority of the scriptures or to inference. Analysis of the circle of nine points would yield the certainty that every scientist desires.

On the subject of knowledge the Shankaracharya spoke of the need for transformation of body, mind and heart, so that they become fit receptacles for the Self. Although the *Atman* is ever-shining, the light of consciousness can be obscured by impurities in the person. For the full measure of its brightness to be evident it needs a fine vehicle, like a jewel in a setting. What may especially bring about transformation is devoted service, which may be a chief feature of work in the School. Meditation also, of course, plays a major part. So too may reason, for by constant rational pursuit of the truth discrimination becomes natural, and the impurity of ignorance is removed.

It is useless to look for the causes of ignorance. How to remove it is the real question. Duality is the worldly condition; even to retain a moment of unity for five minutes is valuable. These moments are like street lamps that are spaced out at intervals. Between them there is sufficient light to move safely.

Atman is pure, conscious and free. It does nothing, but from it the light of knowledge flows out to be available to the *buddhi*. That is the master, not the *Atman*, for it is the *buddhi* that has the power to order the mind and body. It may work according to reason or to create complexity and confusion. *Manas* and the rest are labourers. A vital instance of the master's judgment is in speaking the truth, for that is the expression of *Atman*. Yet sometimes speaking the truth can be harmful to someone, in which case it should be withheld. Often in the world there is also great opposition to the truth. If one persists, even in bitter circumstances, nature will finally give way and lend its support.

In answer to a later question about Jesus extolling the devotion of Mary, who had been berated by Martha for not working at daily tasks, the Shankaracharya gave a warning that devotion in the School must remain essentially to spiritual work. Whilst an organisation is necessary, its needs should not be allowed to override the primary work of the spirit. The moment work on the organisation becomes paramount, the real work is compromised.

MacLaren asked about renunciation. Should School members aim at total renunciation of the world in the pursuit of liberation? Had Sankara enjoined this? This met a very full response, with the introduction of the concepts of *nivritti* and *pravritti*. The former is complete renunciation, retirement from the world with no thought for the results or benefits for others of one's self-discipline and realisation. It is no concern of the follower of *nivritti* if the Sun nourishes the farmer's crop or burns it. All that matters is the Sun of the *Atman*. Very few have followed this severe way. *Pravritti* is participation in the world, which every householder necessarily follows. The way of the School should be *nivritti* through *pravritti*, engagement with the world at the same time as working for liberation. That was the way of such great leaders as Janaka and Rama. Such an injunction was clearly in tune with the original intention of the School in following the teaching of Ouspensky. The Fourth Way of the householder became more defined as *nivritti* through *pravritti*.

Sankara himself was cited as an exponent of this. He had practised *nivritti* to achieve liberation, but had never neglected worldly duties. By discourses, debates, writing and travelling all over India he had won many disciples to Advaita. In setting up the four seats of Shankaracharyas he had ensured the continuance of the tradition. Profoundly intellectual, yet equally compassionate, he had cared for individuals and society alike. When his own mother died, he had ignored the rule for his class of teachers, the *sannyasins*, and attended to her cremation.

In *nivritti* through *pravritti* one applies the universal to the particular. This accorded well with the practices of the School. MacLaren had always insisted on the value of acute attention. Now this was confirmed. Through the precise application of senses and mind to whatever presented itself, the student would be naturally engaged in what the Shankaracharya had prescribed as the way of the School. Internal renunciation is combined with external participation in worldly affairs – in law or art or science, for example. Whilst raising up society is the immediate aim, the ultimate one is liberation. When help is needed it is freely given, but it is not a matter of taking up a mission or looking for opportunities. In the world people may be lost in earning a living or seeking pleasure. The School may bring peace, and remind people of what they truly seek. At the highest level, this is what Krishna means when he says:

> Whatever a great man does, that alone men do; whatever he sets up as the standard, that the world follows.[5]

A modern example of this was given. The first President of India used to recite Vedic hymns at four o'clock every morning in the presidential palace. Some people protested to the Prime Minister, who was a secularist. (India had been founded as a secularist State.) He questioned the President about his partiality for a particular religion. The President replied that he was following the tradition in which he had grown up, which had enabled him to serve the Republic. His duties as President were quite distinct from his personal practices. Fortunately the Prime Minister got some sense of the Vedic tradition, and let the matter drop.

In an earlier conversation the Shankaracharya had said that the School should aim to raise the level of consciousness in the community. MacLaren asked how could this be done. Students in the School, was the reply, by understanding, meditation and service should be able to present themselves in such a way that others are attracted, just as a fine actor with superior speech and emotion may bring people to emulate him. They should be free from the four worldly evils of obsession with sex, uncontrolled anger, greed and showing favour to relatives or friends. By example and by knowledge the desire to realise the Self, which is in fact universal, may be engendered. Those students who are well versed in law, art or science are especially suited to this. They need to have a vision of a glorious future for their subject. The case of the School artists who gave an exhibition at Waterperry of pictures based on scripture, in which they had tried to remove all their own ideas, was approved. Any critical views that were expressed should be considered as possible means of improvement to evolve even better standards.

What can be said about the individual? Any feeling of separate existence brings forth the fear of what may happen in the future. This question elicited a further reference to the elements. Even a mere lump of earth contains, on further examination, all five elements – earth, water, fire, air and space. The subtle elements of scent, taste, form, touch and sound are there also. All these are

5 *Gita*, 3, 21.

universal. Where is the individuality? Each separate thing reflects one single unity, which is the *Atman* itself. Whatever seems to happen to the individual is really happening to universals. So what good or bad thing can happen to an individual? Proper understanding of this eliminates all fear.

This distinction between the individual and the universal appeared in another answer, where the difference between two voices heard in the mind was explained. One is the voice of *ahankara*; the other the voice of *Atman*. Both are heard through the *buddhi*, but the former is affected by worldly sounds, like attachment, hatred or agitation of some kind, whilst the latter is that of a neutral witness. They may be compared with the two birds of the *Mundaka Upanishad*, one enjoying the fruit, the other just watching. Eventually they may converge, leaving only the voice of the *Atman* as the constant guide.

This answer pointed towards the concept a self-realised man. When MacLaren asked a question about *prarabdha*, the Shankaracharya developed the answer in this direction. True enlightenment only happens once, he said, just as a traveller in a desert, on seeing a mirage for what it really is, no longer believes in it. Even in ordinary life, on coming to know a pot we no longer doubt what it is. So, too, *prarabdha*, the situation that confronts us in life at any moment, is really an illusion, existing only in imagination as a result of *sanskara* and present circumstances. On finally waking up to the reality of the *Atman*, this *prarabdha* is destroyed. Its effects in the present lifetime, however, carry on, even though the enlightened man no longer believes them to be true. He meets them with total indifference. Thus he is no longer subject to the passions of anger or hatred, lust or envy and the rest.

Is this self-realisation universal? The Shankaracharya was careful to explain that it was universal in the sense that for the self-realised man his consciousness contains all, like the universal space in which all physical objects exist, but not in the sense that all other people are enlightened simultaneously. When one man awakes from a dream, not all wake up, even though for him who awoke the dream world is there no more. Hence liberation applies to the individual. He it is who knows, feels and acts, and therefore has to work for his own liberation by the dissolution of impediments. Before liberation he thinks of himself as an individual, owing to the imprint on each person's *buddhi* of an image of the *Atman*, which like the reflections of the Sun in pots creates the impression of many, where there is in fact only one. If this image is recognised as an impostor once and for all, then the truth is realised for all time. One is the *Atman*.

The Shankaracharya told a story to illustrate this. A *sannyasin* knocked on the door of a rich man. The man could not be troubled with him, despite the tradition that he should be offered hospitality. When later the man went out to the town, the *sannyasin* transformed himself into the precise form of the man, and called again at the house. The wife, of course, welcomed him. He told her and her children that there was a dangerous impersonator pretending to be himself. If he should come to the house, they should all drive him away. Sure enough, when the man returned, the whole family attacked him and forced him to leave. For a week he was homeless. Then the *sannyasin* went out to meet him, and told him the truth. He would leave, if the man promised never again to turn away a *sannyasin*. The *ahankara* is an imposter. He only leaves when the truth is acknowledged once and for all.

A realised man is unmoved. He is motivated only by the will of the Absolute. He remains the same in pleasure and pain, in praise and abuse, in success and failure. He remains himself. Wisdom is revealed in action. Efficiency, beauty and justice accompany the actions of a wise man. No account can be given of his wisdom; it is by the outward manifestation of it that it is known.

MacLaren asked what happens after realisation. The answer took the ground from under the question. Birth, death, pleasure, pain, purity, impurity, reason, unreason, bondage, liberation and realisation itself are all part of the illusion. All these dramatic events take place in *buddhi* and not in reality. For the real is the *Atman*, and that is alone and unchanging. Ideas of this kind are superimposed, just as a spirit may take possession of a living person. *Buddhi* needs to undo all these complexities, not to liberate that which is already free. The rope never was a snake and never will be.

What then is attracting or drawing out all this effort, asked MacLaren. Injustice has shattered the equity of the *Atman*, was the reply. What is least important is seen as most important. People look for the senses in the body, mind in the senses, intellect in the mind and the Self within the intellect. In truth the complete reverse is the case, for the Self contains them all, and the body is the smallest unit. If things were seen truly, equity would be restored, and thoughts and actions would become just.

Conversations had taken place in 1985, 1987 and 1989. At the end of the first of these the Shankaracharya warned the School against pride in achievements. Detachment is the key to work in the world, for the world is a battlefield, a place of examination that tests the discipline learnt in the School. Have nothing to do with the misery of the world, yet by detachment contribute to undoing it. *Nivritti* through *pravritti* is the way to engage in activities, whilst avoiding danger and difficulty. Keep yourself detached and carry on the work. Four years later the essence of his final message was that spiritual knowledge will never abandon anyone in the dark. It will bring enlightenment and full realisation.

CHAPTER TWENTY-SIX

From Metaphysics
to Medicine

DESPITE its name the School's activities had tended for some while to be artistic or literary rather than scientific. Science teachers had contributed to and learnt from the teachers' group meetings, but there were also other students who had strong scientific interests, with many questions about the bearing that Philosophy had upon modern science. Until the 1990s such questions had, perhaps, been somewhat overlooked.

The Shankaracharya's teaching on the circle of nine points was clearly of great significance. So, too, was his censure of scientists for largely ignoring all but the three tangible elements of earth, water and fire. Confidence in these as scientific evidence in itself confirmed, he said, that there must be some further criterion of certainty, for the tangible elements could not themselves offer proof of their own validity.

With these fundamental words of advice, Leon MacLaren began to meet with a group of School scientists in 1991. They were all mathematics and science teachers at St James' Schools, well qualified and dedicated both to their subjects and to their pupils. For the next ten years they met at first every week and then fortnightly. At the beginning they practised exercises to connect through the senses with the elements. Then they moved on to discrimination between consciousness and what is inanimate; and finally to distinguishing between the gross and the subtle.

One day MacLaren simply asked them what they had to offer. After that they all had to look more seriously into their own interests and research, rejecting commonplace views and developing new insights. Vedic mathematics, music, architecture and many topics in physics, chemistry and biology came within their purview, whilst

MacLaren always brought them back to the standpoint of Philosophy. Occasionally they conducted experiments. The effect, said one scientist, was of liberation, in the sense of being freed from limiting ideas about the world, how it is constituted and the role of scientists themselves. A viewpoint was emerging that could encompass both modern science and Vedantic teaching. Donald Lambie continued with the group in the same vein from 1994. A young scientists group was also formed.

By 1996 the main group was ready to present public lectures. Entitled 'Metaphysics', the series aimed to make the circle of nine points meaningful to a general audience, using a variety of visual aids and demonstrations. These were developed further four years later. Meanwhile three lectures were also given on 'Renaissance and Science', which examined how the modern scientific worldview had evolved from the Florentine Renaissance. Further lectures, enigmatically entitled 'Cloth from Thread, Curds from Milk, Ring from Gold', looked at theories of causality, and how reductionism, evolution and holism can be related to three traditional systems of Nyaya, Sankhya and Vedanta.

'Metaphysics' began with the statement that there is one substance that unfolds in nine states. This substance is consciousness, as referred to in the *Kena Upanishad*:

> That by which one perceives the activities of the eyes, know that alone to be consciousness, not what people worship as an object.

This omnipresence of One is reflected in the generation of numbers by the addition of one at every stage. It is reflected, too, in the one cell from which a complete human being develops. Similarly, each element is one: there is only one water, one light and so on.

In two lies the unmanifest. From a tiny acorn rises the huge oak tree. Where is it in the acorn? Yet from every acorn may arise the very same type of tree, distinct from every other type. For, as the Shankaracharya had said, a law is like a seed, determining all that follows. Here the lecture looked at the chemical analysis of the Sun, given by chemical elements producing lines in the solar spectrum. In a laboratory the same analysis can be reproduced, for the laws are the same.

Nature stands at number three. Here the law of three operates, so that every created thing or event has a threefold character. Everything in nature is governed by the *guna*. Photosynthesis was explained in some detail to illustrate this.

At four the feeling of existence enters, and confronts nature in the realm of mind. Life itself is a series of events, where nature and consciousness appear to meet. Time and space emerge as the twin matrices of experience of the world. This meeting is also the source of energy, or as Heisenberg put it 'the link with the centre' that he discovered on hearing a work of Bach on the violin. Number four can also provide a standpoint, such as that of Mother Teresa, who saw everyone as Christ.

Five is space, which is itself threeold: defined space as in a pot or a cathedral; everyday space in which we draw lines as boundaries, like the walls of a house; and great space, which is immensely big or immeasurably small. Platonic solids give the only possible way of enclosing space equally in all directions. The centre has the knowledge of the form.

Air at six, of course, requires space for its existence. Rather surprisingly, it gives rise to all movement. Sailing boats and steam engines are set in motion by air; so too are birds, whose wings create a pressure differential between air above and air below. Air supports, lends life to things and regulates them. In Vermeer's famous picture of a milkmaid, everything is moving, except the attention given to the stream of milk. Even life is moving.

Number seven – the element fire – is the basic principle of shape. In nature the laws that govern shape often follow from Fibonacci numbers given in the series 1, 1, 2, 3, 5, 8, 13, 21, 34 etc. The ratio between any two successive numbers in the series gets progressively closer to the golden ratio of 1.618 (approximately). Leaves display the golden angle in their development of veins. Beyond this, the Shankaracharya has referred to the light of knowledge that flashes in the mind. What is the light of man, asks the Upanishad. If the Sun has set, it is the moon. If there is no moon, it is fire. If fire is extinguished, it is speech. If there is no speech, it is the Self.

Shapes have limits. A shape creates a boundary, and a bond works through this. Water is the bonding element. At this point the lecture gave examples of the complicated yet elegant bonds formed in molecules of glucose or amino acids. But water also dissolves things. How does it do this? Once more this power comes from its bonding nature, for it forms bonds with something electrically charged, and these are stronger than the bonds that are broken. Einstein thought that there is a binding force that links all things. Jesus spoke to the woman of Samaria of water that would be a well springing up into eternal life. For water, as the Shankaracharya said, is also love. A member of the audience quoted Shakespeare: 'The quality of mercy is not strained; it droppeth as the gentle rain from heaven.'

What then finally is number nine? It is earth, the perfect element, the glorious end of creation. From it comes food, shelter, metals, whatever enables mankind to live on the planet earth. As matter, earth is interchangeable with energy. As one or the other, earth is constant and indestructible.

There is, however, the number ten. For where is the Self in all this? It is ten, one with unmanifest nature by its side. It is the man who forgets to count himself, and thinks that one has drowned in the river. It is the answer to the great question of Philosophy – 'What am I?' So the course of lectures concluded by tracing the elements back from earth (or body) to water, fire and so on to the consciousness at one, in the manner of the practice of *anvaya*.

One example of the fruitfulness of the approach to science outlined in the 'Metaphysics' lectures has been the examination by Dr Peter Bowman of modern scientific views about consciousness. He identified the question, 'What is the biological basis of con-sciousness?' as a leading contemporary issue for many scientists, and found that the great Austrian physicist, Erwin Schrodinger, had some remarkable things to say about it.

Schrodinger rejected the assumption behind the question, namely that the direction of causality is from the physical to consciousness as a subjective experience. Instead he viewed the neural activity of the brain as an effect of consciousness, which is primary.

Not surprisingly then for Schrodinger, the most fundamental question of all was 'Who am I?' In trying to answer this, he realised that, since the individual perceptions that we each have are of the same single world, there must be one final observer or consciousness.

His discovery of Vedanta gave Schrodinger further impetus. The plurality of selves, he learnt, was only an appearance:

> Looking and thinking in that manner you may suddenly come to see, in a flash, the profound rightness of the basic conviction in Vedanta: it is not possible that this unity of feeling, knowledge and choice which you call your own should have sprung into being fom nothingness at a given moment not so long ago; rather this knowl-edge, feeling and choice are essentially eternal and unchangeable and one in all men, nay in all sensitive beings.

He saw this single consciousness as the underlying basis of the continuity of particular species, for the death of a creature is not the end of consciousness. So, too, the continuity of life in a creature, like a hydra, that lives on as two beings when cut in half, seemed to prove that consciousness is one – for how could it divide?

Schrodinger concluded that the consciousness appearing at first sight to be a unique collection of experiences and memories is really 'the canvas upon which they are collected.' The external world is no more than the content of this presented as sense perceptions. But, since modern science excludes this consciousness at the beginning of its investigations into the 'hypothesis of the real world', it can never find consciousness within it. In Shankara's *Brahma Sutra*, Schrodinger found the fundamental distinction between the 'I' and the 'not-I'. Science only looks at the latter, and therefore cannot find the former. Hence the question about the biological basis starts with the physical, and assumes that causality flows from it to the consciousness that it can never actually identify. This conclusion of Schrodinger presents a challenge for all scientists within the School. What scientific insights may arise from the opposite assumption – that consciousness is primary, the one constant starting point for all investigations?

In his exposition of the circle of nine points, the Shankaracharya said that mathematics gives the collection of laws under which the universe works. It follows that the study of mathematics is essential for every scientist. Not long after the conversatons with the Shankaracharya began, the School came across a book on Vedic mathematics written by Shankaracharya Bharati Krishna Tirtha, a pre-eminent scholar in the tradition of Advaita Vedanta. After a long and distinguished academic career, he had spent eight years in profound reflection on the whole field of mathematics. The outcome was a series of sixteen books explaining how Vedic methods could be applied throughout. Unfortunately these books were lost! At an advanced age Bharati Krishna Tirtha then wrote from memory a final volume summarising all his work. This was the book that the School obtained.

Leon MacLaren promptly introduced the study of Vedic mathematics. Students attended early morning classes under tutors of varying degrees of numeracy. The book made challenging assumptions: for example that one knew what terms like 'variable', 'quadratic', 'differential' etc meant. One lady was entirely baffled when the tutor wrote an 'x' on the blackboard. Basically, however, it offered a radically new set of methods that, once understood, greatly simplified most areas of mathematics.

The whole system was governed by no more than sixteen Sanskrit *sutras*. When translated these gave cryptic instructions on how to proceed, such as 'By one more than the one before', 'All from nine and the last from ten', 'Proportionately' or 'The product of the sum of the coefficients in the factors is equal to the sum of the co-efficients in the product'. The key to all of them was that the mind resorted to the nearest available unity to solve the problem i.e. to one, ten, one hundred etc. Amazingly these rules could sometimes lead to one line solutions to problems involving large numbers of digits or variables. Students found some *sutras* very much easier to practise than others. 'Vertically and crosswise', for example, was an easy method that replaced long multiplication. To replace long division, on the other hand, required many hours of practice.

A few well-qualified mathematicians in the School took to all this with gusto. The application to more advanced mathematics provided fertile ground for research. John Allen ran a class for some years that explored aspects like calculus and conic sections. James Glover, who taught Vedic mathematics at St James', even went on a lecture tour of India, making contact with many proponents of the Vedic system there.

Those students who studied the subject seriously found that Vedic mathematics had an effect more profound than an increased ability to solve problems in arithmetic, or indeed in calculus. The practice demanded that attention was centred on a mathematical operation without deviation. If extraneous thoughts, even mathematical ones, interfered, one might have to begin all over again. Essentially it was a system of mental calculation, but it offered a way of spiritual development. Attention improved, and the mind became clearer, quicker and sharper. In quite different areas of life the effect could be observed.

Interest in Vedic mathematics within the School has declined. Early morning classes have ceased. St James' secondary schools have reverted to traditional Western methods. Yet some seeds were sown that may be maturing elsewhere – perhaps curiously enough in India!

In one respect, however, a fundamental principle of Vedic mathematics remains central to continued studies in the School. According to the Shankaracharya, the number nine is the perfect number. In the circle of nine points it represents the culmination of the creative process, where all the nine elements are present. So too it forms the basis of the Vedic system of astronomy, called *Jyotisha*. Questions from Leon MacLaren in 1978 and 1982 had elicited much information on this system. Consequently an astronomy group was formed within the School, led by the enquiring mind of John Allen. After about seven years, the group was taken over in 1986 by Paul Palmarozza, and then in 1994 by Geoffrey Pearce.

It soon became clear that *Jyotisha* embraced much more than the word 'astronomy' now implies. Ancient *Jyotisha* was a science that included aspects of mathematics, medicine, architecture, meteorology and more. At the root of it lay the calculation of time. A work called the *Jyotisha Vedanga*, based on the number nine and including elaborate numerical patterns, is regarded as the definitive text. Having found that the British Library text was poor, the astronomy group obtained a new translation of it from Sanskrit students in the School.

From answers given by the Shankaracharya, it became evident that the real study was astrology , as a science that included not just the movements of astronomical bodies in space but their influence on human affairs. Several members of the group are now serious astrologers, to the extent of having roles in a national association of astrologers. The British Association of Vedic Astrology now holds its annual conference at Mandeville Place. Lectures are also given there entitled 'Laws of Creation and Time'. In dealing with the influence of natural laws on human society, these are in accordance with the founding principles of the School.

What then had been learnt from the Shankaracharya about a subject that is now more or less discredited amongst Western scientists? Persistent questioning from Leon MacLaren yielded some fascinating material. Astronomical bodies do have a significant influence on humanity, he was told. A system was then outlined which seemed, at first sight, to be in opposition to the modern Copernican and Newtonian account of the universe. It became clear, however, that the Indian system was an explanation of the heavens from the standpoint of a human observer, for whom the earth is the central point. Thus the stars, Sun and planets appear to move in circles around the point of observation. Modern astronomy, verified, of course, by space projects, adopts the different standpoint of objective science and mathematics.

Various Sanskrit terms were introduced. A star is a *nakshatra,* but this term also means an area of the heavens containing certain stars. In this latter sense, there are twenty-seven *nakshatrani,* making two and a quarter in each *rashi,* which is more or less equivalent to a sign in the Western zodiac. Sun, Moon and planets pass through the *rashi* and *nakshatrani* in the course of a year. Hence a human birth takes place at a time when a particular set of astronomical bodies is present in the heavens. These exert a powerful influence on the future life. Since the heavenly bodies, as material things, are subject to the *guna,* their influence is *sattvic, rajassic* or *tamassic.* The names of *nakshatrani* indicate their beneficial or baneful effect.

MacLaren asked a most pertinent question: what then of the influence of *sanskara?* This elicited a vital point. Astronomical forces work alongside *sanskara* to determine the course of a person's life, but this is all subject to an overriding principle, namely that consciousness is supreme. Stars and planets only affect the physical world. Human beings can allow themselves to be governed by such forces. The mind can be disposed to accept impulses from the material realm. Yet consciousness is the final arbiter. It may prevail over matter and all that influences matter. A wise man takes account of astronomical forces, which is why the subject requires study, but with the knowledge obtained he arranges his life to take account of the physical determination of things. Both Ficino and Shakespeare were vindicated! 'The fault, dear Brutus, is not in our stars, but in ourselves.' Or as the Economics faculty of the School has often said, more prosaically: the law of gravity is universal; yet Man can build aeroplanes.

In the 1970s the School also took a closer interest in science through the setting up of a medical group under the leadership of Jeremy Sinclair. More recently, the group has been led by Dr Martin Dumskyj. Amongst students there were several doctors and other medical specialists who wanted to know more about the applicaton of Philosophy to their profession. Leading examples of how discussion and enquiry led to practical advances were two questions put to the Shankaracharya on behalf of the group.

The first was about meditation being for the benefit of all. Since it was impractical to expect all the patients that a practitioner met to meditate, how could the universal aspect be understood? The answer was that the doctor or nurse who meditates might use this, together with his or her good *sanskara,* to help the patient. Afterwards meditation might be offered. In the case of children, especially, they might gain from seeing the peaceful act of meditation, and later their own meditation might keep them free from ailments.

The second question was about the use of life-support techno-logy. Should a patient be subjected to the artificial maintenance of essential organs? This produced a forthright answer. Birth, growth, old age, decay and death follow the laws of nature, which are the will of the Absolute, according to a time schedule. A healthy environ-ment, wise living and meditation may lengthen life, but no one should assume the power to inflict death on anyone. Only the Absolute knows when to ring the bell. Support life to the last breath. Everything possible should be done to lengthen God-given life

CHAPTER TWENTY-SEVEN

How Can Freedom be Availed?

T HE FINAL conversations between Leon MacLaren and the Shankaracharya took place in 1991 and 1993. By this time, after nearly thirty years of contact, much ground had been covered, and a great deal of study and work on Advaita had been practised in the School under MacLaren's leadership. Now the questions, though still varied and often idiosyncratic, were perhaps aimed at clearing up outstanding problems, both about the teaching and about the organisation of the School itself. A greater clarity had also developed in the presentation of the answers, probably as a result of the devoted efforts of Sitaram Jaiswal at the hard task of translating.

Appropriately enough the Shankaracharya began with *aham,* I am. *Aham* cannot be doubted. No one can sensibly deny his or her own existence. When this 'I am' meets the objects of nature (*prakriti*), either physical or mental, however, it seems to become no longer pure and simple but complex and troublesome, as 'I am intelligent, or beautiful, young, old, in pain and so on.' This *ahankara,* identification with natural qualities, is a kind of superimposition. The Self appears to be superimposed on nature and vice-versa. A picture of the individual appears and becomes compelling, whereas in truth the individual is a conscious, blissful aspect of the Absolute or *Brahman.* What is spoken betrays the situation. With superimposition the voice loses its natural and harmonious sound.

Reason is the only way to remove the superimposition. For *buddhi,* although itself a natural form of the mind, is always able to discrim- inate between conscious and inanimate, between the Self and what it appears to be identified with. When it is clear, and in particular when it is free from *vikshepa,* the negative aspect of *rajas,* it chooses rationally. 'I' remains, but 'mine', with its power to bind the individual, is cast aside. The ghost of *ahankara* is exorcised.

Later on, in answer to a question about being alone, the Shankaracharya introduced the concept of *kaivalya*. This is the permanent state of complete unity, when nothing other than the Self is recognised. *Aham* no longer seems to give way to *ahankara*. Everything is no more than a form of consciousness, like waves on the ocean, or ornaments made of gold. It is as though the world has become one great dream, in which the situations and people for which one feels affection or sorrow are merely projections of oneself, so that sentiment and worry are dispelled. Yet the bliss of the Self is present in them, included in the reality of oneself. Such illusions as 'I am the doer' have vanished, even though worldly duties are still performed through the means of *prakriti*, which is the real doer. As a hymn of Shankara expressed it: 'I am Shiva alone, harmonious, propitious, blissful, conscious and true'.

MacLaren asked about the limits that prevent full realisation. We introduce limits in order to create identities, was the reply. The limitless is beyond space and time, but identity can only exist within space and time. Ordinary knowledge operates within circles that need to be transcended if real knowledge is to make available the limitless. Yet it is the limitless that comes first; it is pre-eminent, the substratum of everything. There is a natural movement from the limitless to the limited, in which we partake, but by accepting discipline and developing reason one may move the other way towards the limitless.

When one goes up in an aeroplane, the houses, trees, even mountains gradually get smaller and lose their significance for us. So, too, when seen from the unlimited the world of limited things becomes powerless. Identification or association with the problems of life ceases. The *citta,* the emotional centre, bears no scars. The view from the limitless is always with us, though we do not notice it, lost as we are in the circles of limitation. A senior consultant in a hospital is no more than witness, as he supervises the junior doctors, nurses and other staff. He does not rejoice at successes or bewail failures. His staff are the *antakarana*, the instruments of mind; he is the *Atman*.

To look for a purpose in life is to bind the unlimited. True discipline is to remain balanced and to touch nothing. Miraculous deeds are not required. Nor is self-realisation a matter of gaining great powers or fulfilling anyone's desires. A wise man lives like a child without the burden of wisdom. No loss or gain concerns him. Even his knowledge is given up, for it is like a boat that takes one to the far bank and then is left behind. No one carries a boat on his shoulder!

At the beginning of these conversations the Shankaracharya had spoken of the need to find a balance, and then maintain it for a lifetime. MacLaren now pressed the Shankaracharya further on this question of balance. We all experience pulls and pushes in the world, he was told. The main factor that creates an imbalance is *ahankara*. Usually it is the evil forces that are joined by *ahankara*, but if good forces develop *ahankara*, that too will be opposed and overcome. Hence balance is restored mechanically. With discipline and maturity one may avoid being caught up in this constant battle, for then reason may enter the field, so that one may be oneself and find peace, even amidst violent disturbances.

All this must be seen in its true light as a play or illusion. The world and its dramatic events are the sport of the Absolute, which only becomes harsh and painful if we forget that it is only for sport. Balance is like someone dreaming and realising that he is dreaming. For him there is no duality between the forces that act in the dream; it is all one. Duality arises when the dream is treated as real.

This is amply illustrated in the great Indian epic of the *Ramayana*, where Rama, having lost his wife Sita, who represents his natural condition of peace, fights to regain her from Ravana, her evil captor. Ravana has acquired merit and power by austerities, winning the favour of the god Shiva. But he regards himself as invincible, so that this *ahankara* of the demonic forces has to be defeated. Rama's final triumph restores Sita, his peace, to himself, yet at the same time releases Ravana from bondage. Peace restored is the balance that reason may find in every situation. For duality lies in the nature of the creation, in the threefold *guna*. It is present in the *antakarana*, the mind, in the form of resolutions and doubts. Not to be moved by them is the secret of balance.

A question closely related to this was asked. How can this freedom be availed? Freedom is not a state, insisted the Shankaracharya. If it were, it would be subject to change. Only in the Self, in the limitless, is there freedom. Through desire we choose *ahankara*, which creates a screen over the Self. 'Me' and 'mine' crowd out the truth. Yet the Self is ever present as witness in all the states of the *antakarana*, even in deep sleep. Since freedom is not seen, we regard

it as lost or absent. Were we to retain an undisturbed dignity throughout all states, we would become aware of the freedom of the witness
that underlies them all.

Liberation is an idea in Advaita Vedanta. Neither the body, nor
the mind, is liberated, and the Self is eternally free. When body and
mind die, their elements return to their causes in universal elements.
Reason alone gives liberation by showing that the Self is free as
witness, untouched by birth and death. A man acting fully in the light
of reason is not weighed down with knowledge. He is like someone
who has been awarded a degree in a subject, so that when any
question is raised concerning it he knows how to answer. Reason
does not achieve anything special; it just sees things as they really are,
and so knows how to deal with whatever presents itself.

A further elucidation of reason was given. There are two kinds of
knowledge: natural and artificial. The former is not acquired; it is
innate. If a man is called a beast, he immediately denies it without
any thought, for he knows his own humanity without even the
possibility of doubt. Artificial knowledge, on the other hand, has to
be gained by discipline and practice. Take the two elements *aham* and
idam – 'I am' and 'that (everything else)'. *Aham* is always there first,
before knowledge of anything else at all can arise. It is there on
first waking up in the morning, before the knowledge of where one
is or what is there appears.

Knowledge of the Self, in a sense, partakes of both kinds of
knowledge. In truth one has always known the Self as *sat-chit-ananda*
(existence, consciousness and bliss), but this knowledge has become
inaccessible, covered by *sanskara* and desire. Reason is the system
for turning the artificial knowledge learnt from the scriptures, a *guru*
or a School into natural knowledge, for bringing the two forms of
knowledge into conformity. It turns *aham* into *Brahman*. This operation of reason, however, is not automatic. The free will of the
individual must choose it, and be prepared to repeat what it learns
to avoid the fading of the knowledge. Even the wise continue to
practise. Reason is the work of *sattvic buddhi*. If there is a conflict
between what reason prescribes and the needs of the individual or
family, for example, then the *buddhi* is still impure. Under reason
there is no preference and no prejudice. Individuality is replaced by
universality.

In washing a cloth, soap is applied, and the cloth is rubbed and
beaten. This process must be repeated several times, so that all the

stains are gradually removed. Then the cloth is pristine clean, shining with bright colours. So, too, the *buddhi* is only cleansed by many discussions of Advaita that slowly wash away all doubts, until reason recognises the truth without a blemish.

When Leon MacLaren asked about final realisation or *turiya*, the Shankaracharya replied by referring once more to the seven steps on the way of knowledge. His account of the sixth step was of particular interest. The created world consists of words and their meanings, whether causal, mental or physical. At this step in the aspirant's progress words no longer attract him. Their meanings become of no importance; beauty, brilliance, pleasure have lost their lustre. The things themselves remain, but he does not entertain the idea of them in his mind. From this it is one step into *turiya*, where there are no words, no meanings and therefore no relation between them. Differentiation has ceased. He is the limitless Self.

Turiya is the loneliness, the being alone, of *kaivalya*. There is no other, because all is the Self. The world still exists; it is not untrue. But it is not absolutely true; it only has relative existence, so that things pass away, as in a drama. The ignorant believe that the drama is really true, and consequently become attached to people and events. This creates the bondage of the cycle of life and death.

MacLaren asked where love enters into all this. Love and law are always found together was the surprising reply, since the universe is built upon them. Hence love and law are found everywhere. They both treat all with an even hand. Ignorance appears to limit love to small circles, to *vyashti*; in the extreme of selfishness it is limited to 'me' alone. Then love becomes attachment or *moha*, the very same substance but grossly limited. The wise ignore such limits, and view everyone as one family in need of the same happiness, health and freedom. To see the Self in another is an act of love.

On the battlefield of Kurukshetra, Duryodhana, leader of the Kaurava, claimed that all his brave warriors were fighting for him, willing to endure death for his sake. Arjuna, leader of the Pandavas, answered him that his men were fighting for *dharma*, for law and justice. Duryodhana was filled with *moha*, Arjuna with love.

At the core of love lies renunciation or sacrifice. Those on the way of love renounce everything for the sake of love. Thus it works for *samashti* alone. With *moha* things are held on to for private use. In the creation of the world there is no *moha*, which is a product of ignorance alone.

A lengthy and somewhat diverse conversation ensued on a
subject raised by Leon MacLaren in quoting a few passages from
the *Brihadaranyaka Upanishad*. This concerned the relationship
between father and son, particularly the question of what passes to
the son on the death of the father. The Upanishad appeared to say
that the son receives speech, mind and vital force from the father,
and that the father lives on as the self of the son, thus achieving
immortality.

The Shankaracharya was quick to point out that such passages
should not be taken literally throughout. The *Atman* is present everywhere and always, it does not move from father to son, or in
any other way. Poetic licence uses *Atman* for qualities that may be
transferred, such as those that are genetic or educational. Nor can
antakarana or mind be inherited from the father, for if it were the
whole system of *sanskara* and *ahankara* would not operate. Only
the individual is responsible for his own past and present actions
and for the *prarabdha* that confronts him in the present moment.

Even so, the Indian tradition retains a ritual of three promises
made by a son to a father who is approaching death. By these the son
accepts responsibility in three worlds. In the world of the gods he
will endeavour to follow the divine knowledge that leads to realisation; in the world of the fathers he will carry out the sacrifices of
the family tradition; in the world of men he will complete any unful-
filled duties of the father, such as the payment of outstanding debts.

The Shankaracharya was insistent that all that the father can give
the son, in life and death, are his worldly possessions and his blessing for wisdom and prosperity, although certain characteristics are
inheritable. How can he offer his own self? That is impossible. One
cannot transfer something that is already there!

The conversation in 1991 took place at a time when war
threatened in the Middle East, where Sadam Hussain had invaded
Kuwait. MacLaren asked what view School members should take of
these events. There is very little hatred, he said. The issue is mainly
one of enforcing the power of the United Nations to prohibit
aggression. The Shankaracharya's answer referred to the great war
between the Kaurava and the Pandava in the *Mahabharata*. Krishna
had sought to avert it by negotiations, even conceding that the
Pandava would accept five villages only, in place of their just claims
to rule the kingdom. The wise elders of the Kaurava had themselves
blessed the efforts for peace, but Durodhyana was implacable.

He would not give up land, not even so much as is covered by the point of a needle. War was inevitable, if justice were to be upheld

Prayer and meditation may help to preserve peace, but if fighting occurs then the rules of a just war must be followed. Destructive forces, on the other hand, are unpredictable. A man acquires an evil nature by breaking all the rules in the first place

A rare moment of insight into the Shankaracharya's own environment came when he referred to the violence in the dispute over rights to a Hindu temple in India. *Ahankara* at the head of destructive forces, he said, will succeed in so far as the situation is favourable for it. Yet it must be opposed. Negotiations on the basis of law should be pursued as far as possible. If there is war, the fighting should not degenerate into injustice; nor should the victory. Lessons should be drawn from the events and their causes, so that the same mistakes are not repeated. Better knowledge and justice may enable equity to prevail to eliminate the causes of injustice. Was this a warning about a second Gulf War?

Another question on the state of the world was asked. The United States of America, said MacLaren, seemed to be close to breaking up in the manner of the Soviet Union. There are whole areas of Spanish speakers, where English is no longer heard. How can unity be maintained?

This is a common problem, replied the Shankaracharya. In Europe and India similar evil forces are at work to destroy unity. They are often violent, and appear strong from outside, though within they are weak, for *moha* has replaced love. Where love remains, there is an inner strength, even when outwardly a community may look weak because it is peaceful. The circles dominated by *moha* may be mere individuals, families, ethnic groups, even nations or groups of nations. The causes lie in the desire for pleasure through the accumulation of property, wealth, machines and gadgets, regardless of the effects on others.

Only through the spoken or written word can some change be made by those of goodwill. And yet even this requires that people are prepared to listen. If, out of compassion, one gives money to a beggar, he may still spend it on drugs. A holy man once decided to help the poor by refusing to eat unless they were fed. He sat by the Ganges, until the goddess who provides food for all appeared. She said that she would feed all who came and asked, but could not help those who made no effort at all. Were they to be fed also the laws of nature would be broken. The holy man agreed.

Both good and evil forces always exist. The former prevail for longer, because they embody knowledge, justice, compassion and peace. Even when confronted with evil, the good take a rational view and are ready to co-exist. The evil are proud and adamant, refuse to consider any other point of view and seek to eliminate the good. Christ was a man of love, preaching compassion, mercy and charity. When he was crucified he forgave his persecutors. Without suffering, as forbearance, little change is possible. Men and women who remember the words of such a man may follow his teaching. Even those who come near a holy man may change their attitude.

MacLaren asked with reference to this how it is that some new idea, like his starting a School associated with Socrates, comes about. A creative act of intellect requires special circumstances, said the Shankaracharya. The time and place must be propitious. All then depends upon the state of being, *sanskara*, knowledge and devotion of the individual. If a problem lies embedded in his mind, new knowledge may enter to resolve it. Such ideas may change the course of history, but only if the mass of the people do not ignore what is offered. Every man has *buddhi*. That cannot be awoken by brute force. Subtler means are needed, especially reason.

Some important questions were asked about the organisation of the School. The first concerned the position and progress of women. Many, it seemed, despite their devotion to the teaching and to the School, still wanted personal independence, often by opposing their husbands.

The Shankaracharya threw new light on the question of independence. For women to go out to work to support the family was reasonable enough in the kind of social structure now prevalent. Family, society and nation all benefit from the development of female talents. What was important was the kind of independence sought. Real independence is found through reason, not in opposition to it. Since women are naturally gifted with strong emotion and energy, they may need the advice of men whose rational faculties are usually more in evidence. Women need help with reason, men with emotion. From time to time women face critical moments in life, when they cannot protect themselves. At such times they should be able to turn to a man for assistance. Within the School one man should be appointed, a man of good character and clear reason from whom the women can seek advice. MacLaren took action on this when he returned to London.

A question was asked about children who showed an interest in meditation. Those over ten should be encouraged to meditate like adults; those under ten should not, said the Shankaracharya. The younger ones can be asked to sit, preferably with their parents, with their eyes closed and in silence. No other instruction need be given. This would prove valuable later when they take to meditation and the study of Philosophy.

A more challenging question was whether the initiation ceremony for meditation could be amended to take account of the sensibilities of Muslims. As always the answer was unambiguous. The system of meditation was ancient. To change its structure would affect its efficacy. It is available to all religions or beliefs, and has always been beneficial. So why change it? It is designed for the universal spirit of Man.

In the course of the 1993 conversations MacLaren asked about a personal condition that had troubled him for a long time, and which clearly had implications for others in the School. What he called subtle substances seemed to be raining profusely on him, although he knew that the Self is completely detached from this whole experience. A somewhat mixed but illuminating analogy was given in answer to this. From the standpoint of the limitless, the *Atman*, all that happens is a passing show. The situation is like that of a car in neutral gear. The observer is not connected with the show at all. He is the neutral witness. In the *antakarana*, or mind, all that happens is governed by laws of nature. Even the cry for help comes from there. Given the belief that 'I am the doer', one thinks 'I am going through the trouble'. In truth the trouble is unreal, merely a drama to be seen by the limitless observer.

Later on MacLaren admitted that he saw this trouble of subtle substances to be self-inflicted, the result of a wilful act. He was told that there is no need to take over misery in the world by inflicting it on oneself. Help is valid only if there is some way to change the situation, as an act in the drama itself. Taking the drama seriously creates bondage.

Peter Green, who on this occasion had accompanied MacLaren to India, asked whether there was any advice for those who are close to him and wished to help. Do everything necessary without the idea of being the giver, he was told. Even in these conversations it only appears that one is the giver and another the receiver. Look after the body and share the knowledge, for in knowledge there is no other.

In a final message the Shankaracharya offered his good wishes and blessing for Leon MacLaren and everyone in the School. Knowledge may be used everywhere to advance the work of spiritual development. May MacLaren live long and happily to continue guiding the destiny of the School. From these words it became clear that there was to be no release from his worldly duties for the School leader, except through his appreciation of the freedom the Self.

Some time after MacLaren returned home from these conversations, he felt impelled to ask the Shankaracharya one further question. What disciplines were available for the movement from the limited to the unlimited? The reply emphasised the need to maintain discipline throughout life. The difference between the disciple and the master was simply that for the master the discipline becomes natural. It is no longer a duty to be undertaken; rather it becomes a way of life. It is still important to follow essential practices like meditation and meeting in good company (*satsanga*), even where it does not seem to be necessary. There are two reasons for this. Everyone meets events in the world that appear to be false or painful. Discipline reminds one of the truth. Secondly, if the wise do not practise discipline, those seeking wisdom, especially the young, will follow suit and lose direction. When discipline is fully natural, that too becomes a part of the play. Following it is no burden. The wise continue it for the sake of others.

For nearly thirty years Leon MacLaren had been meeting regularly with the Shankaracharya in India. As he grew older and physically unwell, he had not hesitated to undergo these arduous journeys to present questions that the progress of the School had raised. Gradually the answers had been introduced into the Philosophy material. In the case of the senior groups, verbatim passages were presented for discussion. This was the biting edge of School work, where minds were concentrated and new practices undertaken.

A system had evolved whereby the heads of levels in the School met with MacLaren every Sunday in the term to discuss the material they had each prepared. These meetings became an intellectual powerhouse, where the material offered was refined. Feedback from tutors and students could be incorporated, new ideas and sources examined and some elements of Advaita principles introduced.

Yet at the same time the introductory courses were in no way neglected. They continued to draw upon research and experience based upon the teaching of Ouspensky, Plato, the Bible, Shakespeare and many other proven sources. Students described their early days in the School as a kind of brave new world. One had seen himself 'like Pinocchio, manipulated by one's ideas, but then with knowledge no longer a complete puppet.' Another remembered how she had seen people as not separate, with a spontaneous flow of conversation, each person the same as oneself. There was a sense of peace and harmony, an absence of anger.

CHAPTER TWENTY-EIGHT

Changes of Leadership

BETWEEN the fall of the Berlin Wall and the general collapse of the Communist system at the beginning of the decade and the devastating event of 9/11 just after it ended, the 1990s felt indeed like a *fin de siecle*. Britain, in particular, drifted from the bosom of Thatcherism into the molly-coddling arms of New Labour. A kind of rehearsal of the economic disasters of 2008 took place in the early years of John Major's government. Unemployment rose towards two million, interest rates were at record levels of about 14 per cent, and negative equity entered the lives of very many households. Despite this, Major won the election, and led the country through the crisis of Black Wednesday, when the pound left the European Monetary Mechanism – the precursor of the Euro – with dramatic finality.

The first Gulf War and the death of Princess Diana were sombre incidents. Then, typically after nearly two decades of the same party in power, corruption and carelessness made their appearance. By 1997 the scene was set for a decisive takeover by New Labour under the forceful leadership of Tony Blair. The change was soon categorized by cynics as a move from 'sleaze' to 'spin'. Alistair Campbell became a key figure in the presentation of the Blair programme of 'education, education, education', 'tough on the causes of crime', and similar calls to action that did not make a great deal of difference on the ground. In short, politics, especially economic policy, remained largely superficial.

Despite the economic difficulties in the country, the School's financial position remained very sound during the 1990s. The increase in the value of its property could not be precisely measured, as it remained in the books at cost value, but acquisitions and substantial improvements complemented the rise in land values. Brinscall Hall in Lancashire, Chappel Allerton Hall in Leeds, and houses in Edinburgh, Guildford and Croydon were acquired. At Waterperry, a coach house accommodating eighteen was built with considerable craftmanship, and then, after much debate about the use of reconstructed stone, a fine modern extension, called the Elizabethan wing. Some medieval pottery was found during the construction. Nanpanton, too, skillfully converted the stables into a multi-purpose coach house. As for maintenance, in 1995 no less than £85,000 was spent on roofs alone! All this allowed for the expansion and the upgrading of both evening and residential provision. The austere days of Stanhill Court were regretted by only the few who thought that nostalgia was not what it used to be! In the same period, St James' Schools also made significant moves. In 1998 the senior boys left Victoria for Pope's Villa at Twickenham, and all the juniors, plus the senior girls, went to Earsby Street. Financial assistance was given by the School.

These complex property transactions required considerable financial expertise, involving bridging loans from banks, appeals to members and much else. They were undertaken by the new Treasurer appointed in 1991, namely Ian Woods, who replaced James Armstrong. He was helped by Graham Skelcey, a professional surveyor, later in 1999 elected Principal of the School. Peter Green, after over thirty years of devoted service during which the School had evolved into a far-reaching educational organisation of world-wide significance, took on the previously unoccupied position of President.

During this decade the public relations difficulties of the 1980s were eased. For example, the *Guardian* and the *Observer* lifted their advertising ban. Even so, the number of students in London had fallen by a thousand to 1500, less than the 2200 then attending in the provinces. In essence, however, the School was in good health. Part One Philosophy had been rewritten for the first time. New courses were offered in Aesthetics, Metaphysics, Education for Social Responsibility, and Marsilio Ficino. In 1999 the quincentenary of Ficino's death was celebrated with a meeting at Popes' Villa with speakers from a National Gallery conference. The Varanasi Trust began an appeal for a school in India presided over by Mr and Mrs Jaiswal, whilst four Fellowship members also opened an appeal to support the Shankaracharya's ashram. Just before Sheila Caldwell retired, her dedicated service to St James'was acknowledged by a visit from Princess Alexandra to the senior girls.

The Economics faculty was active under its new leader, Ian Mason. The *Economic Monitor* was given a new format. Research was conducted into the economic implications of the Jubilee underground line. Support, both moral and financial, was given to the economist Fred Harrison, a long-standing advocate of land value taxation, for his work in Russia with Dr Dmitry Lvov of the Russian Academy of Sciences.

The early years of the decade witnessed the physical decline of Leon MacLaren, culminating in his death on 24 June, 1994 at the age of 83. At the time when he died – in the early evening – there was torrential rain, thunder and lightening. Sheila Rosenberg had died three weeks before. MacLaren had been ill for some time, and was finally diagnosed with lung cancer. He had not allowed his ill health to interfere seriously with his work for the School, although it made life hard for those who cared for him, especially for Dorine van Oyen, whose constant attention to his needs for over twenty years testified to her recognition of his real stature. An Indian lady from South Africa, Nirmala Jugmohan, also cared devotedly for MacLaren. She had attended him on several trips to India.

For some months MacLaren had lived at the house near Southampton of a generous student, where he greatly appreciated the quiet, the fine gardens and the sea. There he continued to see groups and individuals who came down from London. Despite much advice to the contrary, he began his usual Summer tour of Schools in South Africa, Australasia and America. Soon after arriving in Durban, he had collapsed. When doctors there gave him only a short time to live, he was flown back to London and taken to a private hospital. There he was visited by many students and friends. Several meditated or read aloud from the Shankaracharya's *Birth and Death*. When he died, those present sang the Vedic *Perfect Prayer*. One who was there wrote: 'All is held in this end of breath… It is as if it is held for eternity.'

In accordance with MacLaren's belief that fire helps the physical elements to return to their universal form when the body dies, there was a cremation service. School members were asked to meditate for thirty minutes at the time. Dorine van Oyen arranged for his ashes to be scattered in the Thames some while later. A message from the Shankaracharya had been received that concluded with a prayer:

Homage to the work so far,
Blessings for the work entrusted,
Invocation for the peace of the Soul,
Benediction for the Soul gone free.

MacLaren's death tested the resolve of the School. Many students perhaps had expected to be shocked, and to feel deeply deprived of a leader whose charismatic presence had sustained them for years. In fact, the event passed by with almost no sense of deprivation. It was proof of maturity. It also showed a genuine understanding that the death of the body really is of little signifiance. In essence Leon MacLaren was still there: his spirit, his words, his teaching remained. He himself had been concerned that students might be attached to him personally, until the Shankaracharya had reassured him that it was the truth manifested in him that they sought, not the person. Nor was there an interregnum within the School. Donald Lambie stepped into the role of leadership immediately with no hesitation or disturbance. His way had been well prepared.

The following October a 'Celebration of the Life of Leon MacLaren' was attended by over two thousand people, including many past members, at the Festival Hall in London. The programme included reviews of the various achievements of the School, and – what would have pleased him most – music: *In the Beginning*, *The Eesha Upanishad* and excerpts from Mozart's *Requiem*. At Sarum Chase an exhibition was arranged displaying the work of the various faculties.

Peter Green summed up the man he had served under as Principal for so long:

He was a man of vision, and of great and varied talents. His friends loved and admired him as a truly universal man.

Fearlessness is a universal quality, which the *Gita* puts first in its account of divine virtues. There were countless examples from MacLaren's life: the pursuit of truth and justice through the lean years of the early School; standing for Parliament; seeking a real teaching wherever it might be – in the Fourth Way, in an Indian ashram, in Sanskrit literature – withstanding the setbacks of public criticism; taking responsibility for the lives and souls of so many; above all for speaking, when few others spoke, in a time of spiritual desertion. There is an amusing story of his physical courage. Dorine van Oyen was driving him to Stanhill Court along a winding road in

Surrey, when the brakes did not respond. He was reading a news-paper in the back seat. She cried out that the brakes had failed. 'Well, find a garage somewhere!' he replied.

For the great majority of School students who had not known him in his youth, Leon MacLaren was physically small, a portly figure, stooping slightly, with a bony head and a large, straight nose. His hair was thinning, his face deeply lined. His brown eyes seemed to bulge through very thick lens, but without spectacles there was great kindness in them. He had beautiful hands, those of a pianist, with long fingers. He moved slowly and deliberately. Speech, in particular, was his strength. His voice had a slight Scottish accent, with very clear articulation, resonance and a modulation that could carry both gentleness and great force. Always he spoke spontan-eously, whether face to face or at large gatherings. He had learnt from the Shankarachary to feel the sense of the audience before beginning.

Like the Shankaracharya, also, he seemed to come fully to life when speaking to a group or meeting. Often his sense of humour was to the fore. When taking the senior men's groups, for example, he might begin with a wry comment. One day he sat down, looked at the silent, rather sleepy looking rows, and quoted from Henry V's speech at the siege of Harfleur: 'Or close the wall up with our English dead.' 'Probably the best thing to do with them!' he added. On another occasion, he said to the men that the problem was that everyone thinks they are someone else, instead of being their real Self. Then he concluded, 'It would not matter so much if you thought you were Napoleon!'

Sometimes he told jokes, of which his favourites had often been relayed to him by a Jewish member of the Friday group. One he told with the accent of a Brooklyn Jew. An elderly couple lay awake in bed, unable to sleep because the man, Jacob, was very worried. 'What is the problem?' asked his wife. 'I owe Abraham a thousand dollars, and I can't pay him.' His wife got out of bed, and opened the window. She shouted out to Abraham, whose bedroom window was open across the narrow street. A head appeared there. 'Abraham,' she cried, 'Jacob owes you a thousand dollars, and he can't pay you. Now you worry about it!'

Not long before Leon MacLaren died he was sitting in the high wicker chair that he liked to use on the Waterperry lawn in front of the house, when some youths from the village passed by. 'Hey, you old geezer in that basket chair!' shouted one of them. Telling of this incident was typical of a certain humility that belied his sometimes imperious manner with students. Deeper humility was shown in his attitude to the Shankaracharya, whom he always regarded as his real teacher. The meetings in India were strictly formal, with no exchange of ordinary conversation, only words of thanks and a respectful passing of a gift of flowers.

Beneath the humour the true message always came across. In his recorded lecture on the history of the School, he ended with a brief statement of this. The aim is the truth, beyond creation, the Self of all, for Itself not for any manifestation. Proclaim justice, he went on, for it is the will of the Absolute. Keep moving, with the mind open to the gifts of the wise. Then there will be ideas appropriate to the atmosphere of the time and the power to hold to the course.

He never lost his deep regard for the common law of England. Perhaps this was best exemplified in a simple action when he was in South Africa during the apartheid period. Together with Dorine van Oyen, Nirmala Jugmohan and others, he went to eat in an expensive restaurant in Durban. Nirmala was refused entry, whereupon MacLaren turned round and walked out.

There could be endless accounts of the wise remarks he made to students. One rather beautiful example came from a tutor who had accompanied him on a tour of the South African Schools:

> A powerfully full memory is of sitting by the side of Mr MacLaren, by the Indian Ocean. We were looking at all the stars in the heavens above. He suddenly looked straight at me, and said 'It is all inside you.' This has come back to me many times.

He may never have read the works of Immanuel Kant, but he had encapsulated that philosopher's lengthy exposition of space in five words!

MacLaren did indeed have a kind of direct insight into people and situations that made him give short shrift to ponderous logic or wordy explanations. If he saw the truth within something, then he had no doubts and needed no proofs of its worth. Thus he could select the right person, the right text, the right action swiftly and surely. The system of meditation, the idea of measure, pausing between actions and other fundamental practices were quickly recognised as valuable A more mundane example was of a student who owned a bookmaking firm. One day he was summoned to see

MacLaren. He was frightened that he would be told to give up his job as unsuitable. All that was said was that he should clean up the business of bookmaking.

MacLaren's comments on history were equally to the point. When asked about the English civil war, he replied that when the Constitution is broken civil war follows. Having visited the tomb of the Black Prince at Canterbury, he pronounced that the Prince should have been canonised, not Becket, who had been martyred upstairs in the cathedral. The Romantic Movement, he said, had caused a great deal of trouble. MacLaren's attitude to Christianity is interesting. He once told a student, who asked whether he should read the Bible, that everything in the New Testament was true. On the other hand, when students at Embley Park went to visit Winchester Cathedral, he remarked that God is not found there. From his father he had inherited a dislike for institutionalised religion.

As for financial matters, he took the view that, if the School really needed something, then the money would be found. This proved difficult for some Treasurers who had to find it! Yet one of them said that MacLaren did not approve the purchase of buildings unless the money was available. The growth in School assets was certainly a by-product of the work of the School and in no way the intention of its founder. His attitude to wealthy individuals, however, did undergo a change. In the early days the School had a somewhat puritan air, with almost a contempt for wealth. Later, MacLaren seemed to have greater regard for entrepreneurs and traders who create wealth. At the same time, he was careful to see that they were encouraged to be generous in their contributions to the School. Some indeed were exceedingly so. Success in life attracted MacLaren. For instance, he generally disliked academics as purveyors of ill-founded or worldly 'knowledge', but when a senior student became an Oxford professor of chemistry he was quick to hail his world standing as a renowned expert.

Although MacLaren's judgment was always very greatly respected, there were members of the School who did not view it as above suspicion. Undoubtedly he made some mistakes. The acceptance of the *Gospel of Peace* was one; so too was some of the advice on the marriage of young students. The reputation that the School acquired for secrecy owed something to his own liking for it. For instance, he rarely disclosed his sources. His sense of timing also was sometimes overborne by the intention to take matters in hand. For example, he expected major projects, like improvements of School buildings, to be completed with unrealistic speed. He may also have expected too much from students because he overestimated their strength. The Shankararachya warned him of the weakness of the present generation. This was certainly one cause of his frequent outbursts of anger, which could be ferocious. Anyone who admitted to boredom or laziness, for example, was liable to be excoriated.

A lady in the Friday group, who was a highly talented musician, left the School when he berated her furiously for wearing a skirt that he judged to be too short. That case also illustrated a degree of misogyny, which crept into his treatment of women in the School. He was harsh with them, especially if he detected selfishness, laziness or, worst of all, any attempt by a woman to undermine a man. He demanded the fullest level of service from women. There were some who resented this, perhaps because they lost sight of the principle the Shankaracharya had re-iterated – that all service is ultimately to the Absolute. MacLaren might have helped them by emphasising a little more the need for men to love, support and protect women. He himself was always closely attended by women who were devoted to him. Their devotion was sometimes tested by his severity and exacting demands, yet he could also be most kind and considerate. His care for the young ladies being educated at Waterperry was exemplary, even though it was of necessity delegated.

What most upset some students was MacLaren's tendency seemingly to 'abandon' someone who had previously played a major part or shown special promise. The case of Sheila Rosenberg has already been mentioned. He did this also on one occasion when the School administration was radically overhauled. A Friday group lady, who for many years was in charge of the whole administration, was abruptly dropped from this work altogether without any explanation. Apologies were never part of MacLaren's style. One of the worst cases was during a tour of Australia. The tutor taking meetings had not performed well in the judgment of MacLaren and the School leaders. Instead of drawing him aside or giving him words of advice, he chose to upbraid him severely at the tutors' meeting and then to dismiss him. He did not always see that his own power was not available to others.

This certainly applied in the matter of self-discipline. Having smoked heavily for years, he stopped once and for all at the age of about seventy. Similarly he gave up wine, despite a lifelong liking for claret. He was notoriously bad at spelling, but Sheila Rosenberg said that one day he decided that was not good, and shortly afterwards began to spell perfectly correctly. Once he saw the need for something he did not waver. This applied especially to whatever he found was necessary for the School. When he discovered that he had misinterpreted what the Shankaracharya had said about the mantra, he simply held a large meeting of senior students and told them of his mistake. The corollary of this determination was – as one student put it with a little exaggeration – 'nothing happens without him.'

Self-discipline easily falls over into the avoidance of emotion. MacLaren insisted that emotion was not mere feeling and outward expression, but a deep, permanent feature of one's life, such as love for a profession or art, or the love that is prepared to sacrifice all for another. Few people ever saw Leon MacLaren show signs of the more tender emotions. Yet the presence of love was proved by his steadfast adherence to the search for truth and his care for students. There is, however, an example of another aspect. At one of the final meetings with the Friday group, he was reading Shakespeare's Sonnet 116 ('Let me not to the marriage of true minds…') when, half way through, tears streamed down his face, and he could not continue. It was probably a unique event.

In the running of the School there was never the slightest doubt as to who was master. The early Principals found it difficult to make much impression. MacLaren treated them like any other student. The arrival of Peter Green changed this somewhat. When he was elected he feared that his tenure of office would be as shortlived as those of his predecessors. Nevertheless, he decided not to be a rubber stamp, and sometimes challenged MacLaren on important issues, such as his proposal to make Waterperry the home of St Vedast Boys' School. Green disliked confrontation, and admitted the power of MacLaren, but said that he came to see that the whole situation was ultimately no more than a play!

The most senior group in the School, known simply as the Friday group, had several roles. It was a sounding board for MacLaren's ideas and for the Philosophy material. Sometimes there was open dissent, but more often resistance to his proposals took the form of a wall of silence. Even though his intention was clearly to create people especially able to take command of various sections of the School, and to lead the way with new practices, he did not always appreciate that as the group developed the individuals became both stronger and more independent. Some members saw the Friday group as protecting the School from the excesses of MacLaren!

There were students who found Friday group members somewhat arrogant. *Ahankara* had not departed. Even so, a great deal of work was done selflessly for the School for very many years by the Friday group. One example amongst many was that of Joan Crammond, who gave much 'behind the scenes' help to Sheila Rosenberg, as well as herself being in charge of the senior men for a while. Membership of the group slowly changed, of course, until it was finally disbanded by Donald Lambie.

In some respects MacLaren's attitude to the Friday group was ambivalent. For example, obedience and regular attendance were expected, and fully complied with by some members, whilst others were often absent on business or political commitments. MacLaren still had a lingering attachment to political matters. Once when he was resting for the weekend at a student's house in the country, he phoned Roger Pincham – then a Liberal candidate in Herefordshire – and asked him to come and talk to him, because he wanted some stimulating conversation. Pincham recorded that MacLaren had told him not to do what he had done as a candidate. Rather he should be aware of peoples' sensitivities.

MacLaren presided over the material meetings every Sunday afternoon during the term. He did not interfere unduly, but all recognised the wisdom of his comments and amendments. A minor aspect was his weeding out of unnecessary adjectives. Approved material went quickly into use in both London and the branches. When Part One was finally rewritten by Will Rasmussen, MacLaren made the startling remark that 'Now it is his School!' But it did not turn out that way.

Every Autumn MacLaren gave an annual lecture for all senior members of the School. These were held in Church House, Westminster or in other large London halls. He spoke without notes, and answered questions in the second half. Whilst the range of these lectures was very great, they all centred on the teaching of Advaita that the Self is one. Often students could recognise the Vedantic source of what he said, but always there was a unique choice of words and imagery. For example, clearly inspired by the *Mandukya Upanishad*, this passage from September 1990 makes the essential message familiar to every listener:

You know the famous rhyme: 'As I was going up the stair, I met a man who wasn't there. He wasn't there again today; I wish that he would go away.' Well, there's this character that's not there, but runs the day. That's the curious thing. While we're caught in the dream, he runs the day, and he's quite convincing. There's a very simple way of looking at this. What would you say: you're in a deep sleep, you dream, and you wake up; three distinct steps, and what does it seem like? Do you seem you're the deep sleeper? Are you the same chap as the dreamer? And are you the fellow who wakes up? It's an illusion, all this, because it's the same Self that watches the deep sleep, the dreaming state, the waking state, without changing at all. He didn't change. And the seeming change – and it's very convincing – is evidence of the dream, the dream-like state in which people live.

A description of MacLaren given by a student looking back over some years said that he was captivating to meet for the first time, witty, amusing and wise, with sparkling eyes, exciting, even intimidating. He went to the heart of a problem quickly and kept questioning, with a great gift of attention, never hurried, very determined. He aimed at the truth; the rest did not matter.

Whatever the imperfections, Leon MacLaren was a man of genius, fulfilling a unique destiny at what may prove to be a critical point in history. His task was to create the conditions in which people seeking the truth might discover the one Self to which all are heirs. 'It needed a master man to shake us out of our dreams and idleness', was how one student looked back on half a century in the School. MacLaren never falterd in his attention to the central tenet expressed by the *mahavakya* of Advaita, 'This *Atman* is *Brahman.*' And yet at the same time he saw that the human spirit has many needs. Very few people indeed can follow the way of *nivritti* alone. The way of the School is *nivritti* through *pravritti*. Hence many studies and practices are required for the expression of the spirit in the world. So MacLaren followed whatever presented itself. If he saw a need, he met it to the best of his ability. Many needs appeared: for the study of language, law, government, art, music, architecture, science, mathematics, calligraphy, Plato, for the continued study of economics, for the creation of children's schools, for the translation of Ficino – the list goes on. None of these would have prospered without MacLaren's guidance. He was truly a renaissance man. Remembrance of him is best expressed, as it was with Christopher Wren and his great masterpiece of St Paul's, by an epitaph that could be inscribed amidst the activities of the School of Economic Science: '*Si monumentum requiris, circumspice.*'

In September 1992 a message had been received from the Shankaracharya saying that MacLaren should appoint a successor. That Autumn he called a meeting of a few selected senior students, who indicated that they would be prepared to take on the leadership of the School. During the leaders' conference at Waterperry over Christmas, he announced that Donald Lambie was the designated successor. The following month the Shankaracharya was informed of this, when MacLaren visited him in India. The choice was approved, and the advice given that the new leader would need, especially, to be steadfast, reasonable and compassionate. MacLaren was enjoined to pass on everything he knew.

From that time onwards, until his death, MacLaren made every effort to acquaint Lambie with the knowledge and experience that had arisen from the work of the School. Questions were expected from the incipient leader! Since at this time MacLaren was living at Waterperry or near Southampton, this meant that Lambie travelled frequently from London, usually after a day in the law courts or chambers. This was physically very demanding, though he was perhaps attuned to such a programme, having organised many of MacLaren's Summer tours to North America. Even at the master's bedside in Durban on the last trip and in hospital in London, he imbibed final words of wisdom and advice.

Donald Lambie was born in Newcastle-upon-Tyne in 1955. When he was eleven, his family moved to London. His father died soon afterwards. He was educated at Pinner Grammar School and University College, London, where he took a law degree. After passing the Bar final examinations, he was called to the Bar as a member of Lincoln's Inn in 1978. Pupillage followed and then a tenancy at King's Bench Walk, where he developed a broad common law and Chancery practice.

Having joined the School at the age of seventeen, he had the benefit of participating in the law group at the same time as studying law at College. On joining the youth group he first met Leon MacLaren, who became his Philosophy tutor in 1978. Five years later he married Christine, who had come over from Belgium after being a member of the School in Brussels. Each year from 1986 the Lambies accompanied MacLaren on his annual trip to New York.

It was on their return from this six years later that the providential message arrived from India.

In July 1994 the Executive approved of Donald Lambie's appointment by MacLaren as Senior Tutor. Acceptance by the Friday group, whilst of no constitutional significance, was a vital aspect of Lambie's new position. He was now the arbiter of the School's philosophical development, after almost half a century when this had been the task of Leon MacLaren. For five years he continued to practise at the Bar, but retired from this when most of his time had to be given to the School.

There was no change in the essential teaching. The words of the Shankaracharya, the Upanishads and the *Gita* have remained as prime sources. There has been more emphasis given to the practice of reflection. Reorganisation has helped to unite the School by reducing the sense of a hierarchy. Less formality, for example in dress and speech, has brought the School rather closer to the mores of the twenty-first century.

The main activities have continued to prosper, including its connection with new children's schools in Melbourne, Auckland, New York, Johannesburg and Durban. Donald Lambie has visited and given his support to all of these. Likewise he has followed in the footsteps of his predecessor in tours of overseas Schools around the world. The great majority have willingly accepted his leadership. Only two – Greece and Boston – have gone their own way; whilst new Schools under his aegis have opened in Brisbane, Venezuela, Buenos Aires, Hungary and Israel. In the mid 1990s Donald Lambie helped to resolve the difficulties that arose over the leadership of the School in Amsterdam. From time to time he has also presided over other changes of leadership, fortunately in easier conditions than prevailed in Holland!

The attitudes of people coming into the School have changed radically since the early days of Suffolk Street, when they were coloured, for example, by an upbringing in World War Two. Donald Lambie has been aware of the need to keep the Philosophy courses in touch with the new generation. Accordingly he has rewritten much of the material, and is keen to take account of developments like the use of the internet, as practised in the New York School. He remains insistent that the function of the School is to discover and to pass on knowledge of truth and justice. Its motto, he says, might be 'Learn and teach.' Philosophy involves learning in the sense of discovery, whilst teaching is by living and embodying the principles that have been discovered. Since its inception the School has been inspired by the same impulse. In reality it is common to all.

On 6 December, 1997 Shantananda Saraswati died. Sitaram Jaiswal's wife, Bharati, was amongst those who had cared for him during his final illness. His body was lowered into the waters where the Ganges and Yamuna rivers meet, in accordance with tradition. As Shankaracharya of the North, he was replaced by Vasudevananda Sarasvati. In one sense, leadership in the teaching of Advaita Vedanta had changed; in a deeper sense, it remained precisely the same.

CHAPTER TWENTY-NINE

Wisdom in Practice

IN NOVEMBER 2007 Donald Lambie reminded members of the School that it would soon be the tenth anniversary of the death of Shantananda Saraswati, whose wisdom had directly guided the School for over thirty years. Lambie recalled how, together with Mr and Mrs Jaiswal, he had travelled to the banks of the Yamuna river at Allahabad at that time:

> The boats were just returning from the funeral and after he disembarked, there was the briefest of meetings with Sri Vasudevananda Saraswati. Later we took a boat to the confluence of the Ganges and Yamuna rivers where the body had been immersed. Although the occasion was sad, the atmosphere was profoundly serene.

A few days later Donald Lambie met Vasudevananda Saraswati again, and received a message that provided fresh inspiration for the School. The people of India and those in the West were alike the beneficiaries of the wisdom of Shantananda Saraswati. So it was the duty of his followers in both East and West to proclaim his ideas with dignity to all human beings. Knowledge (*jnanam*), the analytical exposition of it (*vijnanam*) and the establishment of these in one's being as practical knowledge (*prajnanam*) would all be required.

Jnanam is usually gained through study of the scriptures and by experience. Deeper investigation of the whole field of laws of nature may yield *vijnanam*. When this becomes fully practical in daily life, it is transformed into *prajnanam*. This is then no longer a matter of verbal communication, but rather of finding that the individual and the universal have become one, that there is no longer a distinction between inner and outer. It is expressed in the scriptures as '*Atman* is truly all this.'

Two years later, in 1999, Donald Lambie returned to Allahabad to meet Vasudevananda Saraswati once more. He reported on the state

313

of the School, referring to its progress with the study of scriptures and the conversation material, and efforts made to remind people of the rich spiritual heritage available in England. Two problems were mentioned: the lack of commitment of many new students, particularly the younger ones, and the divisions that had arisen occasionally in Schools abroad between the leader and the students.

The Shankaracharya's response was practical. The material may need to be lightened by the addition, for example, of stories and of cases of how the teaching has been put into practice. Too much depth all at once may deter younger people. As for divisions in Schools, these all arise from *ahankara*. The unity of the *Brahman* needs emphasis. Since School work is for the whole of humanity, the ego should be surrendered to *Brahman* to avoid any disruption.

The next question was about the apparent difference between *Atman* at the centre and what is manifested as speech and action. One needs to be truthful in thought, speech and action, so that there is harmony between them, was the reply. If one keeps trying, success will follow. Eventually obstacles will fall away.

A similar question followed. Experience is often of the limited and separate, as though the starting point were wrong. What can be said on this? At the root of this problem is *sanskara*, was the answer. This may give rise to two harmful forces: *avarana* and *vikshepa*. The former is a kind of mental blindness and the latter the negative form of *rajas*. They may be dissolved by the threefold process of listening, reflecting and absorbing the truth into one's being. If the blindness begins to dissolve, it may be replaced by the agitation and doubt of *vikshepa*, but persistent practice of this process will eliminate it. In this discipline, as in others, the three graces of scripture, the teacher and the Self may come to one's aid. One must have a desire for truth and freedom; this is the grace of the Self that precedes all else.

Donald Lambie quoted from the *Brihadaranyaka Upanishad* to the effect that the Self is dearer than everything else, like son or wealth, so that one should meditate on that alone. Why is this? The Shankaracharya replied that whatever one meditates upon one becomes, whether it is a god, a spirit or the Self. But the Self alone is everlasting. Meditation on anything else implies duality, which means division, and in division there is death. Reason finds the Self to be eternal; therefore it may guide emotion to be directed at that in worship or meditation. Otherwise emotion degenerates from love into *moha* or delusion. When the Self is most dear, then one finds it also in son, wealth or any other dear object.

The question was pursued further. Why does the Self sometimes seem to be remote or impersonal? In response the *Eesha Upanishad* was quoted, saying that the *Atman* is both further away and nearer than anything else. Neither by the senses nor by internal means can we perceive it. Yet it is the foundation of all perceptions. An Islamic poem says that the image of the Absolute is sketched on the heart, so that to see Him one only needs to lower the head. To grasp or hold the Self is impossible, for it has no form; but the scriptures tell us that *Brahman* desired to be many, and so created many forms from Himself. In holding these, when eyes see or hands grasp or tongue tastes, we may experience bliss, not of the forms but of Oneself.

If the whole creation is really the play of the Absolute, why then do we take it and ourselves so seriously? This elicited an answer of particular significance for people leading busy lives in the world, whilst working towards liberation in the School. The Shankaracharya made a clear distinction between the real nature of an object and its function. An elephant, a cow and a dog have their respective functions – for ceremony, for milk and for security. Yet, at the same time, all are in truth the Self, so they should be treated without exploitation. Full attention must be given to the functions of things; for example, in work, artistic creation or running a School. So creation is taken seriously within that limit. Cause and effect demand serious attention. The field of Advaita, however, is the limitless. Through emotion one may appreciate the Absolute, even whilst the ego has regard for the affairs of the world.

In answer to a question about *manas*, the Shankaracharya gave a comprehensive account of its role and its relationship to the other organs of mind. It stands between them and the external world of sense perceptions. Principally *manas* deals with resolutions and alternative courses of action. Thus from it stems the freedom of the will, or choice between the desires that present themselves to the individual. What is crucial is whether such resolutions are submitted to *buddhi* for judgment or rational examination. If this is ignored, then actions will be driven by *chitta* with emotional force that acts on the ego, regardless of reason. If *buddhi* is allowed to intervene, then a rational decision is possible. Even so, the state of *buddhi* is still critical. Only under *sattva* will a fully rational action emerge.

Donald Lambie then asked a question that had been in the mind of many students for some while. How may *ahankara* lead towards realisation? One knows how it is binding easily enough. The answer followed what had been said earlier. *Ahankara* has been in disrepute because it is used untruthfully. It is the most important means of action, but it is dependent on the state of the other organs of mind, for it can only use what is offered to it. Clean perceptions, study of scriptures, discipline and good company enable *ahankara* to work for realisation. Purification of mind at all levels is thus essential.

The Shankaracharya had said that the work of the School is for the whole of humanity. What does humanity need today, and what might the School do, were the next questions. They received an unequivocal response. The essence of humanity is the fulfilment of law, and the proper work is to educate people in the law. This has two aspects. At one level law secures the prosperity and wellbeing of the people. At a higher level it leads to freedom. For humanity this freedom is no less than the facility to live a natural life under divine law.

Laws in each land differ according to tradition. In India, for example, people come under the fourfold division of classes and the four stages of life. The ways of action, devotion and knowledge are taught as means of approaching freedom. Philosophical systems vary from materialism and types of dualism to Advaita, which alone states that the Self is *Brahman*. Whatever laws have been handed down in a nation should be honoured, so that people are educated to follow them.

Lambie asked whether there was scope for adding to or refining a tradition. The reply was that the tradition of the land reflected in its culture and religion should be taught, each person being educated according to his or her need and capacity. Yet, at root, education is universal, because all are human. Universality can be achieved only by progressive refinement, but civilisations differ; each stops at a particular level.

At this point Sitaram Jaiswal, the translator, intervened with a question. In the West religion is held so sacred that it cannot be changed, because it is presumed to be revealed by God. How then can the tradition or religion be refined? A remarkable answer followed this. Some traditions presume that the level they have achieved is final, whilst others move on. Some have revealed the basic elements of both human prosperity and freedom. In the *Laws of*

Manu there is a profound definition of *dharma*, which contains ten aspects of law suitable for the whole of humanity.

Patience, the first, reflects the constancy of the Absolute. It is followed by forgiveness, which is especially applicable to the strong or wealthy, since those who are weak or poor can give nothing when insulted or hurt. Self-control, the third, requires discipline, especially for those whose temperaments are wilful. Not to steal comes next; the human law is to be fair and equitable. To take more than one deserves or needs is to steal. After this comes purification of body, mind and emotions, as well as of one's residence and environment. Similarly, there is mastery of the sense organs. Perceptions should be chosen that are conducive to a righteous life, so that depraved sights, sounds etc are to be avoided. The proper use of intellect follows. This means openness to good ideas, their analysis and meaning, and the pursuit of philosophical principles. Spiritual knowledge is said to be another aspect of *dharma*. It is stated by Krishna in the *Gita*, when he says 'I am the spiritual knowledge'. The ninth aspect is the truth. This includes that which really exists, conceiving the truth as it ought to exist, and speaking the truth as it exists in the mind. Finally, there is refraining from anger, not to be agitated or enraged.

These are universal laws, although people may treat them as the preserve of their own particular religion. As for refinement, it is useless to superimpose new beliefs or practices on what is there. Only someone of pure intellect, who truly sees the way of prosperity and freedom, could begin a work of refinement.

Donald Lambie turned to a question about meditation. Some students who practise it devotedly for many years rarely experience its real depth. Can help be given? The Shankaracharya replied that there must be some impediments of body, mind or speech, which should first be seen. Then study of scripture, reflection and *satsanga* may dissolve them. In some cases it requires emotional surrender; in others, intellectual problems need to be resolved. Impediments do not go by themselves.

The translator then asked about the misconception that meditation leads to supernatural achievements. The reply was forthright. Meditation leads to stillness, which is its proper outcome. What happens in the stillness one need not know, but its result is experienced quite naturally. It is against the system of meditation to expect a supernatural result. Realisation of powers has nothing to do with self realisation. Even if the wise acquire powers, they do not use them, and never talk about them.

Could something be said about the School and its general guidance, asked Lambie. The Shankaracharya replied that the School should follow the discourses, advice and meditation given by his predecessor, Shantananda Saraswati, and stand firmly for the system of Advaita. He offered his goodwill and blessings, and added his wish that the School leaders assembling at Waterperry at that time should teach and practise the same wisdom in the spirit of an Advaita family.

CHAPTER THIRTY

The Open Horizon

I N SEVERAL respects the new millennium began with signs that an age of iron was indeed approaching: the terrible event of 9/11 in New York, the invasions of Afghanistan and Iraq and the deeply serious economic crisis of 2008/9 were perhaps precursors of worse to come. To ascribe them all to economic causes would be a simplification, but there can be no doubt that the massive exploitation of natural resources, such as oil, and the private accumulation of claims to wealth in a few hands as a result of huge rises in land values have played their part. When combined with the so-called 'free market in capital' that enables financial operators to gain control of industries throughout the world, these underlying causes have proved lethal. By the end of the first decade there were few indications that real lessons had been learnt on the economic front.

Nevertheless, there have been many references in public life to principles of Economics that the School itself has been advocating for very many years. Care of the planet and restraints on unlimited growth have become watchwords of the green movement. Avoidance of inefficiency and of waste has been accentuated by the acute financial straits of most governments round the world. A few writers, journalists and politicians have even mentioned that taxation could be usefully levied on the economic rent of land. The influence of the School in all this is impossible to quantify, but the effect of its adherence to fundamental ideas of economic justice for over seventy years cannot be gainsaid.

The content of the Economics courses developed in new directions during the decade. Study of the micro-credit system associated with the Grameen Bank founded by Muhammad Yunus led to further material on how vital credit is to every economic system, especially where there is acute poverty. The examination of projects like the London Jubilee Line had emphasised yet more that economic rent is the obvious source for financing public investment. Arguments about free trade and protection have been more closely considered. The conclusion has been established that 'the modern version of a globalised market economy fails to deliver conditions of freedom and prosperity for everyone.' More thorough accounts of basic economic systems, such as classical, neo-classical, Marxist, Keynesian and monetarist are now given. Perhaps the most significant contribution of the School in the field of Economics was summed up in the Waterperry Declaration:

> People prosper where justice and equity are honoured. Today a fifth of the world's population lacks the means to feed itself. This injustice and inequity will be resolved when the recognition of our common humanity becomes the foundation of our conduct.

Conferences have been held attended by like-minded organisations, such as the Land Reform Group and the Henry George Foundation. The publication of a modern version of *Progress and Poverty* was supported by the School. Ian Mason represented the Economics faculty at a conference in Calcutta, where he also gave an interview to the *Indian Times*.

It would be futile to attempt to measure the full influence of the Philosophy taught by the School. Yet how it has developed can be briefly noted. At its heart remain the Conversations between the Shankaracharyas and the School leaders. The earlier parts of the Philosophy course have been rewritten by Donald Lambie. The introduction now makes greater reference directly to Self-knowledge, to experiencing deeper levels of being through stillness, to the central question 'What am I?' and to the Self beyond the universal forces of the *guna*. All this naturally leads on to the offer to students of meditation and study of Advaita Vedanta in greater depth. Since the 1950s Philosophy has been the central practice of the School, on which all other activities depend, and which sustains the life and creativity of its members. No doubt the knowledge and power that it generates will increasingly be felt in the community at large.

In February 2004 a dark cloud appeared over St James' Schools, and at the same time overshadowed the School. A few ex-pupils had set up an internet website on which they posted what the School Executive recorded as 'vitriolic attacks'. These took the form mainly of accusations of unjust or unduly severe punishment. Some of the complainants gave their names; others were anonymous. The School was included in the censure, particularly since the teachers accused were members. David Boddy and Laura Hyde met some of the complainants, and tried to begin a process of reconciliation. When this failed, both the Independent Educational Association and the School sought legal advice. As a result the school governors commissioned a Report by a Queen's Counsel.

After an enquiry lasting over three months, involving written and oral evidence from ex-pupils, teachers and parents, the Report in 2005 contained several firm conclusions. It made no claim to be a balanced account of the overall state of the schools in the period concerned, which was 1975 to 1985. It focussed almost exclusively on questions of discipline and punishment. Despite quoting an Inspectors' Report for 1984 that said caning was 'infrequent', it was critical of the use of the cane in some instances, whilst acknowledging that Nicholas Debenham at no time was influenced by a 'bad motive'. Mistreatment was said to have occurred by other teachers, who on occasion struck boys and used verbal abuse. Three teachers were singled out for criticism, of which two made an apology. In the girls' schools, there had been some undue punishment, including hurtful interrogation. There was no evidence of any form of sexual abuse in any of the schools. Nor was there any medical evidence showing physical or mental damage that could be assigned to attendance at them. It was admitted, however, that some ex-pupils had suffered from the experience.

One serious conclusion was that the governors had not been sufficiently active on their own account in the period concerned. The explanation of this was that Leon MacLaren exerted a strong influence over the head teachers and their policies. The corollary was that Donald Lambie had distanced himself more from the running of the schools, whilst maintaining some say in the appointment of head teachers.

In the nature of the complaints and the enquiry, the whole matter caused considerable trouble, concern and expense to many people, notably the founding head teachers and some staff. It obscured much of the excellent educational work of the early years of the schools. Yet to some extent it cleared the air, even though a few dissatisfied ex-pupils continued to protest. As the Report concluded, the schools in 2005 were in very good shape, offering a fine education and free from any taint of former problems. The bad publicity that attached to the School itself has gradually dwindled.

As for the fabric of the School, one main event stands out, namely the acquisition of No 11 Mandeville Place in the West End of London in the Autumn of 2002. In order to buy this the buildings in Queen's Gate and Chepstow Villas were sold. Mandeville is a listed building dating from 1875, and was bought from the Trinity College of Music, which has moved to Greenwich. It consists of two adjacent buildings, linked by an impressive portico with four Ionic columns. The red brick façade has stone dressings and quoins, and a slated mansard roof with steep pitch at the corner in the French style. The entrance hall has fluted oak columns supporting a plaster entablature. There are stained glass windows depicting Chaucer, Shakespeare, Pepys, Purcell and Fornsete, the composer of the earliest written piece of English music. On the first floor the concert hall has been renamed the MacLaren Room. Many changes have been made to the interior to open it up to light and space. In particular, a large refectory has been built in the basement to accommodate both evening groups and events such as conferences.

The School leader, Donald Lambie, has proposed that the new building should become a 'beacon' of spiritual and practical knowledge, serving the wider community and humanity, whilst the present Principal, Ian Mason, sees the work of the Executive, Fellowship and members as providing moral and material support for this vision. Independent thought and study would enable the School to establish a reputation in the heart of London at a time when fresh ideas are desperately needed in so many fields. Already by the year 2010 some progress on these lines has been made.

Some concentration of group meetings at Mandeville Place has occurred, with the outcome that Sarum Chase was sold in 2005. The funds from this sale have enabled the School to keep a financial reserve, which has proved useful in the economic downturn at the end of the decade. Rooms in Mandeville are now being rented to selected organisations, such as those with medical, educational or spiritual aims. Outside London, School houses have been bought in Stockport and Colchester. Major improvements to the kitchen and laundry at Nanpantan have been made. At Waterperry a new lift has helped older students a great deal, and the roof balustrade has been renewed at substantial cost. A remarkable new project there is the development of a bio-mass power system for the house and grounds, using a wood boiler supplied partly by willow on the site. This may eventually provide power also to the village of Waterperry.

The project reflects a greater emphasis by the School on sustainable and environmentally sound activities.

A great deal of the technical and legal work related to the acquisition of Mandeville and to other property matters was carried out by Graham Skelcey, the School Principal from 1999 to 2008. He inherited the post at a time when the amount of regulation of charities, including matters like health and safety, risk management and employment laws, was growing rapidly. Despite this considerable workload, Skelcey continued to be leader of the branch in Croydon. He has been described as someone who finds it impossible to avoid a task if he sees that it needs doing! This attitude has enabled the School to benefit from his advice on other matters, like a difficult copyright dispute with Dorine van Oyen concerning Leon MacLaren's papers, the tangled issue of the constitution of the School in Amsterdam and the deteriorating financial conditions at the end of his tenure of office.

This latter aspect highlighted the question of why membership of the School has fallen in recent years. Skelcey's view was that people are now less committed to continuing study and practice, so that there is a greater turnover of students. Moreover, there are more institutions offering courses of a spiritual nature, sometimes on easier terms than the School's. He made the interesting comment that the challenge facing Donald Lambie is in some respects more difficult than that of Leon MacLaren, in so far as MacLaren was repeatedly able to provide new inspiration from his latest meeting with the Shankaracharya, whereas Vasudevananda Saraswati had told Lambie to rely upon the existing record of the Conversations, to make them come alive.

Skelcey felt that the School was experiencing an impulse to turn outwards to the community in its work. Where were the six people whom Shantananda Saraswati had said could create a new renaissance? This should not be an explicit objective; nor did it matter whether the School was in the forefront of such a movement or simply offering some kind of guidance. Yet why, said Skelcey with a slight touch of frustration, should we spend so much time on Florence or Mozart when new forms of art or literature and so on are needed? There is a danger, he seemed to indicate, of living in the past, after so many years of practising living in the present! Somewhat paradoxically he suggested that the solution might be to concentrate upon our own tradition.

Despite any falling off in numbers in London, new branches opened in Lincoln in 2000 and in Exeter in 2003. By the year 2009 there were seventeen, operating at no less than 53 locations: Bath, Berkshire, Bristol, Croydon, Devon, East Anglia, Guildford, Kent, Lincoln, Midlands, North East, North West, Oxford, Scotland, St Albans, Sussex and Wessex. Their students continued just to exceed in numbers those of London. Of their many activities, besides Philosophy, one may be given as no more than the tip of a very large iceberg. The Berkshire branch for several years held a very successful annual Shakespeare day, which included excerpts from plays, recitals and discussion. In spirit, organisation and leadership the School in the U.K is a single entity.

Meanwhile in London the new millennium has seen a host of new courses offered to the public. Five public talks under the title of 'A Philosophical Garden' illustrated Donald Lambie's concept of Mandeville as a beacon in the community. On Saturday mornings there have been Sanskrit, Plato, Emerson, Ficino, Christianity in Advaita, Hermes Trismegistus, the *Gita* and calligraphy. Symposiums have been held for first year students. Short courses have included 'The Common Good', 'The Rule of Law', 'Magic of Money', 'Philosophy and Business', 'Feeding the World', 'Spirit of Truth', 'Wisdom Works', 'Parenthood', 'Profession of Humanity', 'Land Issues' and 'Five Great Human Beings'. Residential courses on meditation were introduced for existing students. The Education Renaissance Trust ran a conference on 'Educating for Unity'. In 2004 an exhibition by younger artists in the School was held at Mandeville, entitled 'Art in Essence', refuting the suggestion by Bernard Saunders that School artists were aging!

An important change in the School's constitution was made in 2008, when the Fellowship voted to remove the condition that new Fellows must have completed an Economics course. This condition had been opposed by those who felt it was an undue restriction on some senior Philosophy students, especially those in branches where Economics had not been taught. For those who disliked the change, compensation came in the form of an agreement by the Senior Tutor to include some Economics in the Philosophy material, a step that could lead to interesting developments.

Changes in personnel, besides that of Principal, took place in this decade. Peter Green stood down as President after nine years. Including the office of Treasurer and Principal, his total service amounted to nearly half a century. John Meltzer replaced Peter Watson in 2007 as Secretary on the Executive. Watson had served for nineteen years. Martin Kettle took over from Ian Woods as Treasurer in 2006, and Tommas Graves retired as Chief Accountant after no less than thirty years.

These gentlemen who retired from office were still very much alive and well, but other senior members of the School were ailing. Help was now offered, both in the form of the benevolent fund and with improvements such as the lift at Waterperry. A sub-committee of the Executive was formed to examine the increasing needs of elderly students, such as the provision of Philosophy material and guidance for those who could no longer attend groups. A few who had been employed by the School were offered more specific assistance.

To mark the centenary of Leon MacLaren's birth on 24 September 1910, Donald Lambie proposed a major event to which all School members around the world would be invited. It would be called the 'Festival of Spirit', and would illustrate every aspect of the teaching and practices of the School. The famous London theatre of Drury Lane would be the main venue on the centenary day, with a range of lectures, concerts, exhibitions and other events being held at Mandeville Place and elsewhere. Even so, the best memorial of the work of Leon MacLaren and the host of others who have contributed to the spiritual and creative growth of the School over the years remains the testimony of those who have benefited from it. One such tribute can be summarised, rather incoherently, thus:

> One has changed completely. Crippling ideas have been seen and dealt with. It releases. It is a lifeline. There is a purpose bigger than oneself. In good and bad times Philosophy gives detachment, watching, a connection. The horizon is open to music, words, history, new discovery. If the School stopped enquiring it would be dead. It is a life-long study.

Or, in the more sophisticated words of T.S. Eliot:

> We shall not cease from exploration
> And the end of all our exploring
> Will be to arrive where we started
> And know the place for the first time.[1]

---

1 *Little Gidding* from *Four Quartets*, p.59, Faber and Faber, 1944.

Short Glossary
of Sanskrit Terms

Abhinaya	traditional form of Indian dance
Acharya	teacher
Adhikarana	place and time of action
Advaita	non-dual
Aham	I or I am
Ahankara	I am a thing or an action
Akasha	space
Ananda	bliss
Antakarana	mind or inner organ
Anubhuti	personal verification
Anvaya	correct ordering or synthesis
Apadana	ablative case denoting 'from'
Asura	demon
Atman	Self
Avarana	mental blindness
Avatar	an incarnation
Avesha	possession by demon or ghost
Avyakta	unmanifest nature
Brahman	universal Spirit
Brahmasmi	I am *Brahman*
Brahma Sutra	classic work by Sankara on Advaita Vedanta
Buddhi	intelligence
Chit	knowledge
Citta	heart or emotional centre
Dharma	law or righteousness
Dvaparayuga	silver age
Guna	threefold basic forces of creation
Guru	teacher or mentor
Hita	nerve holding past experience

Idam	this; used for everything except the Self
Jala	water
Jiva	individual soul
Jnaman	knowledge
Jyotisha	astronomy or astrology
Kaivalya	being alone
Kaliyuga	iron age
Karana	instrumental case
Karma	grammatical object
Karta	grammatical subject or agent of action
Kriyamana	the future facing an individual
Kshaya	negative form of *sattva*
Madhyama	penultimate state in expression of speech
Mahattattva	universal feeling of existence
Mahavakya	great sentence in Advaita Vedanta
Mala	negative form of *tamas*
Mananam	reflective hearing
Manas	discursive mind
Maya	universal illusion
Moha	delusion
Nakshatra	star or region of the heavens
Nididhyasanam	absorption of what is heard
Nirguna	beyond the *guna*
Nir-sankalpa	without any resolution
Nivritti	life of contemplation
OM	original creative sound of everything
Papa	bad effects
Para	origin of speech in the individual
Pashyanti	second stage of speech after *para*
Prajnanam	practical knowledge
Prakriti	nature
Prana	breath
Pranava	descriptive term for *OM*
Prarabdha	present experience derived from past
Pravritti	active life
Prithivi	earth
Punya	good effects
Puranas	ancient traditional stories

Purusha	universal person or Self
Rajas	guna of activity or movement
Rakshasa	demon
Rashi	twelfth division of the heavens
Saguna	with or including the *gunas*
Samashti	universal world
Sambandha	genitive case
Sampradana	dative case
Sancita	what is carried forward in *citta*
Sandhi	rules of connecting sounds in speech
Sankalpa	resolution
Sannyasin	enlightened person
Sanskara	characteristics formed in previous lifetimes
Sat	being
Satsanga	philosophical company
Satyuga	golden age
Shakti	power of the Absolute or Brahman
Sattva	*guna* of rest or peace
Smriti	literature of remembered wisdom
Sri	Lord or Holiness
Sruti	sacred literature or the Veda
Sutra	aphorism
Tamas	*guna* of inertia or heaviness
Tanmatra	subtle or finer sense
Tejas	fire or light
Tretayuga	bronze age
Turiya	state of universal consciousness
Upadhi	qualification or limitation
Vaikhari	final, audible form of speech
Vayu	air
Vedanga	six works auxiliary to the Veda
Vibhakti	grammatical cases
Vijnanam	analysis of knowledge
Vikshepa	negative form of *rajas*
Vyashti	individual's world
Vyatireka	separation or analysis

Index

331

By the same author

A NEW MODEL OF THE ECONOMY

THIS BOOK is a radical revision of modern economic theory, but it deliberately follows the broad outline of modern textbooks. Economists today, the author argues, employ 'flat-earth' models which are totally unrealistic. They ignore the huge influence of spatial location, which gives rise to economic, or Ricardian, rent. He incorporates into both micro- and macro-economic analysis this basic and universal feature, thereby bringing economic theory into much closer touch with reality.

Money, credit and interest are also subjected to searching questions. The answers point to a way out of the current confusion over the proper role of the banking system.

Finally, taxation is examined, revealing how present-day taxes inhibit the economy by their damaging impact on the margin of production. This leads to a conclusion which draws together the various elements of the 'new model', and has important implications for policy-makers hoping to remedy today's serious economic problems. The book offers a model for fundamental reform.

'Brian Hodgkinson deftly pulls together many strands of alternative thought and presents them in a format which no economist can easily dismiss ... This is a remarkable book.' Mark Braund, Guardian.co.uk

'If epiphanies can come from text books, unsuspecting readers might expect one here.' Land & Liberty

'... much more relevant to the present state of real-world economies than the models offered by most economics textbooks.' James Robertson, Working for a Sane Alternative

With diagrams, index • Hardback, 368pp, £30
Paperback edition forthcoming; contact publisher for more information

For more books on Ethical Economics, visit
www.ethicaleconomics.org.uk

STANDING FOR JUSTICE

A Biography of Andrew MacLaren, MP

by John Stewart

*'Institutional charity and political expedients
are no substitute for justice'*
ANDREW MACLAREN

ANDREW MACLAREN was a Labour MP who found his inspiration in the philosophy that dominated the great reform movement that swept the Liberal Party to its landslide victory in 1906. The Cabinet of Sir Henry Campbell Bannerman was determined to introduce the radical reform proposed by the American social reformer Henry George. In this attempt they were blocked by the Tories, leading to the constitutional crisis of 1909, when the Liberal Budget was thrown out by the House of Lords.

Born in Glasgow, MacLaren moved to London in 1914 to earn a living as a journalist and cartoonist (examples are reproduced in the book). As a pacifist, he joined the Independent Labour Party to which many members of the first Labour government belonged, including Ramsay MacDonald and Philip Snowden. He first entered Parliament as a Labour member in 1922, losing and regaining his seat twice between then and 1945.

After the First World War, the Georgist reform enjoyed considerable support in the Labour Party and Snowden introduced it in his 1931 Budget, only to have it repealed by the Tories. With the split in the Labour Party, the Fabian socialists gained the upper hand, and income redistribution through taxation and state benefits came to dominate party thinking.

MacLaren was not against helping the needy, but he saw that tax-funded handouts would breed a dependency culture without eradicating poverty. Speaking in the Commons, he likened this to people who 'will shed sad tears when they see men moving down the centre of the stream. They will devise many well-meaning schemes to pull these fellows out of the stream, but they will never think of going up-stream to see who threw them in.'

'John Stewart writes with verve and infectious enthusiasm to give an engaging picture of a man and an issue that both deserve more attention.'
Catholic Herald

32 b&w/colour plates, index • Hardback, 208pp, £12.95

**For more books on History, Biography and Economics visit
www.shepheard-walwyn.co.uk • www.ethicaleconomics.org.uk**

THE LETTERS OF MARSILIO FICINO
Volumes 1-8

Translated from the Latin by members of the Language Department of the School of Economic Science

*'Virtue is a quality of the soul which leads a man
by discrimination to bliss'*
MARSILIO FICINO

'[Ficino] was at the very fountainhead of some of the most characteristic and influential aspects of the Italian Renaissance'
C.B. Schmitt in *The Times Literary Supplement*

MARSILIO FICINO (1433-99), leader of the Platonic Academy in Florence, was teacher and guide to a remarkable circle of men and one of the most influential thinkers of the Renaissance. He put before society a new ideal of human nature, emphasising its divine potential. The ideas discussed appeared again and again in the works of literature and art that followed.

'All that we regard as the norm of Western European art – Botticelli's paintings, Monteverdi's music, Shakespeare's philosophical lovers, Berowne and Lorenzo, Jacques and Portia – has flowered from Ficino's Florence'
Kathleen Raine in *The Times*

'Undoubtedly these letters comprise one of the "spiritual classics" of the past thousand years'
Christopher Booker in *The Spectator*

'From every point of view it is a pleasure to read this perfect introduction to one of the most attractive and influential figures of the Italian Renaissance'
C.V. Wedgwood in *The Daily Telegraph*

'... so well translated, so well annotated and so beautifully produced that it is a pleasure to read and possess'
A. Hamilton in the *Heythrop Journal*

With notes on the letters, Latin text and
Ficino's correspondents • Index • Hardback

Volumes 1-6 £22.50 each • Volumes 7 & 8 £25.00 each
8-volume set £160.00